ON CAPITOL HILL

Studies in the Legislative Process

JOHN BIBBY *University of Wisconsin— Milwaukee*

ROGER DAVIDSON *Dartmouth College*

HOLT, RINEHART AND WINSTON, INC.
New York, Chicago, San Francisco, Toronto, London

to LUCILE *and* NANCY

PREFACE

Something approaching a direct encounter is essential for full comprehension of the life of our national legislature. This kind of experiential knowledge may be derived from a variety of sources: from work or study on Capitol Hill, or from interviews or exchanges with Senators, Representatives, staff aides, and others close to the legislative process. In such ways the observer can confront directly the drama (and boredom) of congressional activities. However, not all teachers, and certainly few students, actually find it convenient to travel to Washington and spend an extended period of time on Capitol Hill.

This book is designed to bring to the reader this experiential element. We make no claim to being the first, or the only, political scientists to have "discovered" Congress first-hand; but our various research interests have led us to spend considerable time on Capitol Hill during the past few years. Our research methods have ranged from the most conventional observational practices to complicated interview protocols and survey techniques. In short, we consider ourselves representative of a generation of scholars who, in the words of journalist Neil MacNeil, have frequented the committee rooms, lobbies, and corridors of Congress "and laid siege to the Congressmen to have them explain their actions and motives."

A word is surely in order concerning our intellectual approach to the subject-matter treated in this book. The "case study" is a familiar technique of scholarship. Its advantage lies in its potential for rich elaboration of the unique factors and relationships which comprise a single event or series of events. Although the case study often presents difficult problems of data-gathering, its analytic demands are somewhat less stringent. It is possible to approach the immediate subject-event without comprehending fully the larger patterns of relationships of which the subject is but a single "case."

The very particularity of the case approach suggests some of its limitations. The case study is by nature micro- rather than macro-analytic. At some point the observer must step back from the events he is describing and ask himself what they add up to. Even an infinite number of case studies will be of value only if they permit comparison and, ultimately, some tentative generalizations concerning the political system itself. The other side of the dilemma is, however, that a "really adequate" number of cases is rarely attainable.

Confronted with this dilemma, the scholar may undertake to collect a very large number of "cases" in the form of quantifiable indicators—votes, for example, or expressed attitudes—from which generalizations on a limited scale may be readily extracted. His other alternative is to collate a limited number of complete case histories and take an analytical "leap" in identifying the sinews of the political system which seem to be exposed in the cases. By specifying the relevant variables ("This happened in X, but not in Y," for example), the analyst is able to draw crude inferences as to what is likely to be the case in Z, of which he has no direct knowledge.

Both methods involve intellectual shortcuts. Qualitative generalization may embrace a totality of variables, but for only a limited number of cases. Quantification, on the other hand, may include an entire universe of cases, but for a necessarily limited number of variables, or indicators. Though either intellectual stratagem represents some compromises with "comprehensiveness," this fact need not deter us. After all, it is not possible to know everything about everything before venturing to say something. At this stage in the development of political science, we can see no inherent advantage of one technique over the other. Both may be considered complementary processes.

This discussion is by way of placing this volume among the various approaches to political events. We have attempted neither a "textbook" nor a series of "anecdotes." The following studies are attempts, through particularistic techniques, to describe patterns of behavior which are typical of Capitol Hill. In each instance we have sought to identify what we conceive to be the relevant variables, and where we think the case fits into the universe of events each narrative to conclusions which are embodied in the best current literature on Congress. The bibliographic essay at the end of the book attempts to direct the reader to a few of these works.

The cooperation of many individuals was instrumental in the preparation of these materials. The necessary restraints of data-gathering prohibit our acknowledging publicly many of our debts, but a few persons must be mentioned particularly. Representative Albert Quie was most generous in permitting us to describe his daily schedule of activities. One of our students, Jay K. Wright, gathered the material on Representative Clark MacGregor's campaign; and Representative MacGregor was kind enough to review the manuscript. Jon O. Newman, formerly administrative assistant to Senator Abraham A. Ribicoff, facilitated the gathering of materials on the Senator's 1962 campaign and contributed his knowledgeable insights. The description of Senator Mike Monroney's office was possible because of the understanding help of Mrs. Joseph Short, one of the Hill's most respected staff veterans. Another of our student assistants, Gerald G. Paul, undertook some of the background research for Chapter 4. The study of the origins of the Economic Opportunity Act of 1964 was completed while one of the authors was a consultant to the W. E. Upjohn Institute for Employment Research. Dr. Sar A. Levitan of the Institute's staff was especially helpful.

Professors Theodore J. Lowi of the University of Chicago and James A. Robinson of Ohio State University read the manuscript in its entirety and made many useful contributions. Our wives not only showed great perseverence during our research, but often contributed willingly of their typing skills and their own insights into the events we were writing about.

For the factual descriptions and interpretations included in these studies, we are happy to accept full personal responsibility.

John Bibby
Roger Davidson

Washington, D. C.
November 1966

CONTENTS

IN PERSPECTIVE: CONGRESS IN THE TWENTIETH CENTURY

1

On August 19, 1964, President Lyndon B. Johnson beamed out over a White House meeting in celebration of the close of the Eighty-eighth Congress:

> This has been a year without precedent in the history of relations between the Executive and Legislative Branches of our Government. This session of Congress has enacted more major legislation, met more national needs, disposed of more national issues than any other session of this century or the last.[1]

The authoritative and usually sober *Congressional Quarterly*, though more restrained, was also stirred by Congress' performance:

> The record of the 88th Congress . . . was indeed impressive. The Congress passed the Civil Rights Act of 1964, a major tax cut, a program to attack poverty, a federal pay bill, a foreign aid bill remarkably close to the Administration's request and a large stack of additional major legislation. At session's end, it had disposed of much of the broad program outlined by President Kennedy. . . . In addition, while President Johnson took over Mr. Kennedy's extensive program, he also added

---

[1] *Congressional Quarterly Weekly Report*, XXII (October 9, 1964), p. 2373.

measures of his own—notably the poverty program. Congress approved some of these also.[2]

Laudatory statements such as these are somewhat outside the mainstream of mid-twentieth century popular and scholarly comments about Congress. More conventional were the criticisms directed toward Congress only a few weeks after the White House ceremony by distinguished politicians, scholars, and journalists. Meeting under the auspices of Columbia University, this group drafted eighteen reforms thought essential for the preservation of a viable and responsible national legislature.[3]

Although there have been persistent demands for the reform of Congress, the pathways to congressional reform are lonely and difficult, as Chapter 8 demonstrates. The existing procedures have powerful defenders both within and without Congress; for these rules are not neutral in their impact, but have a direct bearing on the outcomes of congressional struggles (see Chapter 6). The frequently heard pleas for reform, therefore, are concerned not merely with achieving efficiency in the legislative halls, but also with the basic issue of which bills will pass Congress.

WHY BE CONCERNED ABOUT CONGRESS?

Why is Congress singled out as an object of reforming zeal more than the other two branches of the government? Surely one explanation is the liberals' distaste for the alleged conservative bias of Congress. The liberals want the government to move rapidly with decisive measures designed to meet current social problems. They point out that the executive branch, as the initiator of most major legislative proposals, is typically prepared to act comprehensively and aggressively. Executive activism, however, appears thwarted by a decentralized and conservative Congress that permits small but determined minorities to block or at least temper the will of the majority because of its seniority system, filibusters, rural overrepresentation, localism, and weak party organizations. President John F. Kennedy, for example, saw Congress block his farm bill and his proposals for aid to education, medicare, and the creation of a department of urban affairs.

[2] *Congressional Quarterly Weekly Report*, XXII (October 9, 1964), p. 2373.
[3] American Assembly, *The Congress and America's Future: Final Report of the Twenty-Sixth American Assembly* (New York: American Assembly, 1965).

Another explanation for the criticism focused on Congress is that this body is "psychologically as well as politically a representative body." [4] The mystique of the President, as Chief of State, and that of the Supreme Court, set them apart and protect them from much criticism. Both institutions operate in an aura of dignity and high purpose, unlike congressmen and senators. Plainly visible and expected to handle willingly even the petty problems of their constituents, congressmen are obviously mortal and reflect our own weaknesses and strengths. Such a body of men is a ready-made target for criticism.

Perhaps more serious bases for concern about Congress and its future are that, however strong, the legislative body is losing its vitality to an even stronger presidency and an even more complex bureaucracy, and that it is in need of meaningful roles to play in the late twentieth century, since its role as the *originator* of legislation is increasingly assumed by the executive. It is now established as routine that at the opening session of Congress the President will outline a comprehensive legislative program that will serve as a guide to major congressional issues. Moreover, the President is expected to supply continuing leadership for his program throughout the entire congressional session.

What Has Happened to Congress?

Originally, Congress was much more than a coequal branch. The fears expressed in *Federalist* Number 48 that it would dominate the government seemed well founded. In his famous book on politics of the late nineteenth century, Woodrow Wilson characterized the American government as "congressional government." For Congress not only enacted the laws, it initiated legislative proposals and, through its committees, dominated the administration of the laws it passed.

Even today, the powers of Congress remain impressive. Among the major legislatures of the Western world, it alone is still capable of initiating major legislation. (See the history of the Depressed Areas Act in Chapter 6.) More importantly, Congress has proved that it can modify or alter those measures proposed by the executive that it chooses to enact. There is hardly an aspect of

[4] Ralph K. Huitt, "What Can We Do About Congress?", *Milwaukee Journal,* December 13, 1964.

American public policy that is not significantly affected by congressional action (or inaction). This is true even of foreign policy, an area that the executive has long been acknowledged to dominate. Most administration programs for foreign aid, military defense, and trade must be authorized by Congress, which must also appropriate the funds to carry out executive policy. The central role of Congress in the decision-making process was well stated by Ralph K. Huitt: "Whoever tries to weave a seamless web of American economic policy will find soon enough that all threads lead ultimately to Congress." [5]

Although Congress remains extremely powerful, however, no one today would assert that it dominated even a President like Dwight D. Eisenhower, who was not aggressive in leading the legislature. How did this change in the influence of Congress come about?

The nineteenth century was characterized by the doctrines of laissez faire, social Darwinism, and "strict constructionism" in constitutional law. Government was a passive instrument that imposed minimal restraints on an economy thought to be largely self-regulating and that provided relatively few services (few were demanded). Accommodations of interests, of course, had to take place. These could be accomplished by relatively simple statutory enactments—legislation developed primarily by Congress itself. The government was so small and the sums of money involved were so restricted that Congress through its various committees could with reasonable efficiency draw up the entire federal budget (the Budget and Accounting Act of 1921 transferred this function to the executive).

This traditional role of Congress was to change markedly, however. David B. Truman, commenting on the current state of national legislatures, has observed that the first fifty years of this century were marked by "parliamentary crisis." National legislatures were compelled to cope with the "complexities of increasingly urbanized, industrialized, and irrevocably interdependent societies." [6] This is a different world from the one Wilson was writing

[5] Ralph K. Huitt, "Congressional Organization and Operations in the Field of Money and Credit," in Commission on Money and Credit, *Fiscal and Debt Management Policies* (Englewood Cliffs, N.J.: Prentice-Hall, 1963), p. 408.
[6] David B. Truman, "Introduction: The Problem and Its Setting," in David B. Truman (ed.), *Congress and America's Future* (Englewood Cliffs, N.J.: Prentice-Hall, 1965), pp. 1-2.

about in *Congressional Government*, and, correspondingly, the passive government of yesterday has today become a massive "service state," providing, in varying degrees, assistance to all segments of society and assuming responsibility for maintaining a prosperous economy. In order to provide necessary services to an interdependent society and to guide an economy with an annual gross national product in excess of $735 billion, Congress has been forced to rely increasingly on the expertise of the executive branch. The successful implementation of today's extensive and expanding governmental programs requires continuous administrative supervision and flexibility. Congress, however, is not equipped to administer the day-to-day demands of a "service state." It does not have the time, the manpower, or the knowledge required. Nor can Congress act quickly enough to modify existing laws so as to bring them into accord with conditions that change almost daily. As a result, Congress has delegated to the executive branch vast amounts of discretionary authority over public policy. This delegation has been accompanied, of course, by an increase in the political power of administrators and by a partial shift in the locus of political conflict. How a bill is administered by the discretion of the executive bureaucracy is today as important as the actual content of the bill originally enacted by Congress.

The expanding scope of administrative activity and the concentration of technical expertise in the hands of administrators has resulted in marked attrition of the congressional power to initiate new legislation. The President, with superior informational and technical staff, and publicity resources, has emerged as the chief legislator. It is he who is expected to provide Congress with a comprehensive legislative program. Contemporary pundits and future historians will judge him on the scope and adequacy of his proposals. His batting average in getting his program adopted by Congress will be computed and compared (perhaps unfairly) with that of other Presidents. Gone are the days when Congress could, with wounded pride, castigate a Cabinet officer for the "effrontery" of having his department draft a bill for submission to Congress, as it did to the Secretary of Interior in 1908. Now it is considered the job of high executive officials to supervise the drafting of bills and then to steer them through the Congress.

The formulating of legislative proposals within the executive branch is, however, an extremely complicated and often lengthy process not unlike the one that operates within the legislative branch. The "war on poverty" proposals, for example, directly affected several administrative departments and agencies, each of which represents, in the councils of the Administration, powerful and often conflicting interests within the country. It was therefore necessary for the President to exert strong leadership, if a bill was to emerge from the executive branch. The final package was, however, in reality a treaty negotiated among the various factions within the Administration. (See Chapter 7 for further discussion.)

The massive involvement of the United States around the world and the delicate nature of the present balance of international power has meant that the government must deal with problems—such as the 1962 Cuban missile crisis, the erection of the Berlin Wall, and the war in Vietnam—that arise suddenly and that require decisive action based upon detailed information and a realization of the impact of any action on other governmental policies. As in domestic affairs, the exigencies of America's world involvement have thrust upon the executive initiative in policy-making along with his traditional responsibility of execution.

The functions of the executive and the legislature have steadily come to be the reverse of those the Founding Fathers intended. Congress was expected to propose and enact new programs, with the President acting as the restraining agent armed with a veto. Today, the President initiates most major legislation, while Congress frequently exercises the veto power by defeating or by drastically changing the President's suggestions.

While this may be what some have called an "executive-centered" age, one can excessively depreciate the role of Congress. The President's resources for influencing and leading Congress are great indeed. But it should be remembered that it is still Congress, and not the President, that passes the laws. The centers of power may have shifted in the twentieth century, but the legislative process remains one of bargaining, consensus-seeking, and compromise, as men strive to find a majority on each issue. Congress, alternating between docility and hostility, has impressed this on all modern presidents from Truman to Johnson.

While acknowledging that the role of Congress has changed, Theodore Lowi asserts that its powers, far from declining, have expanded in this century along with those of the executive. In domestic affairs, the constitutional revolution of the 1930s dramatically increased the powers of the national government and, as a direct result, also increased the scope of congressional authority to deal with domestic social and economic problems.[7] There are few areas of national life from which Congress is now constitutionally barred from legislating, as the sweeping Civil Rights Act of 1964 illustrates. Nor has Congress totally lost control of legislative initiative. (As mentioned earlier, Chapter 6 deals with depressed areas legislation, a measure that was born in Congress and pressed forward to enactment by forces largely outside the executive branch.) During the Eisenhower Administration, because the President was not anxious to expand existing programs or to embark upon many new ventures in the social welfare field, it was Congress that, against the wishes of the President, elaborated Administration plans in such fields as housing. In 1965 President Johnson's voting rights bill contained major provisions suggested by Senators Everett Dirksen and Mike Mansfield—the minority and majority leaders of the Senate.

As in domestic affairs, congressional power in the foreign sphere has increased, for a president cannot act without money, material, and manpower, both civil and military. To a large extent, Congress controls the amounts and quality of these resources. Nor has Congress lost altogether its initiative in foreign policy. Involvement in the International Development Association of the World Bank, for example, came about through the efforts of Congress.

A simple list of those government programs due to expire in 1965 that required congressional renewal to prevent their death is ample proof that any attempt to weave the seamless web of American policy does indeed lead inexorably to Congress. Such a list compiled by *Congressional Quarterly* included the following programs:

1. Wheat production and marketing controls
2. Voluntary feed grains production
3. Export Control Act
4. Reduction from $500 to $100 of the duty-free allowance accorded residents returning from abroad
5. Reorganization Act authority
6. Fifty-five percent ship construction differential subsidy

[7] Theodore Lowi, *Legislative Politics, U.S.A.* (Boston: Little, Brown, 1962), pp. xiv-xvi.

7. Veterans education and training benefits under the Korean GI Bill
8. Health services for migratory workers
9. Grants to the states to combat mental retardation
10. Area Redevelopment Administration Act authorization
11. Applications for matching grants for health research facilities
12. Applications for grants for medical, dental, and related facilities
13. Temporary increase in the public debt limit
14. Temporary excise tax rates
15. Authority to issue investment guarantees
16. Labor mobility demonstration projects
17. Authority for interstate highway billboard control agreements
18. A number of FHA general housing programs
19. One hundred percent federal manpower training grants
20. International wheat agreement implementation
21. Higher interest rates on foreign government time deposits kept in U.S. banks
22. Stabilization funds for lead and zinc ore production
23. Interest equalization tax
24. Authorizations for: military construction and procurement, NASA appropriations, foreign aid, Peace Corps, Coast Guard capital construction, poverty appropriation, juvenile delinquency, arms control and disarmament, public works[8]

THE FUNCTIONS OF CONGRESS

Article I, Section 1 of the Constitution declares that "All legislative Powers herein granted shall be vested in a Congress of the United States, which shall consist of a Senate and House of Representatives." This constitutional provision and those that follow say relatively little, however, about the nature and functions of a legislative body. Hence, the basic question remains: What are the functions of a legislature? We would suggest that they include deliberation and law-making, legitimizing governmental decisions, representation, resolving conflicts and seeking consensus, public education, and overseeing the administration.

[8] *Congressional Quarterly Weekly Report*, XXII (January 1, 1965), pp. 6-12.

Deliberation and Law-Making

As the list of expiring legislation indicates, the volume of bills to be considered in a given year is tremendous, particularly if the Administration is aggressive. The complexity and mass of legislation considered during any session of Congress has caused some critics to question Congress' capacity to serve as a truly *deliberative law-making body.* Furthermore, the tendency of the President to act as the initiator of most major proposals has raised the question of which branch, the legislative or the executive, actually deliberates and makes the laws.

Whatever the world outside the Capitol may say, Members of Congress often describe the national legislature as one of the few truly deliberative bodies in the world. Senators take particular pride in citing the thoroughness with which they consider legislation on the Senate floor, where there are minimal limitations on debate. And the members of the House point to the care with which their committees consider bills. "The Tangled History of the Depressed Areas Act" (Chapter 6) demonstrates that these are not idle boasts. The complicated story of the passage of this bill demonstrates clearly that Congress, in committee and on the floor, remains in this "executive-centered" age a powerful and at times creative force in law-making.

It should be noted, however, that it is not just within the halls of Congress that this deliberative process goes on. The President is also a legislator. He and his subordinates throughout the Administration are also involved in study, conflict, and negotiation as they prepare legislative proposals for submission to Congress. (This version of the "legislative process" as enacted within the executive branch is portrayed in Chapter 7, "The Executive as 'Legislator.'")

Legitimizing Government Decisions

Congress then remains, as it has been from the beginning, the official law-maker of the nation. Congress is, however, more than a "bill and resolution factory" whose members are to be graded on a "piecework basis." [9] As a representative assembly one of its functions is to *legitimize* political leadership and political

[9] Ralph K. Huitt, "The Outsider in the Senate: An Alternative Role," *American Political Science Review,* LV (September 1961), pp. 566-575.

decisions. A minimum requirement for every stable governmental system is that its decisions be accepted ungrudgingly by the vast majority of the citizenry. At one time, the doctrine of the divine right of kings was used to induce the necessary public acceptance. The explosion of that myth and the development of democratic ideologies vesting ultimate political power in the hands of the people meant that new justifications for the exercise of political power were required. Theories and devices of representation (such as popular election of delegates to a national assembly and decisions by a majority vote in the assembly) perform the function of providing citizen control over governmental decision-makers in accordance with the dictates of democratic theory. Hence, representation converts a "leader" into a "representative" and converts "power" into legitimate "authority." [10] Any institution that can induce acceptance of its decisions no matter how controversial (the Civil Rights Act of 1964, the Medicare Act of 1965) is indispensable to a stable political system.

The policies emerging from our national legislature may not always be the best solution to a particular problem (though this is difficult to judge objectively), since the process of decision-making in Congress normally involves an almost endless process of negotiation and compromise. Bargaining produced, for example, as Chapter 6 demonstrates, a far different depressed-areas bill than the sponsors intended. But the program, once enacted, was accepted as a piece of "the national consensus." Moreover, the policy commitment to grant aid to depressed areas does not appear likely to be reversed in the foreseeable future, though the administrative instruments and techniques of assistance were modified in 1965. It is important to note that not all modern national assemblies have had as enviable a record as this in serving as a legitimizing agent for the exercise of political power. The French National Assembly of the postwar Fourth Republic failed in this respect and was replaced by a new regime that could command the respect of the populace—the Fifth Republic of General Charles De Gaulle.

Representation

Certainly contributing to the ability of Congress to have its decisions accepted is the widespread assumption by the public

[10] Lowi, *Legislative Politics, U.S.A.*, p. ix.

and the legislators that Congress represents the wishes of the people. *Representation* of society's interests is therefore an important function of Congress. But beyond its significance for inducing acceptance of governmental decisions, a representative assembly is essential for a free society because it keeps the government sensitive and responsive to the society's needs and concerns.

Representation is, of course, a complex phenomenon. For one thing, legislators may perceive the interests of their constituents in quite different ways. Witness the divergent manner in which Senators Paul H. Douglas and Everett M. Dirksen represent the same geographic area, Illinois. What is important, however, is that there is a widespread acceptance that each of these men does, in fact, represent his constituency. In a sampling of House members interviewed in 1963, no less than 84.3 percent viewed their purposive role as one of "determining, representing, and protecting the interests of the people." [11]

Furthermore, insecurity of job tenure caused by popular elections also encourages (perhaps forces is a better word) a sensitivity to societal and constituency needs, especially in an electoral system so decentralized that each member must rely in considerable degree upon his own resources to stay in office (see Chapter 2, which deals with the elections of a senator and representative). In addition, the procedures of Congress permit widespread participation in its decisions. Members encourage their constituents to send them their views on public policy, and spend vast amounts of time, money, and energy maintaining lines of communication with their constituents (Chapter 3 describes how Senator Mike Monroney [D. Okla.] and Congressman Albert Quie [R. Minn.] have organized their offices for this purpose).

With its loosely organized party system, its specialized committees that further decentralize power, and its lengthy and almost unbelievably complex procedures, there are multiple points of access and influence within Congress. Virtually all interests have an opportunity to influence Congress, or to borrow a phrase used in another governmental branch, "to have their day in court." This openness of the procedures also makes it possible for Congress to function as a legitimizing agent.

It should never be assumed, however, that because Congress

[11] Roger H. Davidson, *Congress and the Executive: The Race for Representation* (Washington: American Enterprise Institute, 1965), p. 17.

accords virtually everyone an opportunity to be heard, everyone has an *equal* opportunity to exert influence. For example, one effect of the Founding Fathers' decision to permit equal state representation in the Senate (in an attempt to pacify the fears of small states) has been to increase the influence of interests located in sparsely populated areas—such as farmers, mining industrialists, and southern segregationists. Nor is the seniority system for choosing committee chairmen neutral in impact. Rather this system (as is illustrated by the analysis of the Senate Banking and Currency Committee in Chapter 5) enhances the influence of legislators from safe, one-party areas because a chairman is chosen for having served continuously on a particular committee longer than any other member of the majority party. When the Democrats control Congress, this means that southern members of the party are apt to hold a high proportion of the committee chairmanships; when the GOP is in power, these positions are primarily occupied by members from rural, midwestern and northeastern areas. The extent to which the seniority system bolsters southern influence in Congress can be seen by the fact that in the Eighty-ninth Congress (1965-1966) southerners chaired twelve out of twenty House committees and nine out of sixteen committees in the Senate.

With their many possible points of delay and obstruction, congressional procedures make it easier to defeat a bill (even a handful of men strategically located in the right committee or subcommittee can do it) than to pass a bill. Hence groups or forces on the defensive have an advantage in Congress.[12] The congressional system is obviously not perfect, but people do accept its decisions. One contemporary scholar has therefore defended it in the following terms:

> Congress has the strength of the free enterprise system; it multiplies the decision makers, the points of access to influence and power, and the creative moving agents. It is hard to believe that a small group of leaders could do better. What would be gained in orderliness might well be lost in vitality and in sensitiveness to the pressures for change. Moreover, Congress resembles the social system it serves; it reflects the diversity of the country. There is much to be said for a system in which

---

[12] David B. Truman, *The Governmental Process* (New York: Alfred A. Knopf, 1951), p. 353.

almost every interest can find some spokesman, in which every cause can strike a blow, however feeble, in its own behalf.[13]

Public Education

The activities of Congress are "news" and Congress is a prime subject for national news media coverage. Because of this capacity to generate publicity, Congress performs the function of *public education*. That is, Congress through its deliberations informs the public on issues and raises the level of public interest in current problems.

With its well-publicized committee hearings and floor debates and the press releases that constantly flow from members' offices, there are few matters that do not receive congressional publicity. Often the publicity surrounding congressional activities has helped crystallize public opinion on issues and has thus facilitated the passage of new legislation.

The vocal efforts of congressional Democrats in the 1950s, for example, helped raise the public support needed to permit passage of the Depressed Areas Act of 1961 (see Chapter 6). Similarly, the intense publicity given to allegedly dangerous practices in the distribution of drugs by Senator Estes Kefauver (D. Tenn.) developed pressure for legislation imposing more severe regulations on the sale of drugs. And the Senate rackets subcommittee hearings into the activities of the Teamsters and other unions spurred public interest and demand for what later became the Landrum-Griffin Act to regulate the internal operations of labor unions.

Congress is thus more than an object of public opinion. Its relation to the electorate is reciprocal. Influenced by the voters, it is also constantly engaged in stimulating public interest in current issues and in influencing public thinking.

Resolving Conflict and Consensus Building

Politics invariably involves conflicts of varying intensity. Conflict is the dynamo of politics; yet though indispensable, it can destroy a political system when passions are too intense or when ideological positions are inflexible. An institution for *conflict reso-*

[13] Huitt, "Congressional Organization," p. 494.

lution and *consensus building* is required. Congress is such an institution. Congress must do more than make decisions of staggering proportions; its decisions must be so made that in the process the political system is not torn apart. A political system, then, cannot be judged solely on the basis of the speed with which it deals with matters of public concern; there is also the question of how well the system is maintained in the process. It is simple to condemn the 1964 Senate for being occupied for eighty-seven days with a filibuster against the Civil Rights Bill. (The Administration is less often condemned for taking two years to draft and send to Congress a comprehensive civil-rights bill.)[14] But such criticism ignores the fact that the resulting bill had the overwhelming support of Democrats and Republicans, along with a scattering of southern and border state representatives. Though at first there seemed to be no agreement on the need for certain provisions, such as a ban on discrimination in places of public accommodation, by the end of the deliberations the divergent factions agreed that such a ban was indeed necessary. This bill, like most that emerge from the tortuous legislative halls, was too weak for some and too strong for others. But it did represent a broad area of agreement on probably the most controversial domestic issue of our time. The conflict had been blunted; a temporary consensus had been reached.

Congress is well adapted to serve the conflict resolution and consensus-building function, because it is an arena of decentralized power in which each participant has some means of influencing the outcome of its deliberations. Since, in a democratic system, political parties cannot impose rigid discipline on their members, Congress' decisions are normally the result of extensive bargaining and compromise, as the various congressional leaders —committee chairmen, party leaders, subject-matter experts, state delegation leaders, bloc leaders—negotiate the products of the legislative process. The results may not be entirely satisfactory to all in any given situation, but they are usually sufficient to mitigate conflict until the issue can again be raised in any or all three branches of the government. For legislative enactments are seldom clear-cut or final resolutions of important issues. Rather, they are

---

[14] See Ralph K. Huitt, "Congressional Reorganization: The Next Chapter" (a paper prepared for presentation at the annual meeting of the American Political Science Association, Chicago, September 8-12, 1964), p. 3.

the verbal formulas that "a majority of congressmen find adequate as a basis for their continuing policy struggle." [15] A new law reflects a different balance of forces and provides the ground rules under which the political struggle will continue. But the losing side is seldom so weak that it cannot gain certain concessions, and it seldom has to accept a decision of Congress as inviolate and unalterable. For example, in 1961 House Appropriations Committee Chairman Clarence Cannon did not accept "back-door financing" for the Depressed Areas Act. Though he lost on this issue when the bill was originally before the House, he was ultimately successful through a later appropriations bill in eliminating "back-door financing" (see Chapter 6).

Overseeing the Administration

Long before the rise of the modern "service state," John Stuart Mill expressed reservations about the capacity of legislative assemblies to legislate. He nonetheless believed that these deliberative bodies had an essential contribution to make to the protection of liberty. In 1878 he wrote:

> The proper office of a representative assembly is to watch and control the government; to throw the light of publicity on its acts; to compel a full exposition and justification of all of them which any one considers questionable; to censor them if found condemnable, and if the men who compose the government abuse their trust, or fulfill it in a manner which conflicts with the deliberative sense of the nation, to expel them from office. . . . This is surely ample power, and security enough for the liberty of the nation.[16]

The function to which Mill was referring is commonly called *legislative oversight of administration*. It is a legislative function that most observers believe has taken on renewed significance with the rise of the "service state" and the executive's assumption of wide discretionary powers to make policy within the framework of broad congressional mandates contained in the statutes. Some

[15] Raymond A. Bauer, Ithiel de Sola Pool, and Lewis Anthony Dexter, *American Business and Public Policy: The Politics of Foreign Trade* (New York: Atherton Press, 1963), p. 426.
[16] On *Representative Government* (London: Longmans, Green, Reader, and Dyer, 1878), p. 42.

believe that oversight is now and will continue to be the principal function of Congress so long as mammoth administrative establishments are required. Congress itself formally recognized the significance of oversight by placing a provision in the Legislative Reorganization Act of 1946 that directs each of the standing committees of Congress to exercise "continuous watchfulness" over the agencies under their jurisdiction. This section of the law reflects a fear in Congress that this century's changes in legislative-executive relations have resulted in presidential encroachment on congressional power. Conscientious attention to the oversight function, it was thought, might at least halt the diminution of congressional power.

Though important decisions are increasingly being made by federal administrators rather than by Congress, these decisions are no less political in character. Only the locus for the decisions has changed. Congressmen and senators retain therefore a concern for the administration of laws; it is good politics to know how the administrators are treating interests and constituents. As Roland Young has written:

> Any congressman ignores at his own peril the manner in which the government administers, or who administers it, or the costs involved, for there is, in fact, a close interrelationship between the manner in which the government operates (especially in certain sensitive politically volatile areas) and the election of members to office.[17]

The power of Congress to control administrative acts rests ultimately on its authority to pass laws affecting an agency: granting an agency the right to exist at all or to perform given functions; prohibiting certain agency actions; arranging the administrative structure of the agency; and granting or withholding funds. These powers augment other and less formal techniques, such as committee hearings and investigations, instructions or criticisms in committee reports or floor statements, committee clearance of administrative acts, and informal communications between congressional and agency personnel. The existence of such formal and informal methods of influence forces administrators to develop a sensitivity to congressional thinking and to try to make their decisions as palatable as possible to those members of Congress

[17] *The American Congress* (New York: Harper and Bros., 1958), pp. 164-165.

interested in agency programs. Congress has become a "court of appeals" in which persons and interests adversely affected by administrative decisions seek redress for their grievances with the bureaucracy.

The standing committees constitute the principal agents for performing the oversight function. There is, however, considerable variability from committee to committee in their aggressiveness as overseers. Some, like the Joint Atomic Energy Committee, are extremely active and powerful.[18] Others, such as the Senate Banking and Currency Committee, described in Chapter 5, are more passive toward oversight.

THE NEED TO UNDERSTAND CONGRESS

There is good cause for being concerned about the operation of Congress. Congress has a profound influence on public policy and performs functions essential to a stable democratic order. Congress' future is also the nation's future. Concern for it is widely evident in the apparent readiness of scholars, politicians, and commentators to prescribe congressional reforms for how Congress should act. The views of the reformers and the prospects for congressional reform are analyzed in Chapter 8, "Congress and the Years Ahead."

But if there is a surfeit of reform proposals, there is also a dearth of models telling how a legislature should operate when all its manifold functions and parts are taken into account. Perhaps even more important is the absence of a model for describing how legislatures *do operate*. Without knowledge about an institution that goes beyond the superficial exposition of conventional wisdom, there can be little meaningful reform.

In the past, failures to understand adequately the congressional context have resulted in reforms having unintended consequences. For example, the reduction of the number of congressional committees and the clearer statement of their jurisdictions in the Legislative Reorganization Act of 1946 was intended to make the system more efficient and to reduce jurisdictional conflicts between committees over control of particular bills. Jurisdictional conflicts were indeed reduced, but an unintended conse-

[18] Harold P. Green and Alan Rosenthal, *Government and the Atom: The Integration of Powers* (New York: Atherton Press, 1963).

quence of the change was to further decentralize the leadership structure by reducing the discretionary powers of the presiding officer in each chamber to assign bills to those committees in which they would get the kind of treatment he sought. Consolidation of standing committees also resulted in a proliferation of subcommittees. This was a response to certain basic needs of the legislators: 1) specialization in committee deliberations, and 2) additional power centers where members might pursue their legislative goals.

To be practicable, reforms must be adaptable to various aspects of the congressional environment. They must help the institution and its participants meet their needs. It makes little sense, for example, to propose reforms taken from British parliamentary practice if the American political system lacks the prerequisites to make them work—such as a parliamentary form of government rather than a presidential form, or a disciplined and responsible party system rather than a decentralized party system. Therefore adequate knowledge of the institution is a prerequisite to reform.

Elections: The Threat to Tenure

The ultimate basis of a congressman's or senator's power is his ability to satisfy his constituents at election time. The nature of the process of recruiting, nominating, and electing candidates for Congress obviously has a profound effect on the behavior of legislators. The tendency of the Senate to be more liberal than the House on most issues (civil-rights legislation is an important exception), for example, can be explained in large part by the differing constituencies and electoral problems faced by congressmen and senators. Senators represent whole states, most of which contain at least one major urban center. They must therefore be concerned with urban interests, particularly the activist minorities—labor unions, racial minorities, religious-ethnic groups—that can have a crucial bearing on elections. No senator from a large state, for example, dares appear anti-labor or anti-civil rights if he wants to survive. Coming from smaller and more homogeneous constituencies, a much larger percentage of representatives can be expected to be more conservative than of senators.[19] This is only

[19] See Lewis A. Froman, Jr., *Congressmen and Their Constituencies* (Chicago: Rand McNally, 1963), pp. 69-84.

one more example of how the intentions of the Founding Fathers, who expected the Senate to act as a conservative check on the popularly elected House, have been reversed by the political forces of the twentieth century.

The electoral process also contributes to one of Congress' most salient characteristics—its decentralized power structure. The campaigns of Senator Abraham Ribicoff and Representative Clark MacGregor discussed in Chapter 2 illustrate the loosely structured nature of the party system. Upon each was thrust the major responsibility for acquiring and utilizing the resources necessary for victory at the polls. MacGregor, running in Minnesota where political parties are loosely organized, developed a highly personal campaign organization. Ribicoff, on the other hand, could rely more heavily on the tightly knit Democratic organization led by State and National Democratic Chairman John Bailey. Like most congressional candidates, both MacGregor and Ribicoff conducted campaigns of a highly localized character that reflected the personal backgrounds and legislative interests of the candidates.

The decentralized nature of the American party system is nowhere more apparent than in nominations for Congress in which the national party plays virtually no role. Rather, as V. O. Key has pointed out, each state and congressional district "exercises complete autonomy in the designation of nominees for Senate and House." [20] With the national party's inability to coordinate nominations and select like-minded persons to run under the party's banner, much of the potential for unified and disciplined party organizations within the national legislature is lost. There are few places where state or local party organizations are so strong that they can cast their mantle upon a man and convert him into the party's nominee. The usual pattern of congressional nominations, therefore, is for the candidate to build a highly personal organization and base of support—one that can sustain him through times when his party is in disfavor with the voters or when the party organization leaders may oppose him.

Not only the party system, but also the present legal system of making nominations—the direct primary, which is used in all but a handful of states—works against centralized control of the

[20] V. O. Key, *Politics, Parties, and Pressure Groups*, 5th ed. (New York: Thomas Y. Crowell, 1964), p. 435.

selection process. Evolved in the early years of this century as a reaction against the machinations of party conventions and legislative caucuses in making nominations, the primary was intended to permit more citizen participation in party affairs and to provide a meaningful popular-election contest in those areas where one-party domination had rendered the general election a formality.

The effects of the system, however, have diverged from the reformers' hopes. Participation is lower at the primary than at the general election stage. Moreover, factional lines within the majority party are often highly fluid from year to year. This has meant that incumbents can usually expect to win renomination. Further, the primary has often tended to diminish competition between the parties, as voters and party workers are channeled into the majority party, where the major electoral battles take place. The primary nomination procedure has also weakened party organizations by making it more difficult for them to control and influence nominations. The dependence of the representative or senator on the party organization for political survival has thus been reduced. Representatives and senators with strong personal followings have been able to flout state or local organizations by defeating organization candidates in the primary. The winners then force the organization to accept them as bona fide party candidates in the general elections. The Tammany Hall organization of New York, for example, failed miserably in its attempt to purge Democratic Congressman Adam Clayton Powell because of his support of President Eisenhower, a Republican, in 1956. Similarly unsuccessful were the attempts of the Wisconsin Republicans to drop Senator Alexander Wiley from the ticket in 1956, and those of the Kansas City Democrats in 1964 to oust Congressman Richard Bolling.

The decentralizing impact of the nominating process is partially offset, however, by the centralizing tendencies of the general election. Here, traditional party affiliations, national issues, and, in presidential years, the presidential ticket, can exert a powerful influence on the fate of congressional candidates who may be hurt or helped by grasping the coattails of their party's presidential ticket or by national swings in voter sentiment. For example, one of the foremost problems of Congressman MacGregor in his 1964 bid for re-election was how to handle his relationship with the Republican presidential ticket of Goldwater and Miller (see Chapter 2).

National trends are most important in Senate races, since party competition has become increasingly intense at the state level, and in some highly competitive congressional districts.[21] Most House seats are, however, safe for one party or the other. Indeed, there has been a trend in this century for fewer and fewer House districts to be truly competitive between the two parties. Relatively few seats are apt to change hands even when a party's presidential nominee wins by landslide proportions. Thus, in Lyndon Johnson's sweep of the presidential election in 1964 by the widest margin in this century, the Democrats registered a net gain of only 38 (8.7 percent) of 435 House seats.[22]

In spite of the strong pull of national trends, candidates may be able to fight the current and stay politically viable by building a strong personal following or perhaps by disassociating themselves from their national party. For example, in 1960, though John F. Kennedy carried his native Massachusetts by 60.4 percent of the vote, Republican Senator Leverett Saltonstall was able to withstand the trend. Perhaps even more impressive were the 1964 victories of Republican Senators Hiram Fong and Hugh Scott in Hawaii and Pennsylvania, where President Johnson received 78.7 and 64.9 percent, respectively, of the vote.

Given the importance of satisfactory constituency relations, it is small wonder that legislators are forced to spend vast amounts of time, money, energy, and staff resources on the "care and feeding" of their states or districts. The activities of Congressman Albert Quie of Minnesota and Senator Mike Monroney of Oklahoma, discussed in Chapter 3, and the campaign of Congressman Clark MacGregor (Chapter 2) show that a legislator's mind is seldom far from those who elected him. For the incumbent legislator, the campaign actually never ends.

No two members of Congress face the same electoral problems. Quie and Monroney, for example, have reasonably safe districts where party organizations are weak; others, such as Senator Abraham Ribicoff and Congressman Clark MacGregor, operate in more competitive environments and in Ribicoff's case within the framework of cohesive and well-organized parties (Chapter 2).

[21] H. Douglas Price, "The Electoral Arena," in *The Congress and America's Future*, p. 40.
[22] The effects of the Democratic gains in the 1964 elections are analyzed in detail in Chapter 5.

The very uniqueness of electoral situations within the various states, and the lack of cohesive and disciplined national party organizations to control candidate recruitment and nomination, mean that the leadership of Congress must be loose, because the leadership cannot control a member's job security. The harsh truth of congressional politics is that if a member is rejected by his constituency he cannot, in our system, be given another and safer district in which to run.

The Party in Congress

While the decentralized American party system thus produces legislators who are basically "ambassadors" from their respective districts and states, the congressional party should never be viewed as insignificant or impotent. By virtue of its being the most inclusive group within either chamber, it operates as the major unifying force within Congress. When a party controls the White House, its congressional contingent has a special focus and unity, as is shown by the discussion of the heavily Democratic Eighty-ninth Congress in Chapter 4.

Party membership is for members of Congress a source of personal identity and a matter of emotional attachment and loyalty. Furthermore, the party supplies each member with things he cannot do without—including all-important committee assignments (see Chapter 4), leadership positions, office space, cues on how to vote, reliable political information, campaign assistance, and friendship associations within the chamber. Formal positions of leadership in the party hierarchy in Congress are considered of sufficient importance and power that men will risk a great deal in terms of their standing with their colleagues to gain such positions. This is shown in the struggle for positions of strength among House Republicans in 1963-1965, described in Chapter 4.

Objective proof of the importance of party in congressional decision-making has been demonstrated by studies of roll-call votes in each chamber. These studies show that while each party is torn by internal disagreements, there is a sharp difference between the parties on major issues of public policy.[23] Put more plainly,

---

[23] Julius Turner, *Party and Constituency: Pressures on Congress* (Baltimore: Johns Hopkins University Press, 1951); David B. Truman, *The Congressional Party: A Case Study* (New York: John Wiley, 1959).

on issues usually classified as indices of liberalism or conservatism, the Republicans are clearly more conservative and less liberal than the Democrats. One test of liberalism or conservatism is the extent to which members of Congress support an expanded role for the federal government in domestic affairs. *Congressional Quarterly's* analysis showed the following differences between the Democrats and Republicans in 1964.[24]

TABLE 1   PARTY DIFFERENCES IN 1964

For a larger federal role	Democrats (percent)	Republicans (percent)
Both chambers	70	33
Senate	74	43
House	69	32

Table 1 suggests that neither of the parties is ideologically monolithic. Leading the heterogeneous groupings that make up both congressional parties is an extremely delicate task, as the complaints about Democratic and Republican leadership in the 1960s (Chapter 4) indicate. The problems of leading congressional parties are highlighted in this chapter by the difficulties of Congressman Gerald Ford, the Republican Minority Leader of the House, and the plight of Democratic liberals in the House during much of the previous decade.

Whatever the obstacles may be, the job of party leadership in Congress is to try to hold divergent party elements together and to create a majority on each issue. This often requires picking up votes from the other side of the center aisle that divides the parties. In building majorities, the party leaders have few sanctions available to them. There is no lash to crack over the heads of recalcitrant members who know that the basis of their position as congressmen or senators is satisfying their districts. The leader must bargain with his colleagues and rely on his powers of persuasion, a sense of party loyalty among his troops, his superior sources of information regarding congressional business, and the few favors he can distribute—help in securing favorable committee assignments, assistance in scheduling an important bill for debate, or public recognition for worthwhile service in the Congress. That party leaders lack vast formal powers was made clear by the late

[24] *Congressional Quarterly Weekly Report*, XXII (October 23, 1964), p. 2549.

Speaker Sam Rayburn, when he remarked: "You cannot lead people by trying to drive them. Persuasion and reason are the only ways to lead them. In that way, the Speaker has influence and power in the House." [25] But the Speaker is in a position to hinder or advance the careers of his colleagues through the favors he can bestow upon them. "Mr. Sam" therefore was fond of reminding the junior members of his party that "you have to go along to get along."

Robert Dahl has called the congressional party a "loose alliance of individual congressmen.[26] In similar fashion, David B. Truman has characterized the legislative party as a "mediate group": that is, from the viewpoint of its members it does some things of importance for them; and though its failures are of consequence to them, the retention of their status as members of Congress does not completely depend upon it.[27]

The Committee System

The work load of the Congress is enormous. Over 14,000 measures are introduced in a year. Many of these involve problems of great complexity. Congress has found it necessary to delegate a substantial portion of its responsibilities to smaller units: its standing committees. These committees sort out the bills worthy of serious consideration, a small fraction of which are reported out for final consideration on the floor of the House or Senate. In large part, the content of congressional decisions is shaped in its committees. Such vast powers have made the committees strategic points of influence in the legislative struggle. A corollary result has been that they have become specialized and semiautonomous power centers, further fragmenting power within each chamber. The power of committees and their leaders over the fate of legislation under their jurisdiction has meant that it is frequently necessary for party leaders to try to reach an accommodation with the individual committee leaders.

How a committee functions depends in large part upon who its chairman is and how he chooses to use the prerogatives

[25] *The New York Times*, November 17, 1961, p. 28.
[26] Robert A. Dahl, *Congress and Foreign Policy* (New York: Harcourt, Brace, 1950), p. 51.
[27] *The Congressional Party*, pp. 95-96.

of his office. These prerogatives include the power to call meetings, set the agenda for meetings that are called, appoint committee staff, control the expenditure of committee funds, create subcommittees and appoint their members, control appointments to joint House-Senate conference committees, and formally report bills approved by the committee. These powers must be used within the confines of what a committee majority will tolerate, because ultimately every chairman's power rests upon the support of his committee. The styles of committee leadership analyzed in Chapter 5 clearly show the reciprocal relationship that exists between a chairman and his committee colleagues. The powers of a chairman are sufficiently extensive, however, as to make committee members reluctant to alienate their chairman lest he withhold favors and help from them. The liberal Democratic members of the Senate Banking and Currency Committee, for example, have been reluctant to move against their conservative chairman, Senator A. Willis Robertson of Virginia (see Chapter 5).

The different styles of committee leadership exhibited by the Senate Banking and Currency Committee's two most recent chairmen provide impressive evidence of how a committee chairman can affect the operations of his committee. If he so chooses, a chairman can make his committee an aggressive and active unit in the development of legislation and in legislative oversight of administration; or, he can use his powers as a restraint on his committee and prevent it from acting. The range of possible committee behavior patterns is suggested through the analysis of a Senate committee in Chapter 5.

This specialized and decentralized committee system is well adapted to the needs of the relatively independent politicians. These might be called "free enterprisers," or "political entrepreneurs," since each is engaged in operating a political enterprise for whose prosperity he is primarily responsible. A member with special competence or interest in a certain policy area is allowed to concentrate on this area through membership on the appropriate committee—that is, assuming he manages to get assigned to the committee he desires.[28] Serving on a committee dealing with the interests of the people who elected him is one way for a congressman to help solve the constituency problem. Further, the com-

[28] The politics of committee assignments is discussed in Chapter 4.

mittee system with its many chairmanships, subcommittees, and subcommittee chairmanships gives a substantial number of members an opportunity to gain prestige, publicity, experience, and influence within Congress.

Because the committees can provide these services to the individual member, and because of their pervasive influence on governmental policy, the standing committees of Congress are arenas of intense conflict. Committee rooms are battlegrounds in which propaganda can be generated, substantive and political information gathered, decisions made or postponed, and conflicts resolved. A committee can also perform a cathartic function by allowing various and competing groups to express their views and feelings in a forum that conforms to the expectations of people nurtured on democratic values.[29] The committee can also be used as a device to control administrative agencies as they carry out the laws of Congress. How well a committee performs any of these functions is dependent on a variety of factors: the chairman and his style of leadership, the subcommittee organization, the nature of the membership, the way the members view their job on the committee, the subject matter before the committee, the committee staff, and unwritten norms of committee behavior. The interplay of these factors is discussed in Chapter 5, which deals with the politics of the Senate Committee on Banking and Currency.

The Job of a Member

Membership in Congress is no sinecure. The representative or senator must vote on a series of complex issues of consequence for the nation and the world. Seldom are the alternatives before him clear in their implications. (Note, for example, in Chapter 3, the complex and ambiguous manner in which the Philippine war-claims issue came before the House of Representatives.) Seldom does the legislator consider that the information with which he must make his decisions is fully satisfactory. Yet decide he must, and often in the face of conflicting demands from party, interest groups, constituency, and colleagues. In addition, he must attend to the business of his committee or committees; serve his constituents (answer torrents of letters which may run as high as

[29] Truman, *The Governmental Process*, pp. 369-377.

1000 per day for a senator from a large state, return to the district regularly, meet visitors to the Capital and act as their personal travel agent and guide); handle satisfactorily his relations with party leaders, pressure groups, constituents, colleagues, and reporters; and properly discharge such personal responsibilities as those to his family. These aspects of congressional life are seen in the detailed portraits of Congressman Quie and Senator Monroney in Chapter 3.

In spite of demands upon him, a member of Congress belongs to a "free profession": that is, he makes his own work schedule, defines the content of his job, and sets its standards of achievement.[30] Depending on the individual's objectives and styles, there are many different ways of being a congressman or senator. Some, for example, choose to concentrate their activities on providing prompt and efficient service to the needs of their constituents and on acting as agents of local and state interests; others choose to emphasize the planning and developing of legislation in committee, like Quie; still others specialize in legislative tactics in the well-known fashion of Lyndon Johnson or Everett Dirksen. Some, like Senator Paul Douglas, engage in educating external publics through various forums; some build and maintain powerful state or local political organizations (for example, the Virginia political dynasty of the late Senator Harry Flood Byrd, Sr.); and others are interested in personal aggrandizement and publicity.[31] In other words, each member chooses the kind of job he wants to do or the kind of legislator he wants to be. Made up as it is of persons elected from separate and quite autonomous electoral districts, Congress is very tolerant in that it permits a wide range of interpretations of the legislator's role. There is no one "right" way of being a representative or senator, though there are limits even in this highly permissive environment. For example, the Senate publicly condemned the late Senator Joseph McCarthy (R. Wis.) for behavior unbecoming a senator. Other "deviants" may be ignored or discriminated against in more subtle ways. But such instances are rare.

The member of Congress is forced to be highly selective about what he chooses to do because he lacks the resources to do all the things normally associated with his office. The resources

[30] Bauer, et al. *American Business and Public Policy*, p. 409.
[31] Bauer, et al. *American Business and Public Policy*, pp. 409-410.

of a member include time, energy, staff assistance, information, good will. All these are in short supply. Hence they must be used selectively where they will do the most good—that is, in helping the member maximize his individual objectives from the legislative process. One of the most important decisions any congressman therefore makes is that of how and where he will use his scarce resources of influence. Senator Monroney, for example, who is discussed in Chapter 3, has chosen to devote much of his attention to civil aviation matters and problems of water scarcity in his native Oklahoma. Representative Quie has been an active minority party leader in the field of education policy.

To gain any objective a congressman must depend on the assistance or at least the acquiescence of other members who are equally busy. What develops, therefore, within Congress is a complex set of relationships that requires a great deal of bargaining, cooperation, compromise, and self-restraint if any member is to achieve even a portion of his objectives from the system.

The environment is one of considerable strain for the individual member. There is the uncertainty of tenure and the constant threat of having to take up a new occupation or of having to return to a long-neglected one. This problem of tenure is made more difficult by the ambiguous relationship a member has with his party—one that makes demands upon him and to which he has an emotional commitment, but that cannot guarantee his tenure in office. There are also the conflicting pressures imposed on him by a constituency that does hold the key to job security, but whose sentiments he cannot comprehend fully no matter how much energy he expends.[32] He has to bear also the strains of the great work load and the continuous burden of performing errands for his district while slighting weighty legislative issues.

The pressures of politics are further intensified because Washington is essentially a political city. Not only its values and standards of success, but also the personalities with whom a legislator comes in contact, are political in nature. There is no reprieve from the demands of the job. Even a social event is not without its political overtones, since the congressman is usually in the company of other legislators, or of administrators, lobbyists, or reporters. Such pressures might be eased somewhat if the congressman thought that his was a profession revered and respected in

[32] Bauer, et al. *American Business and Public Policy*, pp. 403-413.

American society, but unfortunately many do not think that this is the case. Rather, the congressman sees himself criticized and even ridiculed by persons who, he feels, do not understand his problems or his accomplishments. Even so, the satisfactions are also many: seeing a cause in which he believes enacted into law, helping people, using power, and participating in exciting and important events.

This neither justifies nor condemns present congressional practices, though the reader has no doubt accurately detected that the authors are basically friendly toward Congress. Rather, this discussion is designed to help toward understanding why Congress functions as it does. The following pages depict and analyze significant phases of congressional life—the campaign, the daily work load, floor activity, committee assignments and committee work, the impact of the formal rules of procedure, intraparty activity, the shaping of legislation, oversight of administration, and the role of the Administration. These aspects of congressional life are presented through discussions of recent and specific events in the lives of congressmen.

CAMPAIGNS AND ELECTIONS: TWO CASES 2

ABRAHAM RIBICOFF OF CONNECTICUT, 1962

Campaigns are the most intriguing public attractions in America's "great game of politics." There are many ways of viewing the game. For the journalist, the campaign is an immediate electoral contest—a clash of personalities, interests, and issues that periodically exposes the sinews of the body politic. Beyond the obvious drama of the political campaign, however, is the vital function it serves in presenting voters with simplified choices through which they may register their current preferences. Campaigns may also be seen as basic or intervening variables in determining the electorate's voting behavior. Or, more importantly from the viewpoint of legislative institutions, one might speculate on the effects that the campaigning process has on the legislator's subsequent perceptions of himself, his constituency, and his legislative roles and tasks. In short, if campaigning is a major part of the legislator's world, it is bound to condition his behavior.

As a case in point, the election of Connecticut's Abraham Ribicoff to the United States Senate in 1962 is of unusual interest. As a former Governor and Cabinet member (Secretary of Health, Education, and Welfare), Ribicoff was a figure of national prominence when he returned to Connecticut to seek the Senate seat then held by Prescott Bush, a middle-of-the-road Republican first elected in 1952. Along with Edward M. Kennedy, the President's brother, who won a landslide victory in neighboring Massachusetts, Ribicoff was one of a handful of candidates favored with nation-wide press coverage during the 1962 campaigns. Yet Ribicoff's victory was surprisingly narrow. Although many careful observers had written off his election as a sure thing, the Republican challenger—an aggressive campaigner with a penchant for distributing thousands of pot holders emblazoned with his name—came within a bare 26,000 votes of victory. The freewheeling competitive politics of Connecticut precipitated the contest, and the cohesive party organizations provided the machinery for the campaign.[1]

The Ribicoff campaign will be described and analyzed with an eye to the larger politically relevant questions surrounding the phenomenon of the electoral campaign. We shall first examine the Connecticut party system, classifying it among the subspecies of American state parties. We shall then turn to the organization, strategies, and tactics of the campaign, noting that it divides itself roughly into two interrelated phases: the nomination (intraparty), and the election (interparty). Finally, we will attempt to interpret the campaign and the vote, examining them from the freshman senator's point of view, to determine what effect, if any, they may have had upon Ribicoff's subsequent behavior on Capitol Hill.

Connecticut: The Politics of Competition

By any conceivable measure, Connecticut politics of the past generation have been among the most closely competitive in the nation.[2] Both political parties are compelled to approach each election with fear and trembling, and state party organizations have traditionally, though not invariably, been tightly organized, internally cohesive, and marked by strong leadership. Following

[1] General information on Connecticut politics is found in Duane Lockard, *New England State Politics* (Princeton: Princeton University Press, 1959).
[2] Two instructive classifications are found in Austin Ranney and Wilmoore Kendall, *Democracy and the American Party System* (New York: Harcourt, 1956), p. 164; and Joseph A. Schlesinger, "A Two-Dimensional Scheme for Classifying the States According to the Degree of Inter-Party Competition," *American Political Science Review*, XLIX (December 1955), pp. 1120-1128.

the era of Republican dominance that ended in 1930, party for-
tunes have remained fairly evenly distributed (see Table 2).
There are several fundamental reasons for this party equilibrium.

TABLE 2   PARTY COMPETITION IN CONNECTICUT, 1930-1962

| | Election won by: | |
Office	Dem.	GOP
Presidential electoral vote	4	3
U.S. Senate elections	7	5
U.S. House elections	47	54
Total Federal Elections	58	62

As one student has observed, Connecticut is divided, like
Caesar's Gaul, into three parts: the larger cities, the rural small
towns, and the newer suburban areas. Although there is little
sectionalism in the state, the varying political characteristics shown
by these three demographic categories form the basis for fundamental cleavages and alliances. Of these, the "small" towns, which
include approximately two-thirds of Connecticut's 169 towns, tend
to display an "old Yankee" bias and are typically found in the
Republican column. The suburbanites of Fairfield County also
tend to vote Republican, as do voters in fringe areas of other metropolitan centers. These GOP majorities are typically offset by
Democratic voting in Hartford, New Haven, Bridgeport, and
Waterbury—the state's four largest cities. Of the twenty largest
cities in the state, in fact, only Norwalk and Stamford typically
vote Republican. Large labor groups and ethnic minorities in these
urban areas tend to be Democratic, though their influence is felt
in urban Republican organizations as well.

This delicate political balance has fostered cohesive party
organization, especially in the Democratic party. Tightly knit city
organizations, sometimes boss-dominated, enter the Democratic
convention with up to forty percent of the 953 delegates. Thus
power within the Democratic party is distributed among a handful of locally based individuals, such as John Bailey, the Democratic leader of Hartford who emerged as state chairman in 1946
and subsequently enhanced his influence until he is now the most
powerful Democrat in the state. In 1961 his base of operation was
broadened further when President Kennedy designated him chairman of the Democratic National Committee. Even though con-

siderable hostility to Bailey's leadership in Connecticut had accumulated by 1962 and threatened to erupt in the Ribicoff-Kowalski nomination contest, Bailey came out of the convention unscarred. The key to Bailey's power—and there has been no serious challenger for his job in two decades—is his ability to bargain for support among the various city bosses. Like Bailey, these men are more organization- than issue-oriented, and patronage plays a key role in their bargaining.

Party unity is further encouraged by the state's system of balloting, a factor often ignored by students of Connecticut politics. Voting machines are used throughout the state, and these machines are set up so that the voter must throw a party lever before making any individual choices. If he wishes to split his ballot, he must then search along the columns of individual levers and locate the column for the relevant office. Having found it, he must then lift the lever over the name of the first party's candidate (it was automatically thrown down when he pulled the party lever) and press down the lever over the name of the alternate candidate.

Another deterrent to ticket-splitting is the bell that rings as soon as the party lever has been thrown—ostensibly to assure the voter that his vote has been registered. But the voter who lingers in the booth after the bell sounds is assumed by the poll-watchers (or "hearers"?) to be splitting his ticket. When confronted by poll-watchers with such audible evidence of disloyalty, voters sometimes try to explain that they remained to vote the constitutional or local referenda questions after the bell sounded. To forestall the poll-watchers' suspicious glances, the practice among those who wish to be considered among the party faithful is to vote the questions first, then throw the party lever and exit quickly when the bell sounds.

Given the delicate balance between the parties, the party-lever device not only encourages party cohesion, but also greatly enhances the so-called "coattail effect." This consideration magnifies the importance of the top of the ticket—the presidential candidate or, in off-years, the senatorial or gubernatorial candidate (for example, Ribicoff in 1958). A popular presidential, gubernatorial, or senatorial candidate transmits his strength directly to the entire ticket. Since ticket-splitting is difficult, anonymous candidates are often swept along with the better-known ones. Thus the Eisenhower vote in 1956 swept six Republicans into Connecticut congressional seats; two years later the Democrats, behind Governor Ribicoff, recaptured all these seats, and in 1960 Kennedy helped retain four of these seats for the Democrats.[3] As the 1962 elections approached, party leaders again faced the problem of finding a popular ticket-leader.

Abe Ribicoff Re-Enters

Abraham Ribicoff's re-election as Governor in 1958 by a 246,368-vote margin established him as one of the most successful vote-getters in the state's history. The 1958 election capped a political career that had begun twenty years earlier, when Ribicoff was first elected to a two-year term in the Connecticut General Assembly. In 1941-1943 and 1945-1947 he served as judge of the police court in his native Hartford. He was elected to Congress from the First District in 1948 and again in 1950. In 1954 the party leadership turned to Ribicoff to challenge Republican Governor John Lodge, brother of Ambassador Henry Cabot Lodge, Jr., of Massachusetts. Former Governor Chester Bowles had indicated his eagerness to avenge his 1950 loss to Lodge, and was supported in this by labor groups; but by this time most party leaders were disillusioned with Bowles and were supporting Ribicoff, who had run well in an unsuccessful race (against Prescott Bush) for a vacant Senate seat in 1952. Their choice was vindicated, for Ribicoff won the governorship—though narrowly, with 50.2 percent of the vote.

During his six years as governor, Ribicoff gained a reputation for direct, efficient, and nonpartisan administration. For example, he abandoned the press-assistant-and-mimeograph approach of his predecessors and held personal conferences with reporters twice a day. If they raised a question he was unable to answer, he simply picked up the phone and called the state official in whose domain the problem lay, thus dramatizing his direct command over his administration. He abolished outmoded county government, eliminated more than two-score state agencies, modernized the lower court system, and put through a $350-million bond issue

[3] In 1964, with President Johnson and senior Senator Thomas J. Dodd leading the ticket, the Democrats again made a clean sweep of the congressional seats, wresting the Fourth District from the Republicans.

for highway construction and safety programs. His spectacular re-election in 1958 by a quarter of a million votes established his position as the state's most prominent political figure.

Along with State Chairman Bailey, Ribicoff was an early supporter of John F. Kennedy's presidential aspirations. The state delivered an impressive margin of some 92,000 votes for Kennedy, and both Bailey and Ribicoff were eventually called to service in the New Frontier.[4] When the President-elect gave Ribicoff his choice of posts, the press speculated that he would accept the first Supreme Court vacancy. As a lawyer Ribicoff toyed with this notion, but as an experienced politician who is primarily a po-litical animal he let the President know that he did not feel he would be happy on the Court. The matter was dropped, and the Supreme Court rumors that persisted after Ribicoff's appointment to the Cabinet were without foundation.

Ribicoff's resignation as governor, which took effect only after he left for Washington, seemed to remove him from the state political picture. For Lieutenant Governor John Dempsey, the move seemed to resolve the problem of succession to the governor-ship: having served the final two years of Ribicoff's term, he was assured of nomination in 1962 and as an incumbent would be in a strong position to win on his own. Incumbent Senator Prescott Bush, who had expected Ribicoff as an opponent in 1962, felt so confident that on December 30, 1960, he announced his candidacy for re-election. Meanwhile, the Democratic senatorial nomination was open to all comers.

Ribicoff, for his part, assumed that his resignation closed the door on his long-standing ambition to run for the Senate in 1962. He candidly discussed the alternatives with his advisors in late 1960, but decided he could not refuse the President's call to the New Frontier. Yet in spite of this interpretation of the alter-natives, Ribicoff was again seriously considering the Senate race by fall of 1961. Meanwhile, the *New York Times* reported confi-dently that Ribicoff would not enter the race. Noting that there

[4] Another conspicuous Kennedy supporter was Bowles, then congressman from Connecticut's Second District. Bowles made little secret of his desire to serve in the new Administration, and even resigned his congressional candidacy abruptly in August 1960 to work full-time for Kennedy. This move ap-parently took state Democrats by surprise and was said to be the source of some subsequent embarrassment for Kennedy, who appointed Bowles as Un-der-secretary of State.

had been some talk of his candidacy, it quoted Ribicoff as saying that "there's nothing to it," concluding that "certain Connecticut politicians can now breathe easier." [5]

The "certain politicians" included several well-known political figures. Former Senator William Benton, a close friend of Bailey and Senator Thomas J. Dodd, hired a public-relations man to keep his name before the public in preparation for a possible campaign. Others mentioned included Congressmen Frank Kowalski (at-large), John Monagan (Fifth District), and Emilio Daddario (First District). But the front-runner appeared at first to be Richard C. Lee, then serving his fourth term as mayor of New Haven. As the vigorous young mayor of a major city, Lee was in an enviable position to make the race. Though most party leaders refrained from making commitments, Democratic National Committeeman John Golden of New Haven endorsed Lee early in 1961. Lee's chances were considerably reduced, however, by his relatively poor showing in the fall mayoralty elections. He won re-election to a fifth term by less than 4000 votes, despite his past margins of up to 27,000 and his expected victory in 1961 by at least 10,000.

Meanwhile, Ribicoff reached a decision: he would run for the Senate in 1962. Because of the need for a strong vote-getter to head the ticket, state leaders from Governor Dempsey to local and town officers were urging him to enter the race. Particularly in view of Lee's poor showing, the Democrats were sorely in need of a candidate if they expected to unseat Bush. (Needless to say, the elected officials—knowing the state's party-line voting tendencies—were also worried about their own jobs.) Bailey agreed with this assessment and urged Ribicoff to run. President Kennedy was inclined to let Ribicoff decide for himself, though it was observed in Administration circles that Ribicoff was probably more needed in the Cabinet than in the Senate. Coupled with these pressures from the state was Ribicoff's increasing restlessness in Washington. As a politician whose entire career had been in elective office, he found the Cabinet somewhat confining and was impatient to be "his own man" again.

Ribicoff continued to deny publicly any interest in the race. Yet his statement on December 6 contained all the signposts of a

[5] The article again speculated that Ribicoff was interested in the Supreme Court. *New York Times*, November 6, 1961, p. 28.

candidacy: Though he did not plan to run, he said, the picture could change.

> You ask me the question today and the answer is "no." What the future holds, I just don't know, and after many years in politics, I know that the future is always hard to predict. . . . I have spoken to no one in Connecticut about it, or asked them to be for me.[6]

Later that month Ribicoff informed several key party leaders that he would run if he were nominated by the convention. Though he maintained his public silence, he found it necessary to indicate this decision because of the other possible candidates. Lee and Benton quickly withdrew; but Kowalski, the only announced contender, remained in the race, charging that Ribicoff was a "ghost candidate."

From Cabinet to Candidate

The decision had been made, but Ribicoff was not yet a candidate. Particularly in view of his resignation from the governorship barely a year before, relationships with party leaders and workers had to be handled carefully. The danger was not that he would lose the nomination, but that intraparty resentments might aid Kowalski sufficiently to force a potentially divisive primary. Under Connecticut law, any candidate receiving at least twenty percent of the vote in the party convention may demand a runoff primary. Fearing such contests, party leaders go to great lengths to reach a consensus on candidates before or during the convention. They have been so successful that there has been no statewide primary since the law went into effect in 1955.[7] Kowalski was thought to have a fair chance of gaining twenty percent of the convention vote, and he had indicated he would go all the way, if necessary, to capture the nomination.

Kowalski, who ran 3000 votes ahead of President Kennedy in 1960, was a two-term incumbent in Connecticut's at-large congressional seat. He apparently believed he had received Bailey's

---

[6] *New York Times*, December 7, 1961, p. 34.
[7] Minority candidates have been known to receive the requisite twenty percent of votes in the convention, however. In the 1958 contest for the Democratic senatorial nomination Chester Bowles elected not to challenge front-runner Thomas Dodd in a primary fight.

unofficial promise of neutrality in the Senate race, although in fact Bailey's encouragement had been of the routine "wait-and-see" variety. As it became increasingly apparent that Ribicoff was going to make the race with Bailey's blessing, Kowalski felt he had been betrayed. An enthusiastic if somewhat erratic campaigner, Kowalski had attracted support from two anti-Ribicoff factions. The Machinists Union felt that Ribicoff had been unsympathetic when, as governor, he intervened during a prolonged strike at United Aircraft's Pratt and Whitney plant in Hartford. The International Brotherhood of Teamsters, which contributed money but not undivided support, had more indirect reasons for opposing Ribicoff. Any member of the Kennedy Cabinet bore the stigma of the Attorney General's vendetta against Teamster boss Jimmy Hoffa. Moreover, though Ribicoff had a pro-labor record, Kowalski was considered a more militant friend of labor. The Congressman also obtained minor though vocal support from the "peace lobby."

Though still avoiding public acknowledgment of his candidacy, Ribicoff spoke to party leaders gathered for a Jefferson-Jackson Day dinner and observed with a broad smile that he would campaign vigorously in the state that fall. Kowalski, who was in the audience, immediately held a press conference and challenged Ribicoff to declare his intentions.

> The Democratic Party of Connecticut [Kowalski said] is being badly hurt by the tactic of playing footsie with something so important as this nomination. The situation is now so ridiculous that Ribicoff buttons are being sold, with the promise that the money will go elsewhere if he is not a candidate.[8]

Kowalski also exchanged sharp words with Bailey, urging him to remain absolutely neutral. To this the Chairman replied, in effect, that he would do what he thought best for the party.

Ribicoff and his advisors took two preliminary steps. In January Louis Harris was hired to conduct a public-opinion poll in the state, and the results seemed to indicate that Ribicoff could defeat Senator Bush handily. Unfortunately, the questions were designed to elicit the respondents' impressions of Ribicoff as an individual and a Cabinet officer, and not as a Senate candidate. Thus, though responses tended to be highly favorable, in light of

[8] *New York Times*, February 18, 1961, p. 50.

subsequent events they were extremely misleading. In addition to the poll, Ribicoff scheduled a series of informal meetings with state leaders during the spring weekends. Beyond that, he accepted every opportunity to appear in the state in order to reassure the party faithful that he was indeed a candidate.

On March 17 Ribicoff announced that he would be "highly honored" to run and indicated that he would resign immediately from the Cabinet if he received the nomination at the July 13-14 convention. Ten days later, a four-man "Ribicoff for Senate" committee was named, and offices were set up a block from the Democratic state headquarters in downtown Hartford. The chairman of the group was J. Walter Kennedy, mayor of Stamford, and the cochairman was Mrs. Helen Case Foster of Cornwall, a member of the state central committee and a highly respected *grande dame* of the party. The secretary was another state committeewoman, Mrs. Dorothy McCaffery of Washington, Connecticut. The treasurer was Archie R. Perry of Fairfield, a veteran of previous Ribicoff campaigns. These four, personally selected by Ribicoff, were to be responsible for contacting local Democratic leaders and convention delegates. Because none of the four was in Hartford, the day-by-day coordination of the office was handled by Herman Wolf, a Hartford public relations executive who had played a major role in Ribicoff's 1954 and 1958 gubernatorial campaigns. Formerly a special assistant to Ribicoff in the State House, Wolf was a long-time friend and one of his closest political advisors. Liaison with the candidate was provided by Jon Newman, Ribicoff's administrative assistant in Washington.

Bailey's organization bore the major responsibility for lining up delegates. Though Bailey remained outwardly neutral, the pressures described above for consensus behind a strong candidate meant that he and the other city bosses had to utilize their influence if they were to prevent the threatened state-wide primary. Though they doubted Kowalski's claim that he held the 190 votes (of a total of 953 delegates) necessary to force the primary, they were seriously concerned about this possibility.

From April through June, party organizations in each of the 169 towns met to select their delegates and endorse candidates; in some cases primaries were held to choose delegate slates. Major primaries were held on May 22 in New Britain and Waterbury, with a total of fifty-one votes at stake. In New Britain, the city party committee had named a delegate slate split eleven-eleven between the two senatorial contenders. Kowalski disavowed the organization slate and filed his own slate of twenty-two members, all pledged to him. By filing a petition containing the names of at least five percent of the city's 25,000 registered Democrats and paying a $15 filing fee for each delegate, Kowalski was able to force a primary. It should be noted that though New Britain was Ribicoff's birthplace, it has the largest Polish-American population in the state and boasts a large laboring group that Kowalski hoped to attract. In Waterbury, the organization-endorsed slate of twenty-nine was believed favorable to Ribicoff, and Kowalski challenged again with his own slate. Kowalski's bid failed, though he did capture New Britain's twenty-two delegates by a wide margin—a net gain of eleven for him. In Waterbury, however, the Ribicoff slate of twenty-nine won overwhelmingly. This left Kowalski with no more than 160 convention votes, considerably short of the necessary 190.

Ribicoff and his advisors refused to become complacent over these developments. Kowalski's victory in New Britain, home of both Ribicoff and Bailey, was of psychological significance, and the Congressman had showed impressive strength among minority voters. Furthermore, there remained the possibility that Kowalski, through a dramatic appeal to the convention, could dislodge latent anti-Bailey sentiment and gain enough votes to force a primary. Ribicoff's aides, however, shrewdly predicted that Kowalski might well destroy himself by going too far in his drive for the nomination. Ribicoff and his committee thus refrained from public comment and continued their quiet campaign of personal contact. To forestall extreme tactics at the convention, Bailey was persuaded to increase the corps of guards on duty at the convention hall.

Though Ribicoff had previously scorned gimmicks, his advisors decided that several should be used to advertise his candidacy at the convention. A donkey and cart were led up to the convention hall entrance, where they were flanked by several "Ribicoff girls." Eyeshades were distributed to protect the delegates' eyes from the glare of TV lights, and there were hundreds of blue and white Ribicoff pennants. On the second morning of the convention, pens with the candidate's name were also handed out. (Only after the convention did union leaders point out that the pens were made in Japan.) The light touch provided by these devices contrasted with the dour Kowalski campaign and, more important, showed Ribicoff as a "live" candidate who was earnestly seeking support.

Most important, however, was the decision to have Ribicoff resign from the Cabinet on Thursday, July 12, the day before the convention opened. Though in 1960 he had delayed resigning the governorship until he was ready to depart for Washington, it was decided that he should make his irrevocable move before the convention assembled in order to refute absolutely Kowalski's charge that he was a "ghost" candidate. The resignation received national headlines, and a TV address and radio interview taped on Thursday were broadcast throughout Connecticut that evening. The TV speech was designed to answer criticisms of his candidacy: "I have made a final and irrevocable decision," he declared, "to serve in the Senate if the people of Connecticut elect me." Though he had been "privileged to serve" in the Cabinet, he explained that he liked "the challenge of elective office."

> I am always willing to face the electorate with my record and views on the issues. I prefer a job that is directly responsible to you, the people of Connecticut. I think I can be of most use to you in the United States Senate. . . .
>
> And—let me confess to you quite frankly—I want to come home. My heart is in Connecticut. I miss frequent contact with my friends and with the people of our state.

In his reply to Ribicoff, the President gave the candidate a near-endorsement. "We need your voice and vote in the halls of Congress," he wrote, "and I congratulate the people of Connecticut for having the opportunity to send you there." Photocopies of the President's letter were circulated at the convention.

The convention opened in Hartford's convention hall on Friday evening, July 13. The first evening was given over to speechmaking, while the balloting took place on Saturday. When Senate Majority Leader Mike Mansfield praised Ribicoff in his keynote speech, his words were met with cheers intermingled with boos from Kowalski supporters, who later demonstrated and sought to obtain the stage. Events on Saturday proved, though, that these tactics had been poorly received by most of the delegates. Kowalski forces lost, by a vote of 762 to 176, on a preliminary move to prevent delegates from switching their votes during the balloting. Kowalski's advisors had feared that if their candidate obtained his twenty percent by a narrow margin, Bailey could force enough switches to snatch away the victory. On the actual balloting, however, Ribicoff won handily by a 786 to 163 margin—with Kowalski twenty-seven votes short of the needed 190. Although Bailey sought to have Kowalski renominated for his congressional seat, he was unable to meet Kowalski's demand that he be presented unopposed to the convention. The nomination finally went to another Polish-American, Bernard P. Grabowski of Berlin, who had been considered for the at-large seat in 1958.

The Republicans, too, were engaged in an intraparty battle for the nomination. After ten years in the Senate, Prescott Bush announced on the day following his sixty-seventh birthday that his health would not permit him to wage a state-wide contest for re-election. The early favorite in the race for the Republican nomination was John Lodge, a former governor and, during the Eisenhower Administration, Ambassador to Spain. Second District Congressman Horace Seely-Brown, a fruit farmer from Pomfret Center, also entered the race and, characteristically, waged an aggressive campaign in which he sought out every accessible delegate to the state party convention to ask for support. This direct-contact campaign paid off, for he won convention endorsement and the nomination in preference to Lodge, whose campaign had been more aloof.

The Campaign Trail

With Ribicoff's nomination, the informal organization that had already been established was augmented and meshed with the state campaign organization. The "Ribicoff for Senate" committee was transformed into a campaign organization. Though the same officers were retained, their actual roles were less comprehensive than they had been before the nomination. The campaign office was moved into the state headquarters one block away, where facilities were shared with the campaign staffs of Governor Dempsey and Hartford Congressman Emilio Daddario. Six Ribicoff staff aides were located in this office. Ribicoff's administrative assistant from Washington, Jon Newman, became his campaign director and was in charge of the office. A woman who had worked in the original campaign office now devoted full time to scheduling the candidate's engagements, and another woman handled most of the candidate's routine correspondence. In addition to a young man who was hired as a general research assistant, there were two secretaries.

As in all of Ribicoff's campaigns, there was little formal organization. Decisions on strategy and tactics were in the hands of an informal directorate of four men. The candidate himself made all the final decisions, especially when differences of opinion arose among his advisors. Newman as campaign director was in charge of coordination and certain day-to-day operations, such as issuing press releases. He was stationed in Hartford and rarely accompanied Ribicoff on his campaign swings. Herman Wolf contributed indispensable advice and expertise, especially in over-all strategy and the preparation of media materials. Finally, Wilbur Randall headed the advertising agency hired by the state party and its major candidates. Randall's office served as agent for the state party and for candidates Ribicoff and Dempsey in contracting radio and TV time, preparing advertisements, planning layouts, and handling the technical work relating to campaign literature and the mass media.

Coordination with the state party hierarchy was informal and flexible. There was little liaison on strategy or issues, apart from casual exchanges with Bailey. Fund-raising was also separate. A cooperative arrangement was worked out for billboard and bus-card advertising: one third each for Ribicoff, Dempsey, and the party ticket in general. Though party leaders considered it, there was no joint handling of radio and TV programs. Time for spot announcements, however, was purchased jointly by the Randall Agency, in order to obtain favorable rates. A woman in the party headquarters served as a "speakers' bureau" to coordinate appearances of the various candidates. Finally, all "election day money" —for poll watchers, rides for voters, and the like—was dispersed directly by the central committee to the town organizations.

Both parties received impressive outside assistance. Former President Truman opened the Democratic campaign at a $100-a-plate fund-raising dinner with an address in which he called for the election of Ribicoff and other party candidates. In mid-October former President Eisenhower endorsed the Republican ticket before 25,000 persons at an outdoor rally in Hartford. Two days later,

President Kennedy made a four-hour tour of the state, delivering three speeches. He repeatedly declared that he needed Ribicoff's vote in the Senate.

The AFL-CIO's Committee on Political Education (COPE) aided the Democratic cause largely through its voter-registration campaign. Union members also helped distribute Ribicoff literature, especially on commuter trains.

The centrifugal tendencies of the American party system are nowhere better illustrated than in campaign finances. Ribicoff's total campaign expenditures in 1962 were estimated at $230,000 —not an exorbitant sum by Senate campaign standards. Of this amount, approximately $15,000 was provided by the Democratic Senate Campaign Committee. Most of the remainder, which had to be raised by Ribicoff and four or five close associates, was solicited largely through personal contacts. Formal fund-raising activities featured two $100-a-plate campaign dinners. "Organizational money" (mainly from labor unions) added about $25,000 to the campaign, exclusive of what the unions did on their own. Ribicoff's close friends tried to impress the unions with their candidate's needs. Archibald Perry, the official treasurer for the Ribicoff organization, who naturally played an important role in contacting potential contributors, also kept the records of income and expenditures. The Connecticut Democratic organization did not contribute directly in campaign funds, though there was a co-operative arrangement for billboard advertising and radio-television scheduling.

According to the figures submitted by law to the Secretary of the United States Senate, Ribicoff *personally* spent $6701 in his campaign. The campaign-disclosure laws, however, require that expenditures be reported only when spent by the candidate himself or by campaign committees operating across state lines. The Ribicoff Campaign Committee, operating only within Connecticut, was not required to file a report.

Ribicoff's usual campaign technique was the "walking tour," interspersed with a few scheduled engagements. Accompanied only by his driver, Ribicoff would go to a town and begin walking up the main street, in and out of shops and stores, shaking hands and talking briefly with businessmen and customers. He also liked to tour factories and greet the workers. If the town was a large one, a whole day would be devoted to the tour; otherwise, several towns might be covered during a day. The driver carried with him a large black notebook filled with information concerning the local political cal scene—town Democratic leaders, city officials, and past voting records of the area. This information would then be relayed "on the run" to the candidate. At campaign headquarters, a volunteer worker plotted out the precise routes that were to be followed by the driver the next day.

The pattern was illustrated on July 26 when Ribicoff opened his campaign, as he traditionally does, in the northwest Connecticut town of Canaan. At 10 A.M. he began making the rounds, starting with a drug store at the town's main intersection. "I always start at that drug store," he told reporters; "I'm superstitious." Then he moved down the street, stopping at an assortment of stores. "Hello, I'm Abe Ribicoff," he would say as he greeted people and shook hands. There were no large gatherings, though the candidate ended his tour with a brief speech. On the stroll Ribicoff was accompanied by Joseph Foley, Canaan Democratic town chairman. This routine was repeated more than a hundred times before the campaign ended.

For the formal speeches, Ribicoff only once worked from a written text. In most cases, a press release containing "quotes" of a general nature was prepared in advance, primarily for the benefit of reporters. Just before a speech, Ribicoff would scan the release to remind himself to include the quotes. Needless to say, the candidate and his aides had agreed beforehand on the themes of these speeches.

Ribicoff and his advisers identified twenty-two campaign issues,[9] but the major themes were dictated to a surprising degree by Ribicoff's experience as Secretary of Health, Education, and Welfare. Education and medicare, along with the commuter problem, civil rights, and air and water pollution, became his most important speech topics. A compilation of Ribicoff's major speeches and statements, as indicated by press releases issued by his staff, shows the predominance of the education and medicare themes (see Table 3). In addition to the formal statements reflected in

[9] These included seventeen domestic and five foreign issues. Domestic: Republican platform; commuters; desegregation; education; Federal Chemical Council; Senate filibuster curbs; industry; medicare; mental health; medical quackery; small business; sports; tax cut; truth in lending; Veterans Affairs Commission; water pollution; women's rights. Foreign: Cuban crisis; foreign aid and trade; health for peace; school for peace; U.N. world food program.

Table 3, the candidate delivered from three to ten informal speeches every day. He touched on educational problems in virtually every speech, with medicare running second. Medicare was also thought to be an especially popular issue: it made superb speech material, and its popularity with labor would help heal

TABLE 3   THEMES OF MAJOR RIBICOFF SPEECHES

Education	10
Medicare	7
Industrial problems	2
Mental health	2
Cuban crisis	2
Foreign aid-trade	2
Desegregation	2
Miscellaneous	15
Total	42

scars left by the Kowalski affair. Union members distributed thousands of mock Social Security cards with Ribicoff's picture on one side and the word "Medicare" stamped on the reverse.

Two special appeals are worthy of mention. An eleven-page compilation of Ribicoff's record on civil rights was sent out to about fifty Negro leaders, and 10,000 copies of a printed clip sheet on the same subject were run off and distributed. On September 25 Ribicoff delivered a major campaign address on civil rights for an NAACP Freedom Fund Dinner in New Haven. The previous day Ribicoff had made a bid for support from Fairfield County residents who commute daily to Manhattan. At a luncheon meeting of the Stamford Chamber of Commerce he proposed a six-point program for commuter service and urged that the Federal Government take a leading role in the mass transportation field. "I believe that getting to work and getting home again is just as important as getting to the moon," he declared. One morning later in the campaign a clever fold-out flier elaborating the proposals was placed on every seat in New Haven commuter trains.

One tactical decision was forced on the Ribicoff camp by the intrusion of the Cuban crisis in late September. Once President Kennedy had spoken to the nation, Ribicoff's advisers decided to cancel all radio and TV spot advertising for several days. Their reasoning was that people preoccupied with an international crisis were not interested in seeing plugs for senatorial candidates. Preceding the resumption of his advertising, on September 26 Ribicoff delivered a television statement pledging support for the President's action in dealing with the crisis.

Another important decision of a different kind was made early in the campaign when Ribicoff and his advisors decided to stage the first telethon in Connecticut history. The idea originated with some Ribicoff supporters in New York, who also outlined its format and furnished a producer. The first program, telecast in Hartford on September 18, served to set the tone for the entire campaign. An estimated 12,500 people tried to call the studio during the hour, and the program was talked about throughout the campaign. Ribicoff was so pleased with the results that he decided on a second telethon—this time broadcast in New Haven as well as in Hartford—to be held a week before the election. The format proved well-suited to the candidate, who is relaxed and informal. A bevy of telephone girls was stationed at a switchboard to take down questions. These were then placed on a table onstage, where they were sifted by two newsmen to avoid repetition and eliminate "crank" questions. Then the slips of paper were handed to television personality, Betty Furness, who asked Ribicoff the questions on camera.

Though the format was designed to produce an orderly, interesting program, only one question was in any sense "planted." After the first telethon an east Connecticut woman, who has a reputation for vocal right-wing sentiments, charged it was a fake and that this would be proved because her question would not be asked on the second program. This was an open challenge to the Ribicoff camp, and in the second show the telephone operators were instructed to relay the question immediately. The question came early in the program and was promptly answered.

A check of the questions received during the first telethon suggests the degree to which they were prompted by Ribicoff's identification with health, education, and welfare issues. Of the 364 questions the 16 operators were able to record, 62 dealt with medicare and 16 more with the American Medical Association's opposition to Ribicoff. Education was the subject of 54 questions. Ninety-eight questions concerned foreign affairs, and almost half of those were related to the Cuban problem.

The two telethons virtually blanketed the state and provided the keynote for Ribicoff's campaign. Ribicoff's aides believed that it provided a meaningful contrast to Seely-Brown, who was repeating the pot-holder campaign that had marked his previous bids for the House seat. It was conceded that the gimmick of distributing some 20,000 pot holders with the candidate's name served to draw attention to Seely-Brown, who was less well-known than Ribicoff. But once the gimmick had served its initial purpose as an attention-getting device, Ribicoff's advisers reasoned, Seely-Brown should have altered the pitch of his campaign so that he would receive exposure as a serious and experienced legislator acquainted with the issues. As it happened, Seely-Brown's campaign changed little from beginning to end, and he continued to be referred to unflatteringly as "the pot-holder" Senator.

Seely-Brown's basic problem was one of visibility. Despite twelve intermittent years of congressional service, he was not as familiar to Connecticut voters as Ribicoff. A poll taken in New Canaan late in October showed that many voters were unable to name any candidates for Governor or Senator. Of those who were able to name any of the candidates, that of Ribicoff seemed to come most readily. Even among those who said they were Republicans, many had difficulty identifying Seely-Brown. And a Ribicoff aide who followed Seely-Brown's campaign trail stopped at a Jewish home for the aged which had been on the candidate's itinerary. He asked a diminutive woman standing in the lobby if she had seen Mr. Seely-Brown. With a puzzled frown, the woman responded: "So, what's a Seely-Brown?" The woman's answer seemed to sum up that candidate's problem.

Ribicoff seemed headed for an easy victory. The confidence of his advisers, supported by the Harris poll of early 1962, was bolstered by the large crowds he attracted wherever he went. Reporters phoned in to say they had never before seen anything like it in the state. Not only were the people eager to see Ribicoff as a national celebrity, but they seemed relaxed and friendly as well.

Yet there remained a certain vague feeling of uneasiness in the Ribicoff camp, even though no one entertained the notion that their candidate was in serious trouble. "We just knew it wasn't going to be another 1958," one of them said. Had they had access to Republican surveys, Ribicoff's advisors would have had greater foundation for their uneasiness: one poll taken prior to Senator Bush's decision to retire had indicated that Bush could have defeated Ribicoff. As it was, rumblings were heard from some lower Democratic echelons because Ribicoff had resigned two jobs within as many years. But was this an isolated grievance, or did it represent a more widespread attitude? Pollster Harris was commissioned to take another reading early in the campaign, in August. Two areas were selected for study: Fairfield County and eastern Connecticut. The results showed Ribicoff doing very well in usually Republican Fairfield County, and the candidate subsequently spent much time in this area. (The strategy appeared effective, for Ribicoff lost the county by less than 1500 votes.) The poll was even more optimistic for eastern Connecticut, Seely-Brown's congressional district. (This proved totally erroneous, however, for Ribicoff lost every county in this region.) With such optimistic portents, Ribicoff and his managers were not seriously troubled. Ribicoff was expected to win by from 20,000 to 50,000 votes, and one Democratic leader privately put the figure as high as 90,000.

Nevertheless, registration figures as of August 31 showed that Democratic voters outnumbered Republicans, 402,932 to 376,617. This spread was not reassuring, since proportionately fewer Democrats go to the polls than Republicans. This phenomenon of American politics occurs because nonvoting is more frequent among persons at the lower social and economic levels, from whom the Democratic party draws a great deal of its support. What was perhaps more important, a plurality of Connecticut's voters—488,064—were not affiliated with either party. With such a delicately balanced political structure the race was still very much in doubt.

Election Day

The use of voting machines throughout Connecticut leaves little time for nervous waiting on election night, and by early evening it was apparent that Ribicoff had been selected by a narrow margin. The official tabulations showed that he had won 51.3 percent of the vote to Seely-Brown's 48.7 percent. The totals were 526,947 for Ribicoff, 500,461 for Seely-Brown. Meanwhile, Governor Dempsey had won re-election by an impressive 66,000 votes over Republican John Alsop. Democrats also captured five of the six congressional seats; only incumbent Abner Sibal won for the Republicans in Fairfield County.

Ribicoff's margin of victory came from the heavily Democratic mid-section of the state, Hartford and New Haven counties. Here he led his opponent by more than 47,000 votes. But Ribicoff's showing in Fairfield County, which includes many upper-class New York exurbanites, was actually more impressive. Traditionally a Republican bastion, it went for Seely-Brown by only 1489 votes. Dempsey also did well in the county, trailing his opponent by only 4500 votes; and political observers wondered how strongly Republicans could count on the area in the future. An influx of voters, mostly Democratic, into industrial Bridgeport gave the party better than a 15,000-vote plurality there. Also, many Republican voters in Fairfield County apparently split their ballots in favor of Ribicoff, whose intensive campaigning and record of "moderate" liberalism were perhaps influential.

Still, the 26,000-vote margin was a far cry from his phenomenal victory in 1958. Observers both in and out of the Ribicoff camp concluded that many voters believed that a candidate who had "walked out" on two jobs was presumptuous in asking them to elect him to a third. In addition, some Democrats may have resented Ribicoff's close association with Bailey and the latter's role in procuring Ribicoff's nomination. Some party observers believed that this made Ribicoff the target for the collective resentments of Bailey's sixteen-year regime. If this were true, it was even possible that Ribicoff helped Dempsey and the remainder of the Democratic ticket by absorbing these resentments. But in the absence of adequate survey data, these were largely matters of speculation.

With the exceptions already mentioned, the state's voting pattern was not greatly different from that of previous years. Ribicoff's margin came from Democratic strongholds in the large industrial areas, while the Republicans did well in the small towns and rural regions of northern and eastern Connecticut. The "neutralization" of Fairfield County was perhaps the most significant new development.

Conclusions

Our analysis of Senator Ribicoff's 1962 campaign illustrates many of the phenomena that mark the electoral process in a competitive two-party state. In the case of Connecticut, the organization of State Chairman John Bailey was a dominating force.

Equally important, however, was the delicate internal composition of this machinery and the subtle counterweights that Bailey's ascendancy had produced. Therefore, the relation of the candidate and his staff to this organizational constituency was crucial despite the over-all cohesiveness of the party. It is significant that Ribicoff's first fence-mending project after becoming senator was to renew his direct contacts with town party leaders. He began with an informal dinner meeting with fifteen local leaders in Plymouth, and he planned to schedule similar sessions in all the state senatorial districts. The success of Ribicoff's project will, of course, be tested in his bids for re-election.

The relation of the campaign to the legislator's total world is of special fascination to students of the legislative process. It has been seen that Ribicoff's previous career and political style determined many of the themes and techniques of his 1962 campaign. In view of his recent experience as Secretary of Health, Education, and Welfare, for example, it seemed only natural for him to stress education, medicare, and related issues during his visits around the state. Whether these were indeed popular issues could not be ascertained without extensive surveying, and in any event the question was probably irrelevant. Ribicoff was too closely associated with these issues, both personally and publicly, to permit any radical alteration of campaign strategy.

The continuity of Ribicoff's interests has been demonstrated in his activities in the Senate. He entered "the world's most exclusive club" as an expert on many issues related to his Cabinet career. After his election, then-Vice President Lyndon Johnson drew Ribicoff aside and advised: "You're not really a 'freshman' senator, Abe. Don't bother to act like one." Ribicoff responded by appropriating several issues from his Cabinet career as his own. In part because of his reputation and Senate contacts, he received a highly coveted spot on the Finance Committee in addition to an assignment to Government Operations. (His assignments were especially impressive in light of the complaints of Senator Clark and others that more senior "liberal" senators were unable to obtain seats on the Finance Committee. See Chapter 4.) Though a freshman senator, Ribicoff was named chairman of his own Government Operations subcommittee investigating water pollution.

Ribicoff's substantive commitments could have been predicted from his campaign themes—education, medicare, urban transportation, and child welfare. As a freshman, he was floor manager for the Mills-Ribicoff bill for maternal, child health, and mental retardation assistance (P.L. 88-156). This measure authorized $282.2 million in federal grants to states for planning programs in these welfare areas. Ribicoff became a major spokesman for medicare legislation, and in 1964 he offered compromise amendments to H.R. 11865 which were thought at the time to meet House Ways and Means Chairman Wilbur Mills' objections to medicare. He spoke for the Mass Transportation Act of 1964 (S. 6) during Senate floor debate. And Ribicoff became known as a champion of legislation dealing with air and water pollution. In speaking for the Clean Air Act of 1963 (P.L. 88-206), the Senator declared on November 19, 1963, that "The air we breathe is free, but when it is filled with filth, it is no bargain."

Ribicoff drew public attention particularly for his support of federal assistance to education. On May 20, 1963, he recommended a six-point program of limited aid to private schools—including tax deductions and aid for "shared time" facilities in local school districts—designed to avoid the religious controversy. With Senator Winston Prouty (R. Vt.), he urged Senate passage in October 1963 of the more liberal House version of the college facilities bill. (The Ribicoff-Prouty amendment to the Senate-passed version of the bill lost by a 33 to 49 vote.) He also pressed for an amendment to tax legislation which would provide a tax deduction for families shouldering expenses of college educations. The Administration rejected this proposal in favor of its own student loan plan. Ribicoff's amendment lost narrowly by a 45 to 48 roll-call vote in February 1964. Nor was this the only occasion when Ribicoff manifested his independence from the Kennedy and Johnson Administrations.

One issue Ribicoff subsequently adopted was not reflected in the campaign, although it was a part of his background. As governor, he was known for his vigorous highway safety program, and in 1965–1966 he became chief sponsor of the Traffic Safety Act.

In Ribicoff's case, then, the Senate campaign provided an important testing ground for the issues and themes that were to mark his early Senate career. The interplay of the candidate's campaign and his previous and subsequent careers is a pervasive phenomenon of political life, and one deserving further attention in the study of political campaigning.

CLARK MACGREGOR OF MINNESOTA, 1964

On July 6 of the Presidential election year 1964, Clark MacGregor filed his affidavit of candidacy for re-election in Minnesota's Third Congressional District. MacGregor, a tall, vigorous man in his early forties, made a brief statement to the press, stressing his experience as a two-term member of the House of Representatives. He touched on several issues familiar to him as a minority member of the House Judiciary Committee. Although the Republican National Convention was two weeks away, MacGregor told reporters that he was confident he could run on a ticket with any presidential candidate his party nominated. Nonetheless, he dismissed the possibility of a significant coattail effect ("Voters in the Third District are very discerning"), attempting to allay the reporters' feelings that President Lyndon Johnson's expected re-election would make it harder for Republican candidates everywhere.

The turbulent presidential campaign was a daily reality for those Republicans seeking to breast the anti-Goldwater tide in 1964. The influence of this larger contest on local candidates of both parties was a major distinguishing feature between this campaign and Senator Ribicoff's off-year effort in 1962. To be sure, the successful outcome of MacGregor's campaign was at variance with the national voting trends that year. While voters returned Lyndon Johnson to the White House and enlarged Democratic majorities to both houses, the Third District's Republican incumbent won a substantial victory. MacGregor's re-election is, therefore, an example of how our electoral system, with its many simultaneous but semi-independent contests, makes possible a base of representation for the minority party even in the face of a great national sweep by the opposition. One of the themes of our narrative will be the extent to which MacGregor's campaign was related to the national party battle.

Again unlike Ribicoff, MacGregor was an incumbent. The 1964 race came at the end of a long and arduous congressional session that kept congressmen in Washington until October 3—just a month before the election. Campaigns waged by incumbents illustrate the interplay between the roles of the congressman-as-legislator and the congressman-as-campaigner. Incumbency carries substantial electoral advantages; but to the harried incumbent the dual responsibility may mean conflicting demands on his time, energy, and resources. We shall therefore want to notice how actions and perceptions in Washington and those in the home base mutually determine and reinforce one another.

The Suburban Third District

Minnesota's Third Congressional District forms a western arc around the city of Minneapolis, taking in suburban Hennepin County, and to the north the entire Anoka County. In 1960 the district had a population of 445,898, a gain of 134 percent over the same area in 1950. Typical of many suburban areas throughout the nation, the district is 94 percent urban (against the state's average of 62.1 percent), and composed largely of upper-middle-class, white-collar residents (three rural counties were lopped off in the redistricting of 1961). Its median income of $7455 is the highest in Minnesota, while the median age (24.2) is the lowest. Median value of owner-occupied dwellings is $15,800, highest in the state. No less than 54.6 percent of the district's workers are classified in white-collar occupations. When midwestern congressional districts are ranked according to median years of school completed (by residents over twenty-five), median family income, and percentage of work force in white-collar jobs, the Third District ranks among the top ten percent in all categories.[10] As these statistics suggest, the Third District possesses a homogeneity of population that is quite striking in comparison with the diverse voters in Senator Ribicoff's Connecticut. It is like shifting one's focus from the entire state of Connecticut to one of its large counties such as suburban Fairfield, adjacent to New York City.

As a relatively prosperous suburban area, the Third District has many characteristics that label it as "Republican." While many factors condition the partisan character of a district's voting habits, observers have identified several demographic features that stand out as most important. Table 4 summarizes some of these features. At least in northern states, Republican representatives—as com-

---

[10] Information from: U.S. Bureau of the Census, *Congressional District Data Book, Districts of the 88th Congress* (Washington: Government Printing Office, 1963), p. 243 ff.; and *Congressional Districts of the United States* (Congressional Quarterly Special Report, August 21, 1964).

pared with their Democratic colleagues—tend to come from districts with low nonwhite populations, high owner-occupied dwelling units, and somewhat lower urbanization. The Third District leans somewhat to the Republican side in most of these categories. Yet the district had elected a Democrat in the five elections pre-

TABLE 4   CONSTITUENCY CHARACTERISTICS AND PARTY AFFILIATION OF INCUMBENT, BY REGION AND PARTY (1960)*

Party of 1960 incumbent by region	Percentage of nonwhite	Percentage of owner-occupied dwellings	Percentage of urban	Number of districts
NORTH				
Republican	3.8	67.0	65.3	162
Democratic	12.7	54.4	79.7	131
BORDER				
Republican	3.3	68.3	60.0	6
Democratic	12.3	63.1	53.4	32
SOUTH				
Republican	8.4	65.0	65.0	5
Democratic	24.7	61.4	51.5	101

* Adapted from: Lewis A. Froman Jr., *Congressmen and their Constituencies* (Chicago: Rand McNally, 1963), p. 33.

ceding MacGregor's victory in 1960. Republican leaders had eyed the district hopefully for several years prior to his candidacy, viewing the rapid growth of suburban Hennepin County as a trend in their party's favor. With a strong candidate, they felt, the district could be theirs; and MacGregor came along at an opportune moment. In the 1961 redistricting (see Figures 1 and 2 in Chapter 3), MacGregor's hold on the district was strengthened by the removal of three rural counties northeast of Minneapolis—a change that increased the weight of the suburban areas and brought the district to its present size.

MacGregor's two victories prior to 1964 were impressive, even considering the "Republican" characteristics of his electorate. In his first try for political office in 1960, MacGregor unseated the five-term Democratic incumbent, Roy W. Wier, winning more than fifty-eight percent of the vote. In 1962 he boosted this margin to sixty percent. Yet MacGregor refuses to regard the district as "safe," and points to the large bloc of independent voters who switch between the parties. No definite estimate of the number of such voters can be made, however, because in Minnesota voters do not register by party.

The Democrats were not without hope. The traditional independence of Minnesota voters seems to confirm MacGregor's spirit of caution. His defeat was not impossible in a state whose political history is dotted with the birth and demise of third parties and protest movements. The Third District, moreover, is a rapidly growing area where many young newcomers settle each year. The influx of such people, many of whom probably lack firm local political ties, tends to keep elections competitive.

The Democratic-Farmer-Labor[11] challenger, Richard J. Parish, was an experienced vote-getter. Elected three times to the school board in his home community of Robbinsdale, Parish served two terms in the state house of representatives and in 1962 was elected to the state senate. Thus, he was a relatively prominent figure in his own community and a proved political candidate. In his 1964 bid for the House of Representatives, Parish would be running with an especially attractive national ticket. Hubert Humphrey, the vice-presidential candidate, had been mayor of Minneapolis and was a veteran of sixteen years in the United States Senate; the state's junior senator, Eugene McCarthy, was expected to have no difficulty in his bid for re-election.

Thus, while MacGregor's re-election prospects looked favorable from the outset, the Democratic candidate could hope for an upset victory. A hard-fought and close contest was expected.

Two Routine Primaries

Congressional candidates in Minnesota are nominated by primary elections held each election year on the second Tuesday in September. Under Minnesota law, any registered person can vote in the primary of either party. Because nominations are usually in doubt as late as September, the parties have difficulty mobilizing their machinery effectively before this date and therefore adopt the practice of endorsing candidates in conventions held well ahead of the primaries. (For congressional nominations, party conventions are held in each district.) In reality endorsement

---

[11] The Democratic-Farmer-Labor Party, or DFL, is an amalgamation of the old Democratic and Farmer-Labor parties. Thus, the DFL is the modern Democratic party in the state.

constitutes nomination, and endorsed candidates are rarely defeated in the primaries.

Once endorsed by their respective party conventions, MacGregor and Parish had, therefore, in effect been nominated, since neither had primary opposition. Nonetheless, their performance in the primary election is a crude method of assessing their relative strength. Of course, the primary was not, strictly speaking, a contest between the two men. But because any registered person may vote for either of the two, the primary is widely considered by local observers as a preliminary test of strength.

The 1964 primary vote was extremely light. MacGregor received slightly more than 25,000 votes in the Republican primary, while his opponent was pulling about 21,500 in the DFL contest. The total vote for both men was less than a third of the 1962 vote cast in the Third District's congressional race. Because of the light turnout, it was difficult to know how much significance to attach to the vote. MacGregor outpolled Parish throughout most of Hennepin County. But Parish had the edge in three Hennepin communities—New Hope, Plymouth, and Robbinsdale—that MacGregor had carried in 1960 and 1962. Parish also pulled better than his opponent in Anoka County, a traditional DFL stronghold that MacGregor had failed to carry in the previous general elections.

MacGregor himself interpreted the result as a warning for Republicans to get busy. He was quoted in the *Minneapolis Morning Tribune* (September 11) as asserting that the vote was a "potential portent for disaster" for the Minneapolis Republican Party. MacGregor's margin of 3500 votes over Parish was far different from 1962, when he was 10,000 votes ahead of his challenger in the primary. He was aware of the close correspondence in percentage terms between his past performance in primaries and the general elections (see Table 5); and his 53.8 percent in the 1964 primary was decidedly an ominous portent.

TABLE 5   MACGREGOR'S VOTE, 1960-1964 (PERCENTAGE OF TOTAL VOTE CAST)

Year	Primary	General election
1960	56.0	58.4
1962	61.0	60.2
1964	53.8	57.0

The Continuous Campaign

Although the formal campaign was compacted into the hectic month following adjournment of the Eighty-eighth Congress, Clark MacGregor's re-election efforts had begun long before. A congressman who wants to remain in office never really stops campaigning. With his seat at stake every two years, he cannot afford to become isolated from his constituency—unless he has the good fortune to represent an extremely "safe" district. While he is in Washington, he must maintain a flow of information from his Capitol Hill office to project the image of a hard-working, effective legislator, and to remind the people at home that he is working on their behalf. This informal campaigning, as important as the more familiar, short-lived contest, tends to give the incumbent a long-run advantage over his challenger.

Each week during the congressional session, for example, MacGregor prepares a one-minute television tape consisting of commentary on a current national issue. The tape is sent to the four stations in the Minneapolis area, and they use it as their schedules permit. At the same time, he makes a weekly five-minute radio tape that is distributed to a number of stations. Two or three of them broadcast the entire tape as part of their regular schedule, while others insert excerpts in newscasts. A transcript of the radio tape is distributed to all Minneapolis newspapers, and several of the suburban papers publish it as a weekly column entitled "Congressman MacGregor Reports."

In June of 1964 MacGregor's office sent to every Third-District resident listed in the telephone directory the "MacGregor Legislative Questionnaire," which requested opinions on ten major proposals before the Eighty-eighth Congress. Responses were tabulated in his Minneapolis office, and each respondent later received a reply from Washington. A summary of the questionnaire results was inserted in the *Congressional Record* and was reprinted and mailed to Third-District residents. A device used by many members of Congress, the questionnaire enhances a congressman's image while satisfying perfectly the norms of representative government.

It is through frequent personal visits to his district that a representative can most effectively keep his name before the electorate, while gauging the climate of opinion among his constituents. Throughout the session preceding the election Mac-Gregor tried to return to the district at least one weekend a month, and by July he was traveling home nearly every weekend.

MacGregor sometimes holds public meetings to inform constituents on legislative issues and to solicit their views. These meetings are usually planned around a specific issue, with his district office issuing invitations to constituents presumed to be particularly concerned. During the 1964 session MacGregor called a meeting of ministers, school superintendents, and school-board members to discuss the Supreme Court's school-prayer decisions and the so-called Becker amendment.[12] Meetings were held on mass transportation and medical care for the aged during the previous session. The typical format of a MacGregor meeting consists of a fifteen-minute speech in which he summarizes the issues and proposals, then answers questions from the audience. Though the press is excluded from the sessions, a stenographer prepares a summary of the discussion.

About four times a year, MacGregor regularly holds a public luncheon in downtown Minneapolis. Invitations are sent to all persons on the district mailing list, and admission is by tickets issued upon request by the district office. Attended mostly by business and professional men who work downtown, these affairs are largely social, although MacGregor sometimes talks briefly on legislative issues.

In view of this constant informal campaigning, the formal electoral contest was in large part simply an intensification of activities taking place throughout the session. The formal campaign did not begin abruptly, but was built up gradually, while Mac-Gregor, pressed by the urgency of the approaching election, devoted more and more time to his district as the Eighty-eighth Congress came to a close.

By the end of July MacGregor was returning to the district for three- and four-day weekends, when the legislative schedule permitted. Frequently he was able to fly to Minneapolis early on a

---

[12] Named for its main sponsor, Representative Frank Becker (R. N.Y.), the measure would have amended the Constitution to exclude Bible-reading and prayer exercises in schools from the First Amendment's ban on religious legislation. House Judiciary Chairman Emanuel Celler (D. N.Y.) was opposed to the measure and managed to keep it in his committee. During the summer of 1964 Becker engaged in widely publicized efforts to discharge the bill from the committee.

Friday afternoon and return to Washington the following Tuesday without missing crucial legislative business. (Notices are sent out each Thursday by Party Whip Leslie Arends [Ill.], informing all Republicans of votes scheduled for the coming week.) Sometimes more lengthy visits were possible: In mid-August MacGregor was able to devote more than a week to campaigning, while Congress was adjourned for the Democratic National Convention.

Campaigning this way had drawbacks, however. When in Washington, MacGregor was deprived of face-to-face contact with the voters. "Many people don't realize Congress is in session, and they wonder why you're not home campaigning," the Congressman explained. In his absence, moreover, his opponent could roam the district freely, making speeches without fear of retort from the incumbent. As a member of the state senate, which had adjourned much earlier, Parish therefore had an edge on MacGregor in meeting the Third-District voters.

The Campaign Organization

Party machinery is often of little help to congressional candidates. Formal party organizations are rarely built along congressional district lines, and workers must campaign for the entire slate. This is especially true in presidential campaigns. The Third District Republican organization was helpful to MacGregor chiefly in performing such generalized functions as registering voters and getting them to the polls on election day.

Fortunately, in 1960 MacGregor had put together an elaborate volunteer organization of his own. The "MacGregor Volunteer Committee" included precinct and ward workers and was headed by a chairman and chairwoman for each village, town, and legislative district. The organization was directed by an advisory committee composed of a chairman, a chairwoman, and five close aides of the Congressman. These seven worked with MacGregor in planning campaign activities and provided a liaison between the entire volunteer organization and MacGregor's offices in Washington and Minneapolis. The committee also served as a clearinghouse for campaign contributions, since MacGregor insists that the identity of donors not be revealed to him.

A handbook, "The Re-election of Congressman Clark MacGregor, 1964," was distributed in September to all volunteers. It described the structure of the volunteer organization, explained the strategy of the campaign, listed some volunteer projects, and gave the background of the two candidates. During the two months of the formal campaign, a weekly newsletter was sent to all volunteers to inform them of coming activities.

The MacGregor volunteers were officially sent into action on September 12, when the Congressman opened the campaign headquarters in Robbinsdale—his first major appearance after the primary. Actually the volunteers had been at work weeks before, distributing MacGregor window stickers, automobile aerial pennants, and lawn signs. Now they were busy mailing the campaign postcard (a photograph of the congressman and his family) to every Third-District voter. Volunteers also handled special mailings throughout the campaign: the legislative questionnaire results, the congressman's voting record, and one of his House speeches.

Volunteer organizations in each locale enjoyed a high degree of autonomy. The chairman and chairwoman in each village or town were expected to recruit precinct volunteers. A form letter to be sent to potential workers was supplied by the Washington office. District organizations operated on their own budgets and planned their own activities. Volunteers could request MacGregor's appearance at particular events by means of a form submitted to the Washington and Minneapolis offices, which were in daily telephone contact. The congressman's activities were coordinated by Bob McCann, his Minneapolis staff man, and Stan Langland, his administrative assistant in Washington. In addition, volunteers were encouraged to make informal personal contacts with voters and occasionally to write letters to newspaper editors.

The Full-Time Campaign

After opening his campaign headquarters on September 12, MacGregor had to return to Washington. Beginning September 18, however, he managed to steal a week for full-time campaigning. His crowded schedule included a kick-off dinner with the Hennepin County Young Republican League; an address dedicating a sewage-treatment plant; an appearance at a steak fry with Wheelock Whitney, Republican candidate for the United States Senate; participation in an assault exercise of the Fourteenth Army Corps (MacGregor is a major in the Army Reserve); and a speech, along with other Minnesota congressional candidates, at the convention of the AFL-CIO Committee on Political Education (COPE) in St. Paul. The highlight of the week was a day of campaigning with Governor William Scranton of Pennsylvania, a close friend of MacGregor ever since the two men were freshmen congressmen in 1961. Scranton also appeared at a MacGregor testimonial dinner in Minneapolis on September 22. The $50-a-plate affair raised about three-quarters of the Congressman's campaign expenses.

The long second session of the Eighty-eighth Congress finally came to a halt on October 3. MacGregor's first full day of campaigning after adjournment was typical of the whirlwind style for which he has become well known. At 7:00 A.M. he stationed himself at a factory gate to greet employees arriving at work, and at 7:45 he attended a breakfast for area Republicans. The remainder of the day was devoted to a series of seven coffee parties. Only a lunch break allowed him a few moments to collect his thoughts.

Scheduled appearances throughout the campaign were interspersed with the congressman's well-known shopping center stops. Often unannounced, MacGregor would pull into the shopping center parking lot in his large campaign van—a delivery truck converted into a mobile headquarters. The large red and blue lettering "MacGregor for Congress" on the sides of the van was frequently sufficient to attract a crowd. Hopping from the van, he would tour the shopping area, greeting shoppers with a handshake and a vigorous, "Hello, I'm Clark MacGregor." If a crowd gathered around the van, he might make a brief speech. Though his remarks were extemporaneous, the subjects were worked out in advance. As many as seven shopping centers might be visited in a single day. The van was equipped with a desk and a cot, and en route he would review speech material, answer mail, or simply relax.

MacGregor's shopping center tours were related to his central campaign strategy, which was to reach the estimated 25,000 persons who had moved into the Third District after 1962. While the candidate himself greeted the voters, local Republican workers were canvassing new subdivisions to compile "Victory Information Program" (VIP) lists. Newcomers were asked to identify themselves as Republicans, Democrats, or Independents. MacGregor workers then moved in to enlist new volunteers in the Republican and Independent categories; and MacGregor coffee hours were held in many new neighborhoods. Special mailings were aimed at these voters during the campaign. In communities in which the mayor supported MacGregor, a letter of endorsement from the mayor was sent to all independent voters.

The Debates

In addition to these routine techniques, the campaign featured a dozen scheduled debates (two televised) between Mac-Gregor and Parish. These confrontations featured prepared speeches by the candidates followed by questions from the audience. Very early in the campaign, MacGregor had decided to stress three themes in his prepared remarks: 1) equal legislative representation for suburban areas; 2) new tax sources for localities; and 3) the conduct of the Vietnamese war. These themes were consistent with MacGregor's background and interests. In discussing Vietnam, for instance, the candidate was able to draw upon his experience with World War II guerrilla warfare in Burma in urging a shift in the war effort. He could also point out that he had urged military action against Cuba before the 1962 missile crisis.

MacGregor devoted, however, most of his attention to suburban problems. Here his interests, his expertise from the House Judiciary Committee, and his district's welfare converged. Following the Supreme Court's state legislative reapportionment decision in 1962,[13] MacGregor became one of the plaintiffs in a local lawsuit aimed at reapportioning the Minnesota legislature. In Congress he introduced a bill to equalize congressional districts,[14] and he had been outspoken in his opposition to the so-called "Tuck" bill —a proposal pushed late in the 1964 session that would have prevented federal courts from hearing reapportionment cases.

MacGregor also called for a more equitable tax program for suburbs. His argument was that suburbanites paid more in federal taxes than they received in federal aid. At the same time suburban

[13] *Baker v. Carr*, 369 U.S. 186 (1962).
[14] MacGregor also played a key role in framing H.R. 5505, which specified that congressional districts deviate no more than fifteen percent (greater or less) from the average size of districts in a given state. The bill also specified that districts be "contiguous" and "compact." Drafted in the wake of the Supreme Court's 1964 ruling that House districts must be substantially equal in population, the bill was authored by Judiciary Chairman Emanuel Celler (D. N.Y.) and passed the House in 1965.

communities sorely needed additional revenues to meet their growing needs for education, transportation, and recreation. Thus MacGregor proposed that the federal government abandon certain revenue sources, especially excise taxes on luxury items, to allow localities to develop new revenues for their own purposes. Both national party platforms had included planks favoring repeal of luxury taxes.[15] The theme of "local responsibility" implicit in this proposal was an attractive one, for it implied confidence in the caliber of community governments.

MacGregor hoped that these themes would present a pleasant contrast with those of his opponent. Taking an argumentative stance, Parish was criticizing the incumbent for a "lack of interest in the suburbs." He also claimed that MacGregor had undermined suburban interests by voting against such Administration programs as mass transit and a Cabinet-level department of urban affairs. MacGregor countered by explaining that federal aid programs would mean more taxes, and hence less local revenue for meeting suburban problems.

The Democrat's central strategy was to capitalize on the presumed appeal of President Johnson in contrast to Senator Goldwater. Whenever possible, Parish tried to link MacGregor with Goldwater. The phrase "MacGregor-Goldwater obstructionism" was employed to point out that both Republicans had opposed such Administration programs as the income tax reduction and the "war on poverty." Like many Republican candidates in 1964, MacGregor's most serious problem was his relationship to the national ticket. The Minnesota delegates had supported former Congressman Walter Judd as a "favorite son" at the San Francisco convention, largely to avoid taking sides. (The delegation's final vote: eighteen for Judd and eight for Goldwater.) But MacGregor had quietly lobbied for his close friend Scranton at the convention. After Goldwater's nomination, MacGregor announced support of the national ticket, and during the early part of the campaign he delivered several "party unity" speeches. To disgruntled Republican friends he cited Scranton's unity speech at the San Francisco convention.[16] As the campaign progressed, however, MacGregor's

---

[15] The reduction in excise taxes finally became effective in July 1965.

[16] An article by MacGregor, "The Moderate Republican's Role—1964," appeared as the lead article in the fall 1964 bulletin of the Minnesota Republican Workshop. In addition to citing the example of Scranton, the article explained Goldwater's civil rights position at length.

references to the national ticket became less frequent. When Parish charged that MacGregor was avoiding the issue, the Congressman would typically reply: "It would be the most blatant hypocrisy for Republicans who supported other candidates [for President] to pretend now that Goldwater was their first choice —but let's remind ourselves that Lyndon Johnson wasn't our choice at all." [17]

MacGregor's position was complicated by one of those unpredictable incidents that sometimes can disturb even the most routine campaign. MacGregor had agreed to do his turn of duty with the "Republican Truth Squad"—a group of prominent Republicans designated to follow the Democratic nominees in order to make "rebuttals" of their speeches. While with the Truth Squad in Atlanta, Georgia, on September 29, he unexpectedly found himself on the same platform with Senator Strom Thurmond (S.C.), a staunch segregationist and former Dixiecrat who had just announced his switch to the Republican party. MacGregor and the other Truth Squad members[18] were unable to avoid being photographed with Thurmond. When the photograph was printed in Minnesota newspapers, Parish charged that MacGregor had repudiated his support of civil rights legislation. A small storm developed in the Third District, and "letters to the editor" columns of local newspapers were filled with indignant letters accusing the Congressman of hypocrisy. Just when MacGregor believed the storm was about over, the nationally syndicated columnists, Rowland Evans and Robert Novak, telephoned that they intended to write an article to point out that it had been a freak accident. MacGregor reviewed the events with the reporters, but he observed that by drawing further attention to the incident an article would hurt more than it would help. Nevertheless, the story appeared and was extremely favorable to MacGregor: Evans and Novak argued that "the acquisition of Dixiecrat . . . Thurmond may cost the Republican Party one of its brightest young stars." [19] MacGregor felt that the article, while written to help him, had merely prolonged public awareness of the issue.

[17] Quoted in *Sunday Suburban Life,* October 25, 1964.
[18] Senators Carl Curtis (Neb.) and Len Jordan (Idaho), and Representative Robert Michel (Ill.)
[19] Rowland Evans and Robert Novak, "Strom May Be Costly," *Washington Post,* October 18, 1964, p. 7.

The Truth Squad incident subsided by Election Day. The anti-civil rights charge against MacGregor had little credibility because his vigorous civil rights record was well known. As a member of the House Judiciary Committee, he had helped draft the Civil Rights Act of 1964 and had managed some of the floor debate. Yet the Democrats continued to exploit the issue. A newspaper cartoon used in many Parish advertisements showed the Congressman's office: MacGregor's picture on the wall next to Goldwater's, and a stack of papers on his desk labeled "unsolved suburban problems." The Congressman's chair was empty as a secretary was shown answering the phone: "Congressman MacGregor? I'm sorry, but he's with Senator Strom Thurmond campaigning for Goldwater's Truth Squad in Georgia!"

If Parish was anxious to link MacGregor with Goldwater, he was even more concerned to ally himself with the Democratic national ticket. His entire campaign was designed to stress that he was a "team player." Cabinet members John Gronouski and Stewart Udall, as well as the national nominees themselves, came to the state and endorsed Parish. There were radio testimonials by Hubert Humphrey and other national figures, and newspaper ads that urged the voters to "Send President Johnson a Supporting Congressman." Parish's problem seemed to be the absence of any real "issue" of his own. Though he attacked MacGregor's record, he offered little alternative except unquestioning support for the Administration's programs. Thus, his speeches had a negative and defensive ring, and his total support of the Administration left him open to charges that he was a "yes man." One of the MacGregor volunteers remarked that "Mr. Parish's bark is starting to sound more like a whimper." [20]

On one occasion Parish's identification with the Administration was turned into a liability. Fridley, a small city in the Third District, is partitioned for postal purposes and is included in the postal zones of other communities. For several years city officials had been trying to consolidate the town into one postal zone and have a post office constructed. When Postmaster General John Gronouski addressed the Fridley Rotary Club on August 12, local civic leaders took the opportunity to voice humorous reminders of their efforts. Responding in kind, Gronouski pointed toward Parish, who was also attending the luncheon, and remarked that

[20] Quoted in *Sunday Suburban Life*, October 25, 1964.

"the way to get a post office here is to send a Democratic congressman to Washington this fall." MacGregor assumed a posture of indignation. On the House floor he declared:

> Is this example of blatant political partisanship to be the hallmark of the Johnson Administration? Mr. Gronouski has lowered the stature and damaged the reputation of our Post Office Department and every public servant in it. Imagine what the American young people must think of their Government when they read of such attitudes expressed by a Cabinet officer.[21]

MacGregor also observed that he himself had written the Post Office Department urging favorable action on the new post office. Copies of the floor remarks were clipped from the *Record* and sent to editors of Third District suburban papers and the Minneapolis dailies. This occasioned a *Minneapolis Star* editorial critical of the Postmaster General. Although Parish later explained that Gronouski's remark had been in jest, MacGregor had succeeded in capitalizing on the incident.

The Taconite Amendment

An inescapable element of congressional campaigns is the intrusion of issues that are strictly local in character. Parish, the Democratic candidate, was entangled with such an issue, the taxation of corporations mining taconite, a low-grade iron ore recently discovered in abundance in Minnesota. Taconite promised to revive the state's mining industry, which was lagging because of the depletion of high-grade iron ore in the Mesabi Range. It was claimed that taconite mining would create 10,000 new jobs in the state. Because the process for extracting taconite is complex and expensive, mining companies had demanded a secure tax policy before making heavy capital investments in mining facilities. A bill was introduced in the 1963 session of the Minnesota legislature to ensure that taconite companies would be taxed no more heavily than other manufacturing firms in the state. The measure passed by overwhelming votes in both houses. In the upper house it was approved fifty-six to nine, with Parish one of the nine senators opposing it.

[21] *Congressional Record* (Eighty-eighth Congress, 2d Session; August 14, 1964, daily edition), p. 9081.

The legislature also approved a constitutional amendment specifying that this tax policy would not be repealed for at least twenty-five years. The amendment went on the ballot for the November 1964 election. A statewide citizens' committee was formed to campaign for adoption of the amendment. Included in the committee were such prominent political figures as Lieutenant Governor Sandy Keith and Attorney General Walter Mondale (both DFL), former Republican Governor Elmer Anderson, and the state chairmen of both parties. The "taconite amendment" had farm and labor endorsements; and Hubert Humphrey and Governor Karl Rolvaag had praised it. On November 3 it received the vote of more than seventy percent of the voters who went to the polls.[22]

During the campaign Parish was pressed about his negative vote on the taconite statute. He refused to discuss the matter, and on at least one occasion his temper flared as he remarked that the issue was not relevant to the congressional campaign. Near the end of the campaign, MacGregor ran a newspaper ad announcing that "Congressman Clark MacGregor Joins All* the Suburban Legislators in Supporting Taconite Amendment." An asterisk beside the word "All" inserted the statement: "The only exception is the man who is MacGregor's opponent in this election."

The Home Stretch

By the final week of the campaign, both candidates had nearly exhausted their issues and themes. MacGregor continued to hammer at the theme of equitable taxation and representation for suburbs; Parish continued to attack MacGregor's votes against Administration measures.

MacGregor's use of the mass media was intensified. Full-page advertisements appeared in the suburban newspapers, sometimes several in the same issue. There were two standard types of ads: one presented testimonials by such national figures as former President Eisenhower, Richard Nixon, Governor Scranton, and Senator Everett Dirksen; the other included endorsements by

[22] Under the Minnesota constitution, all amendments must be approved by more than half of all those voting. That is, a voter who goes to the polls but fails to mark his ballot on an amendment has, in effect, voted against it.

Third District mayors. The ads were directed to the district's twenty-five suburban papers throughout most of the campaign, but in the last week they appeared in the *Minneapolis Star* and *Tribune* as well. During the final week there was at least one MacGregor ad in every issue of each of these papers and in the suburban papers, sometimes several in the same issue.

Spot commercials (thirty seconds for radio, twenty seconds for television) were also intensified. These spots usually consisted of testimonials by "typical citizens"—a housewife, businessman, or a "senior citizen." In some of the television commercials the Congressman himself appeared briefly. Two major television appearances were scheduled. One was an hour-long debate between MacGregor and Parish, sponsored by the League of Women Voters. The other was a joint appearance of Republican congressional and senatorial candidates in the Minneapolis area, sponsored by the state Republican Committee.

MacGregor was fortunate in his endorsements. His candidacy was supported by every newspaper that took a position on the Third District race, including the *Minneapolis Star* and *Tribune*. He also received endorsements from such diverse national groups as the Americans for Constitutional Action (a group that supports conservative legislators), the Ripon Society (a research group of liberal Republican intellectuals based in Cambridge, Massachusetts), and the National Committee for an Effective Congress (a group that supports moderate and liberal legislators).

Election Day

Balmy weather on November 3 meant a record turnout—eighty percent of the registered voters in many Third District communities. MacGregor won re-election by more than 30,000 votes, or fifty-seven percent of the vote. At the same time the Goldwater-Miller ticket polled only forty-two percent in the district. And Senator Eugene McCarthy, the DFL candidate, had won re-election to the U.S. Senate. The Minnesota voters' reputation for ticket-splitting remained intact.

In 1964, as usual, MacGregor lost Anoka County. Blue-collar workers are more heavily concentrated here than in Hennepin County, which comprises most of the district. The area is heavily unionized and has been a DFL bastion for so many years that many Republican candidates have written it off. An influx of white-collar workers is diminishing DFL strength in Anoka County, and a local Republican organization was recently formed. The area was still solidly in the Democratic column in 1964, though MacGregor's percentage improved slightly over 1962.

MacGregor piled up solid majorities throughout suburban Hennepin County, though his margin was cut in most of the areas Parish had represented as a state senator.

MacGregor's over-all performance was three percentage points lower than in 1962, no doubt the effect of President Johnson's fifty-eight percent majority in the district. To the extent that it existed, the "coat-tail" effect for Parish probably worked through an increased turnout at the polls rather than through any mass conversion of the voters. In 1964 nearly 70,000 more Third District voters cast ballots for the congressional seat than two years earlier, a nonpresidental year. The presidential race undoubtedly brought to the polls many "marginal" voters—persons lacking firm political loyalties and regular habits of political participation. It can be assumed that these voters were most strongly influenced by the Democratic tide.

MacGregor's impressive victory did not necessarily imply that his district would be "safe" for all time to come. According to the lore of politics, safe districts are stagnant and uncompetitive; but the Third District is fluid, rapidly growing, and young. MacGregor must maintain continuous informal campaigning to keep in touch with this kind of constituency and to satisfy its expectation of a vigorous and forceful legislator.

The interest in suburban problems and civil rights that MacGregor showed during the campaign continued unabated. As passed by the House, Representative Celler's 1965 congressional districting bill contained a MacGregor amendment providing that states could use special census data (gathered between decennial censuses) to redraw their districts. The amendment also specified that such data could be used by federal courts to validate redistricting plans enacted by state legislatures. This provision was designed to give added voice to fast-growing suburban areas that change radically between the decennial censuses.

The 1964 election, however, conveyed two important messages to Clark MacGregor. First, it was clear to him that his constituents were not satisfied with the national image of his party. Following the election MacGregor issued statements calling for greater participation by younger and progressive House Republicans in formulating party policy. He had long been associated with the efforts to rejuvenate his party's leadership in the House (see Chapter 4); and he now hoped that House Republicans would lead the national party in recovering from the 1964 defeat.

A second but related implication was somewhat more subtle. As an intelligent legislator and a vigorous campaigner, MacGregor himself is regarded as a "comer" in his party. His re-election posed therefore the problem of "where next," and he carefully weighed the alternatives. The Senate did not look promising. McCarthy, now the senior senator, had just been re-elected for a six-year term. To replace Vice President Humphrey, Governor Rolvaag appointed the state's popular Attorney General, Walter ("Fritz") Mondale. This term would expire in 1966, but thirty-seven-year-old Mondale would be a formidable opponent. The gubernatorial picture was somewhat brighter, because Governor Rolvaag, who would be up for re-election in 1966, was reported slipping in popularity.

MacGregor's dilemma was not an unusual one for congressmen in the middle-seniority ranks. Representing the Third District will never be an easy job; but with reasonable diligency MacGregor can expect an extended House tenure, and the accompanying perquisites of seniority within the congressional power structure. Yet the Senate or the governorship—and the resulting national prominence—were tempting alternatives. Leaving his House seat to run for another office could not help but be a risky choice. As the 1964 campaign receded into the background, therefore, MacGregor was considering his political future. On September 3, 1965, the Congressman had reached his decision: He announced to reporters that he would seek re-election from the Third District.

A DAY WITH ALBERT QUIE OF MINNESOTA

Traditional discussions of the job of a legislator have frequently been concerned with whether a man should act as a mirror of his constituents' views, or whether he should, as Edmund Burke prescribed, act independently of their sentiments. More recently, discussions of the legislative role have also been concerned with the extent to which the legislator considers himself a "broker" who attempts to mitigate and resolve conflicts among competing interests. The job of a congressman, however, involves much more than deciding how to represent his district or the national interest (however he may define it) on important votes, and more than determining how to achieve a consensus among opposing forces on a particular issue. He must also establish satisfactory relations with his House colleagues—members and leaders of his party, committee associates, members of his state party delegations, and some persons in the opposition party.

The House of Representatives is not, however, complete unto itself. What the House does affects others. The congressman must therefore develop adequate rapport with persons external to the chamber—with constituents, lobbyists, reporters, and administrators, perhaps even with the President himself. The congressman also has administrative responsibility for supervising the work of his office staff and perhaps of the committee staff. Indeed, there is so much to do that a congressman must choose those aspects of the job he considers sufficiently rewarding to merit the involvement of himself and his staff.

The description of a day in the congressional life of Representative Albert H. Quie will indicate how a legislator can define his job and allocate his energies and resources. It also reveals the broad scope of congressional duties, the heavy work load carried by most members, and the importance of an already large and growing bureaucracy—the congressional staff.

The Congressman: His Background and His District

As is the case with most members of the House, Albert Quie's roots are deep in his native Minnesota and the First Congressional District in the southeastern part of the state. He grew up in Rice County (directly south of Saint Paul) on a farm homesteaded by his grandfather over a century ago. After serving as a Navy pilot in World War II, he returned to the district and attended Saint Olaf College in Northfield (also the alma mater of his predecessor, the late August Andresen), where he majored in political science. After graduation, he purchased and actively operated the family dairy farm. Meanwhile, he became active in community affairs as president of the Rice County Farm Bureau, a member of the Extension Board of the County, and supervisor of the soil conservation district. He was the recipient of the Minnesota Junior Chamber of Commerce's "Young Man of the Year" award and of a Distinguished Service Award from the Northfield Chamber of Commerce.

Quie first entered elective politics by winning a seat in the Minnesota state senate. While a state senator, he ran for Congress when a special election was held to fill the vacancy caused by the death of Andresen, a Republican who had represented the district for twenty-two years. Quie won the special election by a mere 600 votes at a time when there was strong feeling against Ezra Taft Benson, Secretary of Agriculture during the Eisenhower Administration, in his twelve-county district—a rich dairy farming area and center for the raising and processing of corn, livestock, small grains, and soybeans. (Benson felt that rising farm prices were inflationary and therefore favored rigid control based on 1948-1950 parity.) Since winning the special election in 1958, however, Quie steadily increased his victory margins so that in 1962 he gained a plurality of 23,676 votes (fifty-seven percent) over his Democratic opponent.[1]

Although the First District is generally considered a "safe" Republican area, the continuing necessity of winning both primary and general elections means that Quie's job security is constantly being threatened. Adding to his uncertain tenure is the constitutional requirement that congressional districts be redrawn after each decennial census to reflect shifts in population. An adverse redistricting action by a state legislature, or by a court enforcing the constitutional requirement of periodic and equitable redistricting, can summarily end the career of even the most promising or illustrious member of the House.

The harsh realities of redistricting were conveyed vividly to Quie early in his career, when in 1961, he withstood an intense and lengthy redistricting battle. Because Minnesota's population growth has been slower than that of the nation as a whole, the 1960 census decreed that the state's representation in the House of Representatives should be reduced from nine to eight seats. This made it certain that at least one of the incumbent congressmen (six Republicans and three Democrats) would be forced out of office because his district would be combined with that of another representative (see Figure 1, including the list of incumbent congressmen).[2]

For twelve months the Minnesota State Legislature was stalemated over the redistricting issue. Officially, the Minnesota Legislature is nonpartisan, but in reality it has a factional alignment of conservatives and liberals (the DFL), whose views and loyalties are similar to those of Republicans and Democrats. At the time under consideration, a conservative and hence pro-Republican group controlled the state senate and a liberal, pro-Democratic group dominated the Minnesota house. The senate's bill, which

---

[1] Though 1964 was a dismal year for many Republican congressional candidates, Quie maintained a 22,000-vote plurality and gained fifty-six percent of the popular vote.
[2] For an excellent discussion of the Minnesota redistricting struggle, see *Congressional Quarterly Weekly Report*, XIX (December 22, 1961), pp. 1970-1972.

was supported by Republican Governor Elmer L. Anderson, was expected to deprive the Democrats of one seat, which would mean that the GOP would hold its six seats and the DFL would be left with two. By contrast, the bill passed by the liberal-controlled Minnesota House would have caused the Republicans to suffer a net loss of two seats, while the Democrats would gain an additional place.

For three months late in 1961, leaders of the opposing factions of the legislature caucused in an effort to reach a compromise and avert another deadlock like the one that occurred in 1932. At that time the legislature had failed to agree on a redistricting plan, with the result that all incumbent congressmen had to run at large.

Incumbents naturally fear at-large elections because they are forced to run state-wide, rather than in their own districts, where they are well known. The chances of incumbents being swept out of office are all too real in these circumstances. In the 1932 at-large election several incumbents were indeed defeated and the state thereby lost valuable congressional seniority. Also as a result of the 1932 election, some areas of the state were left with no representation in Congress, and others were overrepresented.

Finally, late in December 1961, a compromise was worked out, creating four districts in which the Republicans were thought to hold the advantage and four in which the Democrats would have the edge (see Figures 1 and 2). This expectation was borne out by the 1962 elections, when incumbent Republicans H. Carl Andersen and Walter Judd, a nationally known figure, were defeated. Quie's district was not changed substantially, though heavily Democratic Dakota County was added to his district in order to bring the population of the First District up to the state average. This county contains South Saint Paul, where large stockyards are located and the Packing-house Workers Union (AFL-CIO) is reputed to have considerable influence. The remaining rural counties, however, give Quie and the Republicans an advantage over the Democrats in the district.

Reporting to the District
and a Foreign-Policy Briefing

Quie continually keeps his name in the news, informing his constituents of his activities. On Wednesday, July 31, 1963,

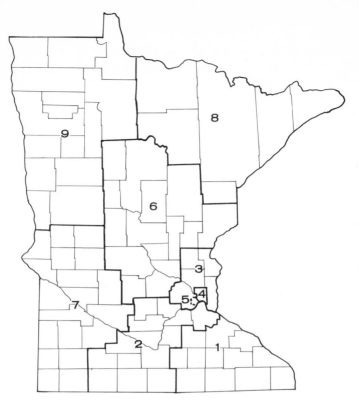

FIGURE 1

Minnesota Congressional Districts Prior to 1961 Redistricting*

District No.	Incumbent	Party
1	Albert H. Quie	Republican
2	Ancher Nelsen	Republican
3	Clark MacGregor	Republican
4	Joseph E. Karth	Democrat
5	Walter H. Judd	Republican
6	Fred Marshall	Democrat
7	H. Carl Andersen	Republican
8	John A. Blatnik	Democrat
9	Odin Langen	Republican

* Source: U.S. Department of Commerce, Bureau of the Census, *Congressional District Atlas of the United States* (April 1, 1960), p. 42.

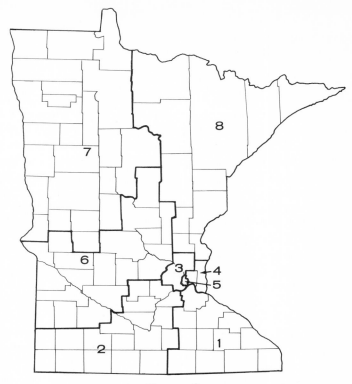

FIGURE 2

Minnesota Congressional Districts After 1961 Redistricting*

District No.	Incumbent	Party
1	Albert H. Quie	Republican
2	Ancher Nelsen	Republican
3	Clark MacGregor	Republican
4	Joseph E. Karth	Democrat
5	Donald M. Fraser	Democrat
6	Alec G. Olson	Democrat
7	Odin Langen	Republican
8	John A. Blatnik	Democrat

* Source: U.S. Department of Commerce, Bureau of the Census, *Congressional District Data Book* (Districts 88th Congress) (1963), p. 243.

for example, he arrived at his office a little before 8:30 A.M. and picked up the script for the program he was going to tape that morning for broadcast over radio stations in the First District. He then went to the recording studio provided for members in the Cannon House Office Building.[3] His broadcast dealt with the Fair Employment Practices Bill that had just been reported out of the House Education and Labor Committee. With several of his Republican colleagues on the committee, Quie was supporting the bill and had been successful in getting a majority of the Democratically controlled committee to support Republican amendments. In the recording studio he completed two different tapes. One was a five-minute program used by five stations in the district, including the state's largest station in Minneapolis; the other was a one-minute tape sent to twelve stations in the hope that they would incorporate it into their regular news programs. Quie used the script as a general guide for his remarks, since he normally prefers to extemporize.

After the taping, Quie rushed to a special secret briefing being given at 9:00 by Under Secretary of State W. Averell Harriman, who had just returned from Moscow where he had been chief United States negotiator for the first nuclear test-ban treaty among the United States, Britain, and Russia. Quie was one of about fifty to sixty congressmen attending the meeting, which was open to members of both parties. He left the meeting generally favorable toward the treaty, but fearful that it contained loopholes that would permit other nations to renew the testing of atomic weapons in the atmosphere. He was also concerned that it might diminish domestic support for continued expenditures for the research and development of nuclear weapons.

Shortly before 10:00 the briefing ended, and Quie returned to his office to check over the morning mail. While doing so, he asked his secretary to call the minority staff member of the House Rules Committee to inquire which of the two bills reported by the Education and Labor Committee would be considered first by the Rules Committee the following day. (Tactics for securing Rules Committee approval on bills dealing with vocational and

---

[3] The three House Office Buildings are named in honor of its most illustrious Twentieth Century Speakers: Joseph G. Cannon (R. Ill.), 1903-1911; Nicholas Longworth (R. Ohio), 1925-1931; and Sam Rayburn (D. Tex.), 1940-1947, 1949-1953, 1955-1961.

higher education were to be discussed later that morning at a closed meeting of the Education and Labor Committee's Select Subcommittee on Education.) The Republican staff member told him, however, that Rules Chairman Howard W. Smith (D. Va.) had not yet made a decision on which bill he would call up first and that he would not do so until just before the Rules Committee met the following day.

Committee Business

By this time it was after 10:00 and the Congressman was already late for a public hearing being conducted by the Livestock and Feed Grains Subcommittee of the Agriculture Committee. The Agriculture Committee divides its work primarily along commodity lines, with members serving on those subcommittees that deal with legislation affecting the commodities grown in their districts. Two of Quie's subcommittees, Dairy and Poultry, and Livestock and Feed Grains, handle the farm programs most important to his district. He also successfully requested assignment to the Cotton Subcommittee, even though no cotton is grown in Minnesota. If he were to be an effective member of the committee, Quie felt, he should learn to work with the members from the South who make up over half its Democratic membership.

Virtually every member of the committee has a strong constituency interest in farm policy. None can be considered impartial or neutral on agricultural matters, because each must foster and protect the interests of the particular type of agriculture practiced in his district. The committee is thus not at all representative of the House as a whole, since an increasing proportion of congressmen represent urban and suburban areas. Rather, it represents a cluster of congressmen who, along with their constituents, have a compelling interest in the outcomes of committee decisions.[4]

This was Quie's first committee post after his election to Congress. His predecessor was considered both inside and outside the House as an expert in dairy legislation, and Quie's supporters in the First District expected that Quie would also become a member of the Agriculture Committee. Some wrote letters to the

[4] For a detailed discussion of the operations of the committee, see Charles O. Jones, "Representation in Congress: The Case of the House Agriculture Committee," *American Political Science Review*, LV (June 1961), pp. 358-367.

Republican leadership urging his appointment. Quie himself was pleased to be assigned to Agriculture because of his farming experience and his concern over its problems. Normally Quie could have expected competition for an assignment to Agriculture. He had no difficulty getting the assignment, however, because in 1958 there was considerable controversy about the Benson farm programs and many Republicans were anxious to avoid being identified with the existing farm programs. Furthermore, assigning him to Andresen's committee seat caused the least disruption of Republican committee assignments in the middle of a session.

Because a House member's committee assignments determine in large part the role he will play in congressional decision-making, the period at the beginning of a new Congress when changes in committee assignments are made is one of intense intraparty maneuvering and conflict. Each member seeks for himself or his allies the most favorable committee slot.

Each party has a Committee on Committees that controls committee assignments. The Democratic Committee on Committees is composed of the Democratic members of the Ways and Means Committee, while the Republican Committee is made up of one Republican from each state that has Republican representation in the House. Each committee member has a vote equivalent to the number of Republican representatives from his state. This gives preponderant influence to the committee members from such large states as California, Ohio, New York, and Pennsylvania. In committee deliberations, the party leader exerts a powerful influence. His ability to grant and withhold desired committee seats from his colleagues is one of his principal sources of power within his party.[5]

Unlike most of his House colleagues, Quie is a member of a second major committee, Education and Labor. He secured this assignment, as he did his Agriculture seat, under unusual circumstances. During the 1959 congressional session, Quie happened to fly to Minneapolis with Representative Carroll Kearns (R. Pa.), the former ranking Republican on the Education and Labor Committee. Kearns suggested that Quie take a vacant seat on the committee. At first Quie was reluctant to do this: he already had a

---

[5] For a more complete discussion of how House committee seats are assigned, see Nicholas A. Masters, "House Committee Assignments," *American Political Science Review,* LV (June 1961), pp. 345-357.

satisfactory committee assignment, and in addition was a member of the nonlegislative Small Business Committee. Yet he had always been interested in education. When the plane landed in Minneapolis, therefore, he and Kearns sent Minority Leader Charles Halleck (R. Ind.) a letter requesting his assignment to the committee. Kearns also later called Halleck to urge Quie's appointment.

At 10:10 A.M. Quie went upstairs to the Agriculture Committee room where a hearing on bill H.R. 4217 was already in progress. This was a measure to grant relief to sheep breeders whose flocks had been seized by the Department of Agriculture because they were infected with a disease called sheep scrapie. Four members of the subcommittee, including Chairman W. R. Poage (D. Tex.), were present along with committee staff personnel. About a dozen spectators were attending the hearing. A sheep-breeder's trade association had lined up a series of witnesses —including several breeders and a genetics professor from Cornell University—to testify in favor of the legislation. Each read his testimony from a prepared text, a copy of which was supplied to all subcommittee members. No questions were asked by the subcommittee members during the presentations, since the chairman had suggested that they be reserved until after the trade association witnesses had testified. While the hearing went on, Quie quickly reviewed the prepared statements of the sheep raisers and conferred briefly with the chairman before leaving to attend a 10:30 executive (closed) session of the Select Subcommittee on Education of the Education and Labor Committee.

On leaving the hearing room at 10:30 Quie was met by a delegation of Minnesota postal clerks attending a convention in Washington. They had come to his office, and his research assistant, Phil Roe, had brought them to the committee room so that they might meet the Congressman before he went to his second meeting. The delegation told Quie of their strong opposition to the new work rules for clerks being instituted by the Post Office. They urged him to support legislation that they felt would rectify their problem. Quie explained that while he was not on the committee handling the bill, he was sympathetic to their problem. Before he departed for his meeting, he was also reminded by the clerks of their support of a bill to increase the salaries of federal employees.

The education subcommittee meeting was in the Cannon House Office Building across the street from the building in which Quie's office was located. On the way to the meeting he met Representative John Brademas (D. Ind.), a fellow member of the subcommittee. Though from opposing parties and having strikingly different voting records, Brademas and Quie share a common interest in higher education and especially in church-related institutions. Both had previously been affiliated with such schools—Quie as a student at Saint Olaf (Lutheran) and Brademas as a professor at Saint Mary's College (Roman Catholic) in South Bend, Indiana. Brademas showed Quie some literature on higher education he had just received. Later in the day Quie asked his secretary to get him copies of the literature Brademas had recommended to him. The two congressmen also discussed the Harriman test-ban briefing and remarked about the unusually "hot" discussion between Harriman and Representative John Pillion (R. N.Y.).

The subcommittee's executive session was held in a small, ornate, carpeted room on the fourth floor of the Cannon House Office Building. The members settled around a heavy mahogany table covered with blue felt. The Chairman, Mrs. Edith Green (D. Ore.), presided. The majority and minority staff assistants also attended. The meeting was conducted on a friendly and informal first-name basis. The first item discussed was the strategy to be used in pushing the bills to aid vocational schools and higher education through the House Rules Committee.[6] Quie was personally committed to both bills and, with his Republican committee colleagues, had effected changes in the bills that they thought essential. When the Rules Committee considered the bills, it was agreed that Mrs. Green would be the first to testify in favor

---

[6] Before major legislation can be considered on the House floor, it must normally gain the approval of the House Rules Committee. This committee has the unique power to introduce special resolutions, or rules, that call up a particular piece of legislation for House consideration. These rules also determine the conditions under which the bill will be debated: the amount of time allotted and whether or not the bill will be amendable on the floor. After the House approves the Rules Committee's rule (as it normally does), debate on the legislation begins. Its strong influence on the House agenda makes the Rules Committee an important power center of the House. See Robert L. Peabody, "The Enlarged Rules Committee," in Robert L. Peabody and Nelson W. Polsby, *New Perspectives on the House of Representatives* (Chicago: Rand McNally, 1963), pp. 129-164.

of legislation; Republican members of the subcommittee would also testify for the bills in order to demonstrate bipartisan support.

The subcommittee also discussed the possible effects of an amendment barring those areas practicing racial discrimination in public education from receiving the funds authorized by vocational and higher education bills. Such amendments are popularly known as "Powell Amendments," because their principal sponsor in the past had been the flamboyant Negro congressman from Harlem, Adam Clayton Powell. "Powell Amendments" have contributed to the defeat of previous aid-to-education bills because they have deprived the bills of southern and border-state support needed to secure final passage. Interestingly, the support for such amendments has come from very different sources: from persons who as a matter of principle believe that segregation must be eliminated quickly, and from persons who see "Powell Amendments" as a means of defeating aid-to-education bills.

A majority of the Republicans on the Education and Labor Committee favored the inclusion of such an amendment, not because they felt that it would help kill the bill, but because they opposed segregation and were desirous of dramatizing the Democratic party's division on racial issues. Southern members of the subcommittee were naturally opposed to the amendment, as were some of the northern Democratic members who thought that it would endanger the passage of the bill in either the House or the Senate.

Since Democrats had a majority, the bills, as reported from committee, contained no antisegregation provision. The Education and Labor Committee, however, does not function by resolving its conflicts internally and then acting with unanimity on the House floor when its bills are being considered. Rather, the committee's internal conflicts are carried onto the floor by members dissatisfied with its decisions,[7] who hope that the full House will reverse actions of the committee or that they will be able to intro-

[7] For a detailed discussion of the internal workings of the House Education and Labor Committee, see Frank J. Munger and Richard F. Fenno, Jr., *National Politics and Federal Aid to Education* (Syracuse: Syracuse University Press, 1962), Chapter 5. This committee stands in marked contrast to the well-integrated House Appropriations Committee which has evolved techniques for solving its problems internally with a minimum of conflict. See Fenno, "The House Appropriations Committee as a Political System: The Problem of Integration," *American Political Science Review*, LVI (June 1962), pp. 310-324.

duce floor amendments that will embarrass the opposition. Republicans on the committee, including Quie, therefore later supported an amendment to the aid-to-higher education bill barring the use of federal funds in states that discriminated in their educational practices. Their amendment, however, was defeated by southerners and northern Democratic liberals.

The subcommittee also decided that the membership would oppose a move to use the higher-education bill as a vehicle to increase the student-loan authorizations of the National Defense Education Act. Subcommittee members thought that raising the student-loan issue would endanger passage of the bill, because the question of increased student loans was closely related to the highly controversial matter of a federally supported college scholarship program. The subcommittee spent the remainder of the morning discussing a bill to set up a pilot project in the District of Columbia to assist juvenile delinquents and what action should be taken concerning the renewal of existing legislation on juvenile delinquency.

Activity on the House Floor

The Education and Labor meeting ended at 12:15 P.M. Bells had already rung at noon, indicating that the House was in session. Quie and Representative Charles Goodell (R. N.Y.), along with the minority staff assistant, stayed after the meeting to discuss Republican strategy on the juvenile delinquency bills. They continued their discussion as they walked to the House Chamber in the Capitol building via an underground passageway. As they walked, bells rang again to summon congressmen to a quorum call that had been requested in the House. (A quorum call requires each congressman to appear on the floor to answer when his name is called.)

Quie spent the next two hours on the House floor and in the cloakroom and lobby outside the chamber. The business before the House was a bill to pay the Philippines for damages incurred by the United States during World War II. As is true of much activity on the House floor, consideration of the Philippine claims bill was complicated by procedural questions. In this case, the House was being asked to approve a conference report, or compromise bill, worked out by a conference committee of senators and representatives. The conference committee procedure was necessary because the House and Senate had previously passed quite different versions of the legislation.[8]

The bill itself had obtained considerable notoriety because of revelations concerning the large retainers that a lobbyist for the Philippine interests was scheduled to receive under legislation passed in 1962. Quie had already made up his mind to oppose the Philippine claims bill. The United States, he thought, had neither a legal nor a moral obligation to pay the claimants. He did not think it necessary for him to spend much time listening to the debate. Rather, he utilized the opportunity of having a large number of his colleagues present to discuss legislative and political business.

The first person Quie sought out was the Republican Minority Leader, Charles Halleck. From him, Quie received assurances of support for the vocational and higher education bills. Next, he spoke to Representative William Avery (R. Kan.), a member of the Rules Committee, which was scheduled to consider the two education bills the following day. Quie was anxious to obtain GOP support for the bills in the Rules Committee because there were doubts about whether the bills could reach the House floor without minority party support.

Quie also met with Representative Peter Frelinghuysen (R. N.J.), the ranking Republican member of the full Education and Labor Committee. He asked Frelinghuysen's assistance in arranging a meeting of Republicans interested in educational matters to discuss the two bills. This proved to be impossible because no mutually agreeable time was available so late in the week. As a result, Quie went to Representative John Byrnes of Wisconsin, the Chairman of the House Republican Policy Committee, and asked him to call a Policy Committee meeting so that the minority members of the Education and Labor Committee could explain the bills to a cross section of the GOP House membership and urge the Policy Committee to adopt a resolution supporting the bills. Byrnes agreed to call a meeting for the following Monday.

The House Republican leadership normally calls a meeting of its Policy Committee to discuss important legislation before it

---

[8] For a detailed discussion of the impact of the procedural rules on the outcomes of congressional contests, see Chapter 6, "The Tangled History of the Depressed Areas Act."

is considered on the House floor. At these meetings, Republican members of the committee that has considered the legislation explain the bill to the members of the Policy Committee. Discussion follows, and the committee normally takes an official Republican position on the legislation. The committee's decisions are not considered binding on any member, but rather are a means of communicating its sentiments and leadership to the rank-and-file GOP members of the House.[9]

The House Democrats have no institution comparable to the Republican Policy Committee. A Steering Committee was created in 1965, but it has remained an inert organization (see Chapter 4). The Democrats at present, however, have less need for this kind of an institution because their party controls the White House and it is the President who formulates his party's legislative program.

While the Philippine claims bill was being debated, Quie also caucused briefly with the other Republican members of the Minnesota congressional delegation—Representatives Ancher Nelsen, Clark MacGregor, and Odin Langen. They discussed what course they should take regarding the 1964 Republican presidential nomination. Their decision was to support former Representative Walter Judd as Minnesota's favorite son at the National Convention. They also exchanged news on Minnesota politics. The Minnesota Republican congressmen meet regularly for lunch on Tuesdays and, as they did on the day under discussion, gather periodically off the floor. These meetings are considered a valuable means of exchanging reliable information—a commodity that busy congressmen are always seeking. Since the Minnesota Republicans are on different committees, they can advise and inform each other about the issues before their respective committees. As a result, on many matters the delegation tends to vote together. When he first served in the House in 1958, Quie helped institute the regular meetings of the Minnesota delegation.

As he moved about the floor and cloakrooms, Quie also chatted casually with other members. On this day the main topics of conversation were the flare-up between Harriman and Pillion (with most members being rather surprised about Harriman's

---

[9] For a thorough discussion of the House Republican Policy Committee, see Charles O. Jones, *Party and Policy-Making: The House Republican Policy Committee* (New Brunswick, N.J.: Rutgers University Press, 1965).

quick temper) and the baseball game the night before between the Republican and Democratic members of Congress—a game the Democrats won 11-0. Quie also discussed with Mrs. Catherine May (R. Wash.), arrangements for a trip members of the Agriculture Committee were going to take the following day to Uniontown, Pennsylvania, to observe the operation of a food-stamp program being used to distribute government surplus food to needy families. In the midst of his discussions with other members, Quie caught a quick sandwich and glass of milk in the cloakroom.

While Quie was moving among his colleagues, the House debated the Philippine war-claims issue.[10] The first matter considered was whether the House should adopt House Resolution 453, a resolution (or rule) reported by the Rules Committee calling up the conference report for consideration. Under the complex rules of the House of Representatives, unless this were approved, the Philippine war-claims conference report could not be considered on the floor. In this case, opponents of the conference report had elected to contest the procedural issue of whether to accept the resolution of the Rules Committee. An opponent of the conference report and the ranking Republican on the Rules Committee, Clarence Brown of Ohio, stressed in debate that the prerogatives and rights of the House were at stake, because the conference report contained provisions that were in the Senate version of the bill and that would not have been germane to the bill had they been offered as amendments on the floor of the House. He therefore urged his colleagues not to vote to take up the conference report; if they did, they would be allowing the Senate to force on the House provisions to which it was opposed. Because the question involved the prerogatives of the House, opponents of the report thought they had a better chance of blocking it at this stage than later on the substantive question of agreeing to the report.

A roll call was held on the question of considering the report. Approximately thirty-five minutes were consumed as the clerk called the names of the 435 members of the House in alphabetical order and then repeated the names of those who did not answer. Members not present when their names were called then

---

[10] For a verbatim account of the events of the House floor on July 31, 1963, see *Congressional Record* (Eighty-sixth Congress, 1st session; July 31, 1963; daily edition), pp. 13043-13067.

filed into the "well of the House" and cast their votes orally, as the clerk recognized them. Quie voted "nay" on whether to approve the resolution to call up the conference report for consideration. He would have preferred to vote against the conference report itself, but since he had learned that the opponents intended to ask for a roll call only on the question of the rule, he voted against the rule in order to be on record against the war claims. The motion to take up the conference report passed, however, 234 to 166. After a short period of debate, the conference report was agreed to by a voice vote. Following this vote at 2:30, Quie left the House Chamber and walked to his office—this time going outside and using the sidewalk between the Capitol and the Longworth House Office Building.

The Congressman's Office Staff

While Quie had been on the floor and in committee meetings, his staff had been working in the crowded outer office of his two-room suite in the Longworth Building. Quie has six full-time employees. During the summer he also has a college student intern who assists him by doing research work in the Library of Congress. The congressman's administrative assistant, Reynold Berquist, previously worked for Quie's predecessor and was retained by Quie. Berquist had twenty-seven years' experience working on Capitol Hill and was a resident of the First District. Because of his long Washington experience and familiarity with the district, he handles most of the constituent requests for assistance in dealing with government agencies. This "case work," as it is called, covers a wide variety of requests—ranging from help in securing passports and aid to servicemen having trouble with the military to assistance to veterans and older persons in their dealings with the Veterans Administration and the Social Security Administration. On this day, Berquist had spent much of his time on the problems of several grain-elevator operators who had sold soybeans to the Department of Agriculture. The operators had received a reduced price because of alleged contamination and foreign matter in their beans. They wrote and called Quie to ask his help in securing a clarification of Department policy and a reversal of the administrative decision. During the day Berquist made several calls to the Department to determine why the operators suffered the reduction in their price and to request that the beans be re-inspected.

In addition to Berquist, Quie has a research assistant, Phil Roe, who came to the office after graduating from Saint Olaf College (Quie's alma mater), where he had been active in the Young Republican organization. Roe was principally responsible for preparing material to be sent to constituents, party organizations, newspapers, and radio and TV stations in the district.

Quie has taken pains to keep his constituents informed of what he is doing in Washington and of his views on issues before Congress. He sends out a two-page newsletter entitled "Congressman Al Quie Reports" about six times per session. His July newsletter contained a long article explaining his position on civil rights legislation and several short items, including one critical of the Administration's handling of the impending rail strike and another expressing concern about the future of NATO and free world unity. Because of his concern for NATO's future, Quie had just been appointed by the Republican Policy Committee to head a twelve-man subcommittee to study the problems of North Atlantic unity. In addition to his radio broadcasts to the district, Quie also writes an article for several of the weekly and daily papers in his district. Earlier in the session, he had sent a questionnaire to 120,000 residents of the district, asking them how they felt about the issues before Congress. Roe helped him prepare the questionnaire and process the results.

The Congressman also has made a special effort to keep in touch with Republican officials in the district. He periodically sends a special newsletter called "In the Family" to members of his personal campaign organization, the Quie Volunteers. Quie organized this group during his first congressional campaign in order to provide a unified campaign organization. He thought such an organization was essential because there was no regular Republican party organization in Minnesota at the congressional-district level. The basic units of the party were instead the county GOP organizations. Since his election, Quie has been successful in integrating his own volunteer organization into the regular party structure and has secured the cooperation of the county organizations in raising campaign funds. Quie also sends a special news-letter, "The Party Caucus," several times each session to the active members of the county Republican organizations in the district, and he writes articles for the newsletters that some of these organizations distribute.

In addition to the two men on the staff there are also four secretaries. Judy Edblom, another resident of the district, is Quie's personal secretary; she handles dictation, appointments, and some of the mail the office receives. The other secretaries type replies to letters drafted by Quie and Berquist and do the more routine case work that Berquist may delegate.

Much of the staff's time is spent assisting Quie in answering the steady flow of mail that his office receives from constituents. Since the mail is one of the few direct contacts a member can have with his constituents, Quie wants his constituents to receive prompt replies and, whenever possible, positive responses to their requests. Quie himself quickly scans most of the mail. Each evening he examines and signs each letter the office sends out. Quie does not, however, attempt to gauge his voting in the House by the majority viewpoint expressed in the mail he receives. He feels that since the voters of southeastern Minnesota had sufficient confidence in him to send him to Congress, they expect him to exercise his own judgment. There are times, however, when thoughtful letters from well-informed persons and individuals whom Quie respects can influence his decision on how to vote. On some issues, interest groups stimulate huge volumes of mail, as during congressional consideration of withholding taxes on dividends in 1962. Quie's office has learned to identify "pressure mail" quickly. Such mail, Quie feels, has little effect on how he will vote, though he is interested in it because it provides him with a gauge of how active interest groups are on a particular issue.

In order to keep in touch with his district, Quie also attempts to get back to Minnesota approximately every four to six weeks while Congress is in session. When Congress is out of session, he opens an office in Faribault, which he uses as his headquarters while he is in Minnesota. He also receives in his Washington office all of the papers published or circulating in his district. This includes the four daily Minneapolis-Saint Paul papers, seven other dailies, and forty-five weekly papers. Quie personally reads one of the metropolitan papers thoroughly while his staff go through the rest for matters that will be of interest to him.

Quie tries to see his constituents when they visit Washington. Often he has his picture taken with the visitors on the steps of the Capitol by a photographer who regularly performs this service for members and is paid by the members personally. Quie normally sends one copy of the picture to the visitor and another to the hometown newspaper of the constituent in the hope that the paper will print the picture.

The Congressman's Office

As Quie entered the outer room of his office at 2:40 on the day being considered, he stopped at Roe's desk and helped him identify several constituents in pictures taken the previous day on the Capitol steps, suggesting that a special note might be sent to the newlyweds in one picture. Next he went into his own office and started to go through the day's mail. His office is furnished with a large mahogany desk and several blue leather chairs and a couch. On one wall are about thirty autographed pictures of some of his colleagues in the House, along with several pictures of himself with such prominent Republican leaders as former President Eisenhower, Richard Nixon, and John Foster Dulles. Behind him on one side of a window is a picture painted by his wife and on the other side of the window is a large portrait of Lincoln. On the wall to Quie's left hang several pictures of his family. There are also several pictures of Quie at his farm near Dennison, Minnesota, along with several citations, including his Distinguished Service Award from the Northfield Chamber of Commerce.

Among the letters received that day were a request for tickets for the guided tour of the White House and a letter complimenting Quie for the stand he had taken on civil rights legislation in his last newsletter. A director of the maternity ward of a hospital in the district wrote requesting an additional supply of the government booklet entitled *Infant Care* that the hospital distributed to all new mothers. Unlike many congressmen, Quie does not send these books automatically to all new mothers in his district, but rather sends them to the hospitals in the district for distribution. Each book is stamped with a greeting from Quie. He also received an invitation from a rural cooperative power association in Elk River, Minnesota, to attend a luncheon at the May-

flower Hotel in Washington in August. Quie called in Judy
Edblom, asked her to take care of the mail, and told her to inform
the cooperative people that he would attend their luncheon.

While reading his mail, Quie also received several phone
calls. One was from a reporter who asked him about the status
of the aid to education bills and whether the bills would get
through the Rules Committee. Quie said that he was very optimistic about having Republican support in the committee. A
representative of the grain elevator operators association also called
to express his concern about the possibility of a rail strike as a
result of the failure of the railroads and rail unions to reach an
agreement on work rules to end "featherbedding." Such a strike
would have dire effects on the elevator operators. Quie talked
frankly and told the trade association official that he was sure Congress would not let the trains stop running. Another member of
the Agriculture Committee called about the forthcoming trip to
Uniontown to view the operation of the food-stamp program.

At 3:00 a Minnesota lobbyist for the trainmen's brotherhood met Quie in his office after having arranged earlier in the
day through Judy Edblom to see the congressman. He first reviewed quickly the major proposals before the Congress for dealing with the impending strike of the railroad brotherhoods. In
particular, he stressed his strong opposition to the President's proposal that Congress authorize the Interstate Commerce Commission (ICC) to settle the work rules dispute. He explained
that the unions were opposed to this because it meant compulsory
arbitration and a loss of the unionman's right to strike. He noted
also that the ICC had just authorized discontinuing passenger
service to Rochester, a city in Quie's district that needs good transportation facilities because of the Mayo Clinic. Quie agreed that
compulsory arbitration was a bad precedent to start. The lobbyist
then explained the merits of the proposal the union hoped would
pass Congress. This measure called for Congress to appoint a
special "watchdog committee" of congressmen and senators to see
that the railroads and unions would again sit down at the bargaining table and bargain in good faith. He said repeatedly that he was
convinced that agreement could be reached under these circumstances. Asking Quie to be a cosponsor of the resolution embodying the union proposals, he said that Quie's support would be

extremely influential with other members of the House. Quie again expressed his fears of compulsory arbitration, but said that in a matter as serious as this he wanted to study further. He also said that before deciding he wanted to talk to Representative Nelsen of Minnesota who was on the committee (Interstate and Foreign Commerce) considering the rail problem. The informal talk was conducted throughout on a first-name basis.

At about 4:00, after the lobbyist had left, Quie's secretary brought in for his signature the letters being mailed that evening. He carefully read each letter and took care to sign either his full name or just "Al" depending on how well he knew the constituent. As he was signing the mail he received a long distance call from a friend who operated a grain elevator in Austin, Minnesota. This constituent, too, was having trouble with the Department of Agriculture regarding the price he was receiving for his soybeans. Quie assured him that he would try to see why elevator operators in the district were having this problem and said he would see if the beans could be reinspected to be sure the operators were receiving a fair price. Following the call, he continued to sign his mail until Berquist brought in a draft of a letter to be sent to another of the elevator operators having trouble with the Agriculture Department. Quie went over the three-page statement carefully and consulted with Berquist about how best to handle the situation. He also called the Washington representative of the feed and grain dealers association to ask him if dealers outside his district were having the same problems his constituents were having. He was assured that they were. The trade association man gave Quie further information on the problem and agreed to send him pertinent literature.

Shortly after 5:00 Quie began picking up material that he wanted to read or work on at home that night. This was an unusually early time to leave, but the House had recessed early that day. Furthermore, Quie had special reasons for wanting to spend a few extra hours with his family this day. Congressional duties would require him to be away from Washington for the next two days. In addition, he and his family were in the midst of a home-improvement project in the backyard of their Washington home and this was one of the few opportunities he would have to work on it.

Conclusion

Congress constitutes a social system that gives wide latitude to its members in determining the type of congressman they want to be. That is, to a considerable degree each member defines for himself his congressional goals and how he will allocate his time and resources. Albert Quie has chosen to emphasize the job of lawmaker as he has sought to play a constructive role in the shaping of educational and agricultural policy. As a member of the minority party, he believes his job is not merely to be opposed, but also to have alternatives to the proposals of his Democratic colleagues. He was not, however, totally free in allotting his own and his staff's energies. The various forces impinging on the congressional scene have made Quie more than a legislator. As his constituents came to him to appeal what they considered unfair administrative decisions by their government, Quie assumed the role of the constituency servant. With elections always just around the corner for members of the House, Quie was constantly concerned about creating a favorable image of himself in Minnesota and with having a gauge of his constituents' sentiments on the issues. He also sought to keep his ties to local party leaders in good repair. Others external to Congress whose actions could affect his career, such as lobbyists and reporters, were also given considerable time and attention in the course of his work day.

Within the House, long hours were spent on the floor and in committee debating, planning, listening, and chatting with his colleagues, as he sought to influence policy decisions and establish satisfactory relations with party leaders, committee colleagues, and other members of the Minnesota Republican delegation. In addition, he was administrative director of a six-man office staff. Quie's was but one interpretation of the congressional role, but it illustrates the complexity and strains of the job.

THE OFFICE OF MIKE MONRONEY

NSOB 6205 boasts one of the most inspiring panoramas in Washington. Located on the southwest corner of the new Senate office building's sixth floor, its windows look out to the south on the gleaming marble of the Supreme Court and the

Capitol. Its view to the west takes in the entire length of the Mall, with the Washington Monument rising in the background to break the horizontal monotony of the federal buildings along Constitution Avenue. Inside, the paneled office appears to the visitor somewhat small by Senate standards. On the walls are pictures of family and political associates, and the windows and tables are crowded with trophies. Conspicuous on the large desk is a model of the Wright brothers' first airplane, the 1961 Wright Brothers Memorial Trophy for service to aviation.

The aviation trophy is symbolic, for the occupant of NSOB 6205 is Senator A. S. Mike Monroney, chairman of the Senate Aviation Subcommittee and principal author of more than half a dozen major laws relating to air transportation. Known on Capitol Hill as "Mr. Aviation," the senior senator from Oklahoma has been fascinated by flight ever since he became aviation editor of the *Oklahoma News* (Oklahoma City) in 1924. Three years later, when Charles Lindbergh returned to St. Louis after his nonstop solo flight to Paris, Monroney interviewed him on the possibilities of commercial transoceanic air service. And in 1933 he contributed $12.50 to a fund to finance the solo round-the-world flight of Wiley Post, a fellow Oklahoman.

After nearly three decades on Capitol Hill, Monroney has never lost the enthusiasm of those early days of aviation history. He often campaigns by air, calling himself "the world's most enthusiastic air passenger." The 1961 Wright Brothers Memorial Trophy, one of aviation's highest awards and one of many such trophies adorning Monroney's office, cites the senator's "continuous emphasis on air safety, his pressure for further advancement in the art of air navigation and traffic control, his leadership in the field of air cargo development, and the foresight which has put him in the vanguard of airport development throughout the country. . . ."

Monroney was born in Oklahoma City in 1902, five years before Oklahoma Territory was admitted to the Union. In 1924 he was graduated Phi Beta Kappa from the University of Oklahoma. After five years as a newspaper reporter and political writer, he took charge of his father's small retail furniture business. He was elected to Congress in 1938 from Oklahoma's Fifth District (Oklahoma City), and since then has never lost an election. During his twelve years in the House of Representatives (1939-1951), he gained national prominence for his leadership in Congressional reorganization. The LaFollette-Monroney Act of 1946 remains a permanent monument to his efforts. In 1950 Monroney entered the Democratic senatorial primary to challenge thirty-year Senate veteran Elmer Thomas, winning in a runoff by 60,740 votes. Until recently, Democratic statewide primaries in Oklahoma have been tantamount to election; and in 1956 and 1962 Monroney won reelection by 87,000 and 26,000 votes, respectively.

During his first twelve years in the Senate, it appeared to some observers that Monroney was laboring in the shadow of his senior Oklahoma colleague, Senator Robert S. Kerr—whom journalists were fond of calling "the uncrowned king of the Senate." Kerr's rise to power within what Senator Joseph Clark (D. Pa.) called the "Senate Establishment" [11] was consummated very swiftly —largely after Lyndon Johnson left the Majority Leadership in 1961. Though his quiet and good-natured personality contrasted sharply with Kerr's more mercurial temperament, Monroney was invariably considered an intelligent and knowledgeable senator who could be counted upon for comment and information on legislative business. With Kerr's powerful personality removed from the Senate by his untimely death on New Year's Day of 1963, Monroney began to exercise more of the prerogatives of a senior senator.

In addition to aviation matters, Monroney has maintained other specializations during his Senate career. As coauthor of the Legislative Reorganization Act of 1946, he is considered an expert in congressional organization and procedure. In 1965 he proposed the creation of a Joint Committee on the Organization of Congress (S. Con. Res. 2); he became cochairman of this committee in March of that year. Upon the death of Senator Olin Johnston (D. S.C.) in April 1965, Monroney was elevated to the chairmanship of the Senate Committee on Post Office and Civil Service. Finally, as the representative of a major oil-producing state, Monroney has been a staunch supporter of oil depletion allowances.

In early 1965 Monroney was a candidate for the position of Majority Whip vacated by then Senator Hubert Humphrey

[11] For a discussion of the "Establishment" controversy, see the account of the Senate Democratic party in Chapter 4.

(D. Minn.). Though he does not consider himself a member of the "Senate Establishment," Monroney believed that his good personal contacts with other senators would make him a compromise choice between the two other candidates, John Pastore (D. R.I.) and Russell Long (D. La.). The anticipated stalemate failed to materialize, however, and Long was elected to the post by the Senate Democratic caucus.

The complex of seven offices, of which NSOB 6205 forms the apex, both reflects Monroney's institutional position and conditions his operations on the Hill. His staff is organized to complement his background, style, and legislative interests in performing the many functions surrounding the office of senator. Indeed, his staff is designed to play many of the roles of a United States senator with a minimum of personal intervention. The Senate is an intimate institution when compared with the larger House of Representatives, but the offices of individual senators display precisely the opposite characteristics. While the average congressman expects to exercise strong personal direction over his small staff, the senator heads an organization that must run largely on its own impetus.

Yet a senator's interventions at strategic points in his staff operations remain crucial. These interventions both reflect and condition his approach to his job. More than many of his colleagues, Monroney prefers to exercise strong personal supervision over the activities of his staff. As one of his staff members puts it, "The Senator's direction is continuous: some member of the staff, though not every member, gets strong direction each day from the Senator himself." For one thing, Monroney is the most important single source of outside information for his office. "He is constantly being educated," one employee explained. "On the floor, in committee meetings, and elsewhere, he is being exposed to information that we don't have." Much of this information is interpreted by Monroney as it is passed on to his aides.

The full dimensions of Senator Monroney's job can thus be measured only by exploring the nooks and crannies of NSOB 6205 and the auxiliary offices located elsewhere. To recreate accurately the view from NSOB 6205, we must look carefully at the functioning of Monroney's staff organization, which is in effect the formal structure of the Senator's job perceptions and performances.

The Senator Himself

On a pleasant August day in 1963, Senator Monroney got off the elevator at the sixth floor shortly after 9:00 A.M. and entered his suite of offices. Passing through a small reception room, he paused briefly at the desk of Mrs. Betty Lund, his personal secretary. As usual, Mrs. Lund had prepared a schedule of the day's formal engagements: Monroney follows the schedule if he can, but less important items often must be shunted aside as the day proceeds. Copies of the schedule are distributed daily to key staff members. In addition to keeping the schedule, Mrs. Lund handles Monroney's personal correspondence and serves as chief receptionist. Another woman in this room assists with these duties while serving as secretary to the senator's administrative assistant.

Monroney's schedule for this particular day was relatively simple. The Commerce Committee's Aviation Subcommittee, of which Monroney is chairman, was holding all-day hearings on the future of feeder air service in New England. Earlier in the summer, the Civil Aeronautics Board had refused to renew Northeast Airlines' lucrative New York-to-Miami run, a decision that imperiled the airline and alarmed New Englanders who depended upon it for air service. Shortly before 10:00 Monroney left his office for the hearing, which was to be held in the old Senate office building.

After conferring briefly with committee staff members, Monroney banged his gavel to open the session. Although the hearings had opened four days earlier, Monroney spent several minutes reviewing the purpose of the investigation for the benefit of witnesses and spectators attending for the first time:

> The Committee will hear testimony on the economic impact which possible discontinuance or interruption of air service will have on the communities, businesses, employees, and other affected parties. The Committee will also hear testimony and consider what may be done to provide continued, adequate, and, if possible, improved service to this region.

Monroney stressed that the CAB's decision was not specifically under review. While the committee could hardly fail to take note of the CAB action, he explained that the appropriate appeals were petitions for reconsideration and appellate review in the courts. "I do not believe it would be proper for this Committee to inquire into the merits of that case at this time," he concluded.

Throughout the morning the subcommittee heard a series of witnesses, mostly mayors from small New England cities. One by one, they reiterated the importance of air service to their communities. The witnesses had been recruited by the subcommittee staff in cooperation with the New England Council, a lobbying group which services the six New England states. At noon Monroney declared a recess until 2:00 P.M., when another set of witnesses would be heard.

Returning to his office shortly after noon, Monroney greeted two constituents from Ketchum, Oklahoma. They asked his help in a personal problem, and Monroney later made a phone call on the matter. He also greeted three young men from Muskogee, Oklahoma, one of whom was the son of a friend. At 12:30 he went to lunch with John Burzio, a Commerce Committee staff counsel assigned to work with Monroney on aviation issues.[12] They discussed progress and plans for the subcommittee hearings. On his way from lunch to the afternoon hearings, Monroney stopped to greet a family from McAlester. (During the day he missed four other sets of Oklahoma visitors, who were entertained by staff members in his absence.)

Monroney reconvened the Aviation Subcommittee at 2:00 to hear a long succession of witnesses. Among those testifying were executives of Eastern and Northeast Airlines, the chairman of the New England Council's aviation committee, and the spokesman for a stewardesses' group. As the afternoon wore on, Monroney left the room at one point to seek out Majority Leader Mike Mansfield. In Mansfield's chambers in the Capitol Building, just off the Senate floor, they discussed scheduling of the airport bill, which Monroney would manage on the floor. They decided to schedule debate four days later, on a Friday. Two hours would be devoted to consideration of the bill, with one additional hour for each germane amendment. The time would be equally divided.[13] With this

[12] In the Commerce Committee, staff counsels are appointed personally by Chairman Warren Magnuson (D. Wash.) and are not typically assigned to subcommittees; but in practice they develop a specialization and work with the relevant subcommittee chairman. Burzio, for example, works from desks both in Monroney's office and in the committee offices.

[13] The bill, S. 1153, "to extend the Federal Airport Act and to authorize funds therefore, with amendment (S. Rept. 446)," was reported the next day. The

single exception, Monroney continued to preside until the witnesses had finished and the subcommittee was recessed at 7:00 P.M.

At no time during the day did Monroney actually go to the Senate floor. The Senate convened at noon; but since it was a Monday and many members were spending a long weekend in their home states, the session was relatively brief. The business began with the "morning hour"—a period when senators are free to introduce bills, insert material into the *Congressional Record*, and speak briefly on matters unrelated to the measures currently pending.

Following the morning hour, the Senate resumed consideration of the nuclear test-ban treaty. Senator Barry M. Goldwater (R. Ariz.) delivered a speech opposing the treaty, while Majority Whip Hubert Humphrey interjected the Administration's answers to Goldwater's arguments. Debate on the nuclear test ban followed the classic Senate pattern of "advising and consenting" to treaties. The sporadic debate began on August 5, when the treaty was signed in Moscow by representatives of the United States, Great Britain, and the Soviet Union. Finally, on September 24, the Senate was ready to vote. The treaty was ratified by a vote of eighty to nineteen (Monroney voted for ratification), fourteen more than the two-thirds required by the Constitution. During the intervening six weeks, Monroney was able to absorb the arguments and form his opinion; and as we shall see, some of his constituents were already asking where he stood. On this day, however, he chose not to listen to the debate.

Wearily, Monroney checked in at his office. When he departed at 7:15 P.M., his briefcase contained about 150 letters to be signed. The next morning Monroney returned the letters—signed and ready for folding and mailing.

Like the first day, the second workday began around 9:00 A.M. Within fifteen minutes Monroney was talking to a constituent about a large accelerated public works project for street improvements in Okmulgee, Oklahoma. As he left the office for a 9:30 committee session, he shook hands with another constituent and his college-age son.

Monroney hurried down one floor to a meeting of the full Commerce Committee which had been called the day before by

---

date and length of time determined by Monroney and Mansfield were adopted by unanimous consent.

the committee's chairman, Senator Warren Magnuson (D. Wash.). It was an executive session, that is, limited to members, relevant staff people, and invited witnesses. The committee first approved the nomination of Ashton C. Barrett to the Federal Maritime Commission, along with twenty-six routine nominations to the Coast and Geodetic Survey. Then the senators turned briefly to the public accommodations section (S. 1732) of the President's civil rights legislation, which had been referred to the committee. Secretary of Labor W. Willard Wirtz finally joined the group to discuss the threatened nation-wide strike of the railway brotherhoods. Under immediate discussion was S.J.Res. 102, a desperation measure providing for compulsory arbitration to avoid the strike.

With the railroad dispute and the public accommodations bill, the Commerce Committee had its hands full during the late summer of 1963. (It was at this time that the press was complaining about the "do-nothing" Eighty-eighth Congress, and indeed many of Monroney's colleagues on other committees found their schedules less demanding. Monroney's third committee, Post Office and Civil Service, was fortunately relatively inactive at this point.) On this particular day, the Commerce Committee agreed to reconvene at 2:00 on the railroad labor bill. In addition, two meetings were scheduled for the next day: another session on the public accommodations measure was planned, and three members were delegated to meet once again with Secretary Wirtz on the railroad labor question.[14]

The bulk of the Commerce Committee's agenda made Monroney late for his second committee meeting, an open hearing of the Defense Appropriations Subcommittee scheduled for 10:00. Deputy Secretary of Defense Roswell Gilpatric was on hand to continue his testimony on the fiscal 1964 defense budget.[15] The hearing was adjourned at noon. Subcommittee chairman Richard Russell (D. Ga.) scheduled an executive session for 2:00, at which time General Maxwell Taylor, chairman of the Joint Chiefs of Staff, was to explain certain classified items in the budget. Monroney was not able to attend that session.

At noon Monroney rushed to the Senate radio-TV studios

---

[14] Chairman Magnuson, Senator John Pastore (D. R.I.), and Senator Norris Cotton (R. N.H.).

[15] The federal fiscal year 1964 had already begun more than a month and a half earlier, on July 1.

in the Capitol basement, where he was to be a guest on a regular half-hour TV show filmed by Senators Joseph Clark and Hugh Scott for distribution in Pennsylvania. During the unrehearsed interview, Monroney was questioned at length about legislative reorganization. He explained the proposals then pending before the Senate Rules Committee and reminisced on the passage of the LaFollette-Monroney Act of 1946.[16] He also fielded questions concerning issues before the Commerce Committee. He reviewed the railroad labor dispute and predicted that the President's public accommodations bill would reach the Senate floor in some form.

From the studio Monroney rushed to the New Senate Office Building for a 1:00 P.M. briefing of the Aviation Subcommittee. Officials of the North American Aviation Company reported on progress of plans for the supersonic RS-70 aircraft. In midafternoon the meeting was adjourned so the senators could go to the floor and vote on a three-month extension of the existing temporary $309-billion ceiling on the federal debt. The proposal (H.R. 7824) was passed by a fifty-seven to thirty-one margin, with Monroney voting with the majority. After the vote, Majority Leader Mansfield asked for and received unanimous consent for consideration of Monroney's Federal Airport Act later in the week. The terms of the unanimous consent agreement were those that had been worked out the day before between Monroney and the Majority Leader.

Monroney's Senate appearance on this day was not typical. Often, his committee responsibilities left him no time to spend on the Senate floor. The legislative body, however, had convened as usual at noon. During the morning hour, Senator J. William Fulbright (D. Ark.) delivered a stinging attack on a recent *Life* article on "pork-barreling" that had slurred an Arkansas River navigation project in which Fulbright (as well as Monroney) was interested. Terming the article "a libel of the entire Congress," Fulbright

---

[16] Earlier in the session Monroney had presided over a five-man *ad hoc* committee appointed by the Democratic leadership to make recommendations. The committee recommended a) a "rule of germaneness" for regular Senate debate; b) automatic permission for Senate committees to meet during the "morning hour"; and c) specified recesses, including a fifteen-day late summer "vacation." The Senate Rules Committee later held its own hearings, and Monroney made a highly publicized appearance during which he counseled avoidance of such highly charged issues as cloture. Later in the summer, the committee reported out the first two proposals, along with another proposal to give former Presidents limited rights to appear on the Senate floor.

observed that with current deficits in the Post Office Department, the government was furnishing the publishers of *Life* with a "pork" subsidy amounting to $14.5 million a year. Then Senator Lee Metcalf (D. Mont.) delivered a detailed exposé of what he considered improper lobbying activities of private power companies in the upper midwestern states. Senators and representatives are sensitive to attacks on the integrity of Congress, and the *Record* is often filled with such rejoinders to outside criticism as these.

Following the morning hour, the Senate resumed its sporadic consideration of pending bills. Senator Norris Cotton (R. N.H.) rose to support the nuclear test ban treaty, after which Senator Sam Ervin (D. N.C.) continued his series of "extended remarks" opposing the Administration's civil rights bill. Other southern senators engaged Ervin in a colloquy to support his position. (The civil rights legislation was not passed for another ten months.) The extension of the debt limit was the only legislation actually consummated that day.

At 5:30 Monroney returned to his office and consulted with John Burzio on the railroad labor bill and plans for floor debate of the airport bill. Then he returned the eight telephone calls that had accumulated during the day (two to Oklahoma businessmen, two to government departments, one to NBC radio, one to United Press International, and two to senators concerning legislation). The day's mail was then signed, and the day on the Hill ended at 7:00 P.M.

The Staff Carries On

The schedule just described is relatively typical of the late days of the congressional session, when committee and floor work is at its peak. Task follows task and Senator Monroney is able to check in at his office only sporadically. While he was occupied with his schedule, however, his staff continued to perform a variety of functions. No description of Monroney's "senatorship," then, would be complete without attention to these tasks.

On one side of Monroney's private office are the offices of his administrative and legislative assistants. Carter Bradley, the administrative assistant, joined the staff early in 1963. A former Oklahoma newspaperman, Bradley handles political matters and important constituency case work requiring personal contact. He represents Monroney on all types of matters and deals with many constituents who assume they "have to see the senator" concerning their problems. (Bradley's predecessor was a lawyer who handled many legislative matters, including aviation bills. His replacement by a non-lawyer has shifted emphasis of the job to constituency relations and case work.) The aviation specialist, John Burzio, is a young lawyer also new to the staff; his duties are roughly comparable to those of Bradley's predecessor and center around Commerce Committee business. A third man in the office, Harold Messenger, specializes in Appropriations Committee affairs and applications for appointments to the military academies.

On the other side of Monroney's office is a series of four rooms, strung out like a railroad flat. The reception room is immediately adjacent to the senator's office. Next is an office occupied by Don McBride, a special assistant for natural resources; after that the office of Miss Mary Ellen Miller, who handles the bulk of the legislative mail. The final office is devoted to the press secretary and also holds current correspondence files.[17]

Keeping Up with the Mail

The incoming mail, which averages 350 to 500 pieces a day, first goes across the desk of Jack Yocum, whose small office adjoins the reception room. Yocum joined Monroney's staff in 1946, and as a "clean desk man" he has developed mail-answering into a fine art. First, in- and out-of-state mail is separated. Constituent mail is answered as soon as possible, while out-of-state letters are given lower priority. Letters are opened by an automatic machine that was purchased several years ago when an important issue brought several thousand letters a day. Glancing at the first sentence of the letter, Yocum classifies it and puts it in the appropriate pile, to be directed to the various staff members.

Much "casework" is handled by Yocum himself, though many matters requiring personal intervention are referred to the administrative assistant. "Casework" includes all manner of requests for assistance of one kind or another: servicemen asking for

---

[17] Files from previous sessions are relegated to the attics of Senate office buildings, where Senator Monroney is assigned storage space, or to the National Archives, which accepts files in the hope that they may be added to its permanent collections.

transfer of assignments; citizens with Social Security claims; veterans wanting to establish eligibility for Veterans Administration benefits; people seeking help in bringing friends and relatives into the nation under immigration quotas; and a thousand similar demands. Yocum attempts to answer, or at least acknowledge, such requests the same day the letter arrives. Because the constituent may have written to other legislators, Monroney's office is in a sense competing with other offices.

"Legislative mail" goes to Miss Mary Ellen Miller and her assistant. She prepares replies for everyone who writes in about pending legislation. These replies invariably express the senator's appreciation for the constituent's sentiments, then explain the bill's status, and finally assure the writer that his views will be kept in mind. Whenever possible, Monroney prefers to state his position on the issue being inquired about.

Though Miss Miller tries to prepare individualized replies whenever possible, form letters must be used if a large volume of mail is received on a given subject. One such issue was the nuclear test-ban treaty signed in the summer of 1963. After about ten letters had been received, Miss Miller drafted two letters—one for those who favored the treaty, another for those who opposed it. The second letter was somewhat longer, since many who opposed the treaty did not seem to understand it and some explanation seemed in order. Both letters indicated that though the senator had reservations concerning the treaty, he was inclined to vote for it. It was explained, however, that he wanted to study the treaty and the subsequent hearings of the Senate Foreign Relations Committee before making a final decision. Monroney approved Miss Miller's drafts without change, and they were run off on the two robotype machines owned by the senator and located in a basement office of the old Senate office building. Another machine signs the senator's signature to the letters. Similarly, a "position paper" was prepared in 1964 for constituents inquiring about civil rights, a particularly controversial issue in a border state such as Oklahoma. (Monroney supported civil rights legislation in 1964 and 1965.)

In addition to Miss Miller and her assistant, a young woman is employed to handle all requests for government documents and publications. Another employee takes care of simple requests pertaining to appropriations and tax matters.

With the exception of the robotyped letters, which he has already approved in draft form, Monroney himself reviews each letter before it is sent out. Each letter is worded so that he can note its contents by scanning the first two or three lines. Sometimes he will affix comments and send the letter back to be re-drafted. If the letter is satisfactory, he signs it personally in green ink—a long-time Monroney trademark. (As in most senatorial offices, one staff member has learned to copy the senator's signature, in emergencies, for robotyped materials.)

"The Third Senator from Oklahoma"

Don McBride, Monroney's special assistant for water resources, occupies a somewhat unique place in Oklahoma politics. Though he has never held elective office, McBride has been so successful in promoting the state's interests during more than a generation on Capitol Hill that he has been described as "the third Senator from Oklahoma." Few people are more knowledge-able on reclamation and public works programs. A former Oklahoma state engineer, he was appointed head of the state's Planning and Resources Board by Governor Robert S. Kerr. Then he became director of the National Reclamation Association. In 1949 McBride accompanied Kerr to the Senate, where he served first on Kerr's personal staff and then on the staff of the Senate Public Works Committee. After Kerr's death in early 1963, McBride and his secretary were brought into Monroney's office.

McBride serves as a kind of independent agent on reclamation issues. His responsibilities to Monroney include handling all mail and casework pertaining to natural resource development—that is, any federal program involving soil, water, natural resources, public works, area redevelopment, highways, recreation, and the like. Such programs are considered "bread-and-butter" issues by legislators from southern and western states. About twenty-five percent of McBride's time is spent consulting with Oklahomans who need advice on how to deal with federal agencies. He either accompanies them to the agency or arranges their appointment and tells them how to proceed. He has extensive knowledge of the laws and programs, not to mention friendships with Washington officials from Cabinet members on down. McBride also maintains liaison with state and local officials in Oklahoma, averaging seven trips a year (each of a week to ten days in length). While accompanying Monroney to Oklahoma in July 1963 for dedication of a new reclamation dam, for example, McBride consulted with several local development groups and spent an entire afternoon talking with the Regional Engineer of the Army Corps of Engineers.

Nor do McBride's activities stop there. He serves as an informal consultant to all members of the Oklahoma delegation and occasionally to other legislators from the seven-state region of the Arkansas-Big Red drainage system. A listing of most of McBride's phone calls during the first of our two days illustrates the dimensions of his job:

1. with a Soil Conservation Service official, discussing a report on recreational development of Four Mile Creek at El Reno, Oklahoma;

2. with a Public Health Service official, discussing natural salt pollution program in Oklahoma and Texas and plans for an interim report on the subject;

3. with a legislative assistant of Senator J. Howard Edmonson regarding a difference between the Coast Guard and the Grand River Dam Authority in Oklahoma. (Later in the week the two senators and the relevant congressman introduced a bill to straighten out the dispute.);

4. with an Oklahoma congressman's administrative assistant about a job for a constituent who wanted to come to Washington;

5. with a Senate Interior Committee staff member about disposition of certain hearings of the Senate Select Committee on Water Resources;

6. with an administrative assistant of an Oklahoma Congressman about an application from Jay, Oklahoma, for Area Redevelopment Administration assistance to increase the town's water supply;

7. discussed same problem with ARA's southwest division representative in Washington;

8. with a staff member of an Oklahoma congressman, who inquired whether or not the Corps of Engineers had under authoriza-

tion any projects in the vicinity of Alva, Oklahoma, which could be used for municipal and industrial water supply. (McBride advised that they did not.);

9. with Alva, Oklahoma, businessmen (long distance). Since the Corps of Engineers had no reservoir available to Alva, the businessmen wanted to know how to apply for a P.L.566 water project to supplement the town's water supply (information was given);

10. with the press secretary of another senator, who wanted the names of the ten largest hydroelectric power projects in the nation;

11. with a clerk of Senate Appropriations Subcommittee on Agriculture, to find out for Monroney why the agriculture bill had not yet been reported out. (The clerk said that the committee was awaiting a report on REA loans from the General Accounting Office.);

12. the clerk called back later in the day to say that the GAO report had been received and that the subcommittee would mark up the bill later in the week.

Since Kerr's death, McBride's scope of operations has narrowed somewhat. This stems primarily from the fact that Monroney does not have Kerr's unique institutional base of power in this policy area. Kerr was acting chairman of the Senate Public Works Committee during the long period when the actual chairman, Senator Dennis Chavez (D. N.Mex.), was gravely ill with cancer. Monroney is not a member of that committee, though he has been on the Public Works Subcommittee of Appropriations since 1961. McBride's functions, however, will not become obsolete so long as Oklahoma, like other western states, depends on federal funds for the development of its natural resources.

Relations with the Press

As a former newspaperman himself, Monroney takes an unusual interest in his relations with the press. He is available to the press and has staffed his office to supply newspapers with competently prepared "copy." Like professional newsmen, however, he is suspicious of "public relations" and prefers not to "spoon-feed" reporters with publicity releases every time he delivers a speech. Rather than writing a press release, Monroney's press aide prefers to show the reporter the relevant documents and allow him to prepare the story on his own.

In charge of press relations is Mrs. Joseph Short, an Oklahoman who once covered Mrs. Eleanor Roosevelt for the Associated Press and who served as correspondence secretary to former President Truman.[18] Mrs. Short has been with Monroney for six years.

A mimeographed collection of short news releases is sent out every two to three weeks. Though written primarily for small daily and weekly newspapers, copies are also sent to the wire services and special correspondents. They must be sent out by Saturday to reach Oklahoma in time for Wednesday or Thursday deadlines (the days when most weeklies go to press). Only two or three newsletters for the general public are put out in a year.

News releases are frequently sent out on special subjects. The stories may pertain to Monroney's activities, or they may announce a federal grant or project. (Federal agencies often allow legislators [especially those of the President's party] to announce such things, and a lively competition has developed among many Hill offices to get first crack at these announcements.) On this particular Monday, Monroney's administrative assistant received word that the Farmers Home Administration had approved the first rural water system loan for Oklahoma, a $380,000 loan to the Sapulpa Rural Water Supply Corporation. Monroney was advised of the loan, and a joint release was sent by wire to Sapulpa newspapers and officers of the local corporation. (Under the practice of "joint releases" instigated some years ago by Monroney, each federal project is announced under the names of the two senators and the congressman from the relevant district. This applies no matter which office actually sends out the information, and the courtesy extended to the state's lone Republican congressman, Page Belcher of Tulsa.) As a result of inquiries to the FHA, the office obtained more details on the project, and later in the day a comprehensive press release was sent air mail to all newspapers in the county involved (Creek County). Although sent from Monroney's office, the releases were in the form of a joint announcement by the two senators and Congressman Tom Steed. The preparation of a formal

[18] Joseph Short served as President Truman's press secretary. After his death in 1952, Mrs. Short was appointed to the White House staff.

written release was fairly unusual, for announcements of federal grants or projects are usually relayed by the office directly to the papers (and the recipients) by phone or wire.

In addition to the newspapers back home, several Capitol correspondents include Monroney's office on their "beat." The two Tulsa papers, the *Tribune* and the *World*, have Washington reporters, and a third reporter represents the two Oklahoma City dailies, which are under joint management. In addition, the two major wire services have regional correspondents on the Hill who handle stories pertaining to Oklahoma and surrounding states. Mrs. Short maintains close contact with these five reporters, sometimes even covering floor debate when they are unable to attend. When Monroney is involved in floor debate or committee work of a generally newsworthy nature, the regular wire service staffs take over.

Press releases are rarely employed during Monroney's tours of Oklahoma, except during campaigns. Reporters in the smaller cities invariably cover his appearances, and the senator's news sense often enables him to assist local reporters in extracting newsworthy "leads" from his speeches. The big city papers, which rely more heavily on press releases, give Monroney's tours somewhat less coverage.

The Oklahoma Delegation

The eight members of the Oklahoma delegation have developed an unusually close working relationship. In addition to the cooperative arrangement on news releases, the delegation has meetings from time to time. There is a rotating chairman and secretary to coordinate activities (Monroney was chairman in 1963). Visiting dignitaries are sometimes invited to meet with the entire delegation. Each spring the legislators and their staff assistants attend a dinner staged by the 150 or so Oklahomans attending the U.S. Chamber of Commerce convention.

If a large delegation of constituents is known to be coming, Monroney's staff sometimes reserves the Senate Post Office Committee room across the hall and orders an urn of coffee from the Senate cafeteria. Monroney then drops in briefly to speak to the group.

Conclusions

Our accounts of the day-to-day environment of legislators are designed to illustrate the variety of tasks performed by senators and representatives. In general, these are hyperactive men whose daily schedules are cut up unmercifully into discontinuous five- and ten-minute segments. In the case of Senator Monroney, we have deliberately focused as much on the staff as on the senator himself to reflect the critical importance of staff personnel on the Senate side of Capitol Hill.

The activities of Monroney's staff encompass practically the full range of the senator's responsibilities. Most senators are inclined to stress their roles in policy-making, and their staffs can assist them by gathering information, doing a limited amount of research, and even writing speeches pertaining to policy issues. Because Monroney is a senior member of several committees, he enjoys committee staff support on such matters as aviation or post office and civil service. In fact, it is difficult at times to separate the work of his personal and committee staffs.

The most time-consuming activities of the senator's personal staff are a function of constituency interests and demands. Constituency work, as we have seen, ranges from answering legislative mail to the varieties of "casework" chores. Because senators have a state-wide constituency, the volume and variety of their tasks are quite large in comparison to those of their House colleagues. Considering Oklahoma's median size and distance from the nation's capital, Monroney's constituent work is probably about average in volume; but like most senior members, he has seen a sizeable increase in constituent communications during his legislative career. His staff expects this volume to increase further as government becomes more involved with the personal lives of citizens, and as the citizens' level of education rises.

Some senators and representatives complain that "errand-boy" functions for constituents detract from legislative deliberation. But most members nonetheless work diligently to answer constituent requests. A congressman is often in a position to give real assistance to a bewildered or troubled constituent; and a job well done can produce a grateful and loyal supporter (not to mention the constituent's family and friends).

A further function performed in part by staffs is support for the senator's communications with the public. Dissemination of news to the media is an increasingly distinct task of Capitol Hill staffs. Every legislator is newsworthy in his home state or district; but senators are more often able to command national publicity. And a senator's greater staff resources make possible the cultivation of this national exposure on a more regular basis.

The operations of NSOB 6205 are in a real sense, therefore, the expression of Monroney's "senatorship." Monroney's office staff shares this characteristic with the staffs of his ninety-nine colleagues; and, as we have intimated, his staff is probably about average in size, work load, and degree of specialization. Though many routine functions are performed without the senator's personal intervention, the office itself is heavily dependent upon his personality, organizational skills, legislative interests, and even his political style. As for NSOB 6205, Monroney's own informality and genial manner do much to preserve the loyalty, not to mention the sanity, of his staff. As in every senator's office, the work load is highly uneven and produces periods of frantic frustration. But when all is said on the matter, most staff members would not choose to work anywhere else.

HOUSE REPUBLICANS ELECT A LEADER

Critics of the American party system are fond of deprecating Congress for its undisciplined and disunited party organizations. Yet in spite of their limited powers, the Democratic and Republican parties in Congress are the principal agents of centralization in a decentralized political arena. This is especially true in the House of Representatives. Because the average representative is less in the public eye than his corresponding senator, his party label and how it is perceived by the electorate is apt to be crucial to him. Also, in so large a body as the House it is not possible to build up as personalized a communications system to keep in touch with all House business as it is in the Senate. Rather, one must rely on more regularized sources—principally the party leadership. The leadership is also in a position to advance or retard the member's career by influencing the allocation of important committee assignments.

Who the party leaders are and how they manage the party's machinery in the House are important determinants of what the party's record will be and to what extent individual members will achieve their legislative career objectives. This power in the hands of the party leadership has meant that turnover among leaders is low and that overt challenges are few. The organizing sessions at the beginning of each new Congress are therefore normally quite routine affairs at which incumbent leaders are usually re-elected. This quiet pattern has been disturbed recently by revolts resulting in the involuntary retirement of party leaders. The intraparty leadership struggles among the House Republicans in 1963 and 1965 provide an opportunity to learn more about the nature of the legislative party (particularly about the minority party, which does not get as much publicity as the majority) and about the methods used to influence House decisions.

A Recent Precedent for Leadership Change

On the day after the House Republicans met to organize for the Eighty-eighth Congress, *The Washington Post* in a front-page story announced a seemingly minor change in the House Republican leadership. The *Post*'s story stated:

> By an 86-78 vote, the House GOP Conference elected Representative Gerald R. Ford (Mich.) its chairman, ousting Representative Charles B. Hoeven (Iowa), old guard chairman for four years. The position is largely symbolic, but it was an impressive show of muscle by the junior members. It will give them an articulate voice in leadership circles and was viewed as a first step toward trying to change the party image in the House.[1]

Here was a public manifestation of a feeling shared by an important segment of the House Republicans that their party was not functioning as it should.

Such expressions of discontent with party organization are not without parallels in the recent past. In 1959, following an election debacle in which the GOP suffered a net loss of forty-seven seats in the House, the House Republican Conference elected Charles Halleck (Ind.) as Minority Leader. Halleck ousted Joseph Martin (Mass.), the long time Republican leader (1939-1959) and former House Speaker. It was an extremely close contest that required two ballots before Halleck emerged the victor. At the same meeting, John Byrnes (Wis.) was chosen to assume Martin's duties as chairman of the Republican Policy Committee. Charles Hoeven became chairman of the Republican Conference,

---

[1] Richard L. Lyons, *The Washington Post*, January 9, 1963, p. A1.

while the venerable Leslie Arends (Ill.) was re-elected Republican whip. Halleck's election was not a reflection of ideological differences within the party, since his candidacy was supported by liberal and conservative Republicans. Rather, his defeat of the aging Martin reflected a desire on the part of the newer Republicans to bring younger and more aggressive members into the leadership.[2]

Halleck was particularly aggressive when marshalling his forces against the New Frontier. He had built a reputation as a tough, partisan "gut fighter," ready with the quick and often caustic retort in debate, often abrasive in manner but willing to act quickly and decisively even if it meant wounding the sensitivities of his party colleagues. Under his leadership, party unity increased. The *Congressional Quarterly* reported that during 1958, Joseph Martin's last year as minority leader, the average Republican in the House had a party unity score (the percentage of times he voted with a majority of his Republican colleagues against a majority of the Democrats) of sixty-five percent. Under Halleck's tutelage, this index of GOP unity jumped to seventy-seven percent in 1959. Halleck's record of marshalling support for the Administration's programs in the House led President Eisenhower to express publicly his admiration for Halleck's legislative skills.

Similarly, new life was breathed into the Policy Committee under John Byrnes' leadership. The committee acquired a small staff and met periodically to deliberate and issue statements of party policy on bills due for floor consideration. These official Republican statements gained wide circulation among partisans and hence contributed to the increased party unity under Halleck. Two special study committees were also organized by the Policy Committee, and they issued lengthy reports entitled, "Meeting the Challenges of the '60's" and "American Strategy and Strength."

When a Democratic President was elected in 1960, the relation of the Democratic-controlled Eighty-seventh Congress to the White House was changed. The minority party leadership again began to express criticism. The absence of a Republican in

[2] Halleck, who had served as Republican Majority Leader during the Eighty-third Congress, was reported to have been the third choice among Republicans seeking to replace Martin. The insurgents' first choice was reported to be Byrnes, with Ford and Halleck, second and third respectively. Halleck, however, made it clear that he was going to run regardless. In a three-way race, Martin would be assured re-election, so Halleck became insurgent candidate and Byrnes was named to head the Policy Committee.

the White House espousing specific programs meant that Halleck and his counterpart in the Senate, Senator Everett McKinley Dirksen (Ill.), became the chief national spokesmen of their party. They used a joint leadership press conference—soon dubbed the "Ev and Charlie show" by the Capitol press corps—as a means of presenting the views of the Republican congressional party.

During the Eighty-seventh Congress the seeds of discontent with party functioning in the House were sown, mainly among the junior Republicans. The fruit of this dissatisfaction was Gerald Ford's election to the Conference Chairmanship in January 1963 and his defeat of Halleck as Minority Leader in January 1965.

Bases of Discontent Among the
Younger Members, 1963

Disappointments of the 1962 election   The 1962 Congressional elections left many Republican House members disgruntled. Whereas the normal pattern in midterm elections is for the President's party to suffer substantial losses in the House, in 1962 the Republicans registered a net gain of only two seats. The reason for this small gain is undoubtedly the fact that while John F. Kennedy won the presidency in 1960, his margin of victory was small, and the Democrats actually lost twenty House seats. With few Democratic congressmen owing their 1960 elections primarily to Kennedy coattails, Republican opportunities to pick up seats in the 1962 off-year elections were diminished. Even so, many House Republicans, already unhappy with their minority status, were disappointed by the meager gains of the 1962 elections.

Need for an improved party image   Both liberal and conservative Republicans were unhappy about the public image of their party in Congress. They were aware of the rather low esteem in which the "Ev and Charlie show" was held by the press.[3] One member commented:

> We needed a fresh and dynamic leader to project to the public. I believe that the Republicans have some tremendously capable men here in the House—in the statehouses, too—but we weren't getting that picture across.

[3] The head of *The New York Times* Washington bureau, for example, had drawn painful comparisons between the youthful President Kennedy and Dirksen and Halleck whom he said looked "like a veteran Shakespearian actor and W. C. Fields." See James Reston, *Boston Herald*, January 9, 1963, p. 17.

The only three leadership positions in the House anybody knew anything about were in the hands of old midwesterners. We had Halleck, Arends, and Charlie Hoeven—those old midwesterners—making all the decisions.

Another Republican said that it was essential to change the image of party members as "crusty, old obstructionists." In a similar vein, an insurgent said after the 1963 Ford election:

Too often we Republicans ended up cowering defensively in a corner even when we were completely right. Too often legislation was shaped by Republicans but we didn't get the credit because our people weren't articulate. Instead, the President, who is articulate, would get the political glory.

We decided to push the very articulate and vigorous people in our party from the second echelon into the leadership.[4]

Lack of participation in party policy decisions   The younger members (in terms of service) thought that they were being left out of GOP policy formation. Representative Charles Goodell (N.Y.), a leader of the group of insurgents who helped elect Ford in 1963 and 1965, gave an explanation for his activities in the 1963 drive to elect Ford in a newsletter to his constituents:

Of the 176 Republican Congressmen, 83 had been elected in the last *four* years. We are a YOUNG party in Congress, with many hard-driving, articulate, intelligent and attractive Congressmen who should be speaking for us frequently as a party. In the seniority-conscious House, these Congressmen of high leadership caliber were under-utilized, chiefly because they had only been here 10 or 15 years.

There was also dissatisfaction with the party's internal communications system within the House. A Republican elected in 1960 complained:

The basic problem was that the leadership was not getting through to the troops on strategy and policy. We were not being consulted and too frequently there seemed to be no policy at all. It was not that we ex-

[4] Quoted by Lawrence Stern, *The Washington Post*, January 10, 1963, p. A4.

pected to be important all at once, but we did feel that
the organization was not working as it should. Perhaps
the leadership was a little complacent and too secure.

In addition to the rather widespread feeling of frustration
among the younger members of the party stemming from not being "in" on party decision-making, there were more specific complaints about the work of the party's two chief organs in the House,
the Republican Policy Committee and the House Republican
Conference.

Criticism of the Policy Committee   The Republican
Policy Committee was created in January 1949 by a resolution
passed by the House Republican Conference. Prior to 1963 the
committee had thirty-three members with a chairman elected by
the conference. There were ten *ex officio* members: the floor
leader, chairman of the conference, secretary of the conference,
the Republican whip, and the five Republican members of the
Committee on Rules. Fourteen members were elected to represent
nine geographic regions. Meeting in secret caucus, Republicans
from these regions chose regional delegates to the Policy Committee, with one delegate allotted for each twenty GOP congressmen in the region. Three members of the committee were at-large
members, recommended to the conference by the Committee on
Committees. Finally, each of the five most recent "classes" (year
of election) elected a nonvoting representative.

While Congress is in session, the Policy Committee normally meets each Tuesday to discuss the major issues about to be
decided by the Congress. Following a period of discussion, if
there is substantial agreement among the participants, the committee issues a statement of policy. Votes are not normally taken
in the committee. Rather, it usually reaches a consensus without a
formal vote. A copy of the policy declaration is sent to each Republican in the House as a guideline rather than a command. The
committee was formed because busy congressmen (see Chapter
3) need fast and reliable sources of information and cues on how
to vote on complex issues. The Policy Committee helped meet
these informational needs. One of the effects of its creation is
thought to be an increase in party unity.

The criticisms of the committee made by the 1963 insurgents were not directed toward the work of its chairman, John
Byrnes, who was very popular with the insurgents. Rather, the

basic structure of the committee was the target. The geographic basis of representation was especially irksome, because the newer Republican members believed that it accorded too much weight to the older members, while leaving the last five "classes" with only nonvoting representation. The result of the system of apportioning representation, some thought, was that the younger members were being effectively blocked from participation in one of the most important phases of party policy-making, and further, that many of the decisions reached by the Policy Committee were not representative of the views of the party rank and file.

Some also thought that the tendency of the committee not to take stands on legislation until a bill cleared its legislative committee left the minority party little time to formulate an alternative it might then sell to the country. Policy Committee statements issued prior to legislative committee consideration of pending bills would, however, have stripped Republicans on legislative committees of their traditional role as party spokesmen on issues before their respective committees.

Criticism of the House Republican Conference   The House Republican Conference consists of all the Republican members of the House. Under the chairmanship of Charles Hoeven (1959-1963), the principal function of the conference had been to elect the floor leader, Policy Committee chairman and its own officers—a chairman, vice chairman, and secretary—at the beginning of each new Congress. It also ratified the nominations of the Committee on Committees for Republican whip, at-large members of the Policy Committee, and Republican legislative committee assignments. The conference had met rarely for other than organizational functions. On the rare occasions when it did meet, it was normally just prior to an important House vote. Its gatherings then served as a means of mobilizing Republican support for a position adopted by the leadership and Policy Committee. The conference was not used as a forum for discussion of what party policy should be.

Because the conference rarely met, other than just prior to a few crucial votes on the floor, several Republicans complained that it was of little use to them. They said they needed information on pending legislation earlier than just before it went to the floor, if they were going to answer their constituents' questions and make intelligent decisions on what stand they themselves should take. Some thought that more regular meetings of the conference would be extremely valuable, not only as an information source, but also as an aid to promote party unity.

This expectation was in sharp contrast to that of a member of the Republican leadership who commented after Ford's election about the impossibility of utilizing the conference to work out policy positions. He said:

> They [the insurgents] thought they could make the Conference active and important—but you can't get agreements from 170 different guys. It just can't be done. That's why the Policy Committee is so important. There, where you have 30 to 40 people, you can thrash things out and come up with a position—as on the ARA [Area Redevelopment Administration] last week. We took a strong stand on that.

Although Chairman Hoeven was acknowledged to have used the conference in accord with the wishes of Floor Leader Halleck, still there were complaints about the way he had conducted meetings. There were complaints that he had been "heavy handed with the gavel" in arbitrarily preventing members from bringing up certain issues for discussion.

Lack of constructive Republican alternatives   Among those who initiated the movement to elect Ford, there was also a strong feeling that the party was not coming up with positive programs as alternatives to those of the Democratic Administration. Instead, they feared that their party appeared merely as an opponent of whatever the Democrats were proposing. A member of the class of 1960 commented:

> It [the movement to elect Ford] was not an ideological thing at all. The best way to characterize it was the 'activists versus the negativists'. . . . It was led by people who wanted the party to have a position and alternative programs. We wanted to show that we could assume the responsibilities if we were to get a majority in the House. I don't think that the older people like————are prepared to do that.

An example of negativism on the part of the leadership cited by the insurgents was the handling of the 1962 Trade Expansion Act, a measure that had high White House priority. In keeping with custom, Halleck had allowed Noah Mason (Ill.), the ranking minority member of Ways and Means, to offer the only Republican recommittal motion permitted under the rules. Mason's motion was simply that the committee report out a simple one-year extension of the existing program that the Administration was seeking to revise extensively. The Kennedy trade bill would thus have been killed. John Byrnes and other GOP Ways and Means members would have preferred to offer an amendment to the new bill that cut out certain objectionable provisions but left the bill otherwise intact.

A related criticism of the leadership was its failure to support a movement led by Thomas Curtis (Mo.) to increase the size of minority staffs on congressional committees. The leaders of this movement thought that additional staff assistance was essential if the party were to discharge its responsibility of acting as a constructive critic of Administration programs.

The original leaders of the insurgent movement were able, restless, and ambitious young men chafing under a system that seemed to reward mainly older members. They were also worried about the party image and its ability to present constructive alternatives. The insurgent movement was not, however, without its ideological overtones. Liberal and conservative spokesmen within the party were critical of the leadership on policy grounds. On the one hand, some conservatives thought that the leadership had not been sufficiently aggressive in unifying the party to fight the New Frontier. For them, the party had been too moderate. In Gerald Ford, they saw a hard-hitting critic of the Administration. By contrast, liberals in the party were concerned about what they called the "obstructionist tactics" of the party and they thought that with Ford in a leadership post, their cause would receive a fair hearing.

Choosing a Course of Action

By January 1963, there was substantial feeling among House Republicans that the party's operations in the House had to be improved. This viewpoint was particularly widespread among members who had served less than five years. As Table 6 indicates, the younger group was in a numerically advantageous position. The members elected since 1956 constituted fifty-five percent of the Republican membership of the House, while Republicans elected

TABLE 6   HOUSE REPUBLICAN MEMBERSHIP GROUPED ON THE BASIS
OF LENGTH OF SERVICE IN THE HOUSE, JANUARY 1963

Year of election	Number	Percent of total GOP membership
1962 (88th Club)	31	17.6
1960 (87th Club)	31	17.6
1958 (86th Club)	21	11.9
1956 (85th Club)	14	8.0
1954 (84th Club)	9	5.1
1952 (83rd Club)	21	11.9
Prior to 1952	49	27.9
Total	176	100.0

since 1952 included seventy-two percent of the party's membership.

Although there had been considerable discussion during
the Eighty-seventh Congress concerning the need to improve the
operation of party machinery, there was no advance planning for
the events of January 1963, which resulted in Ford's election as
conference chairman and the enlargement of the Policy Committee. These results were obtained through intensive efforts by a
small group of men working in a brief time-span of seven days—
January 2 through January 7, 1963.

On January 2 Representatives Charles Goodell and Robert
Griffin (Mich.) met for lunch at the Capitol Hill Club (a Republican meeting place near the Capitol) to discuss the upcoming
work of the Committee on Education and Labor. They quickly
decided, however, that some action had to be taken that session to
revitalize the whole Republican operation in the House. They continued their discussions that afternoon in Griffin's office and were
joined by several other members who had also just returned to
Washington from their respective congressional districts.

These discussions at first centered about what structural
changes might be made in the party's organs in the House. It was
agreed that the system of representation in the Policy Committee
should be changed to give the newer members a more prominent
voice in party councils. Specifically, they wanted an eight-member
expansion of the Policy Committee, with the seats allotted so that
the three newest classes would have two representatives each and

the classes that had been elected six and eight years before would each gain one additional representative.[5]

The insurgents also considered ways of making the conference more active. Among these were a requirement that the conference meet on a regular biweekly basis and a reduction in the number of member requests that would automatically call a conference. They wanted to use the conference as a forum in which party policy might be discussed and worked out in advance of floor action on a bill, rather than as a means of enlisting rank-and-file support for a position already adopted by the leadership.

Some of the insurgents thought that changes along the lines mentioned above would be sufficient. They would avoid the unpleasantness of attempting to remove senior members from party office. Others, however, felt that an attempt should be made to put a younger member in an elective leadership post. Otherwise they thought structural changes would be unsuccessful. Little serious consideration was given to attempting to oust Halleck, an extremely difficult task, especially on such short notice. Nor was removal of John Byrnes considered, since he was popular with the younger members. The insurgents did seriously think of attempting to remove the whip, Les Arends of Illinois. The party's Committee on Committees, however, nominates the whip and its choice is then ratified in a routine way by the conference. Thus, with the choice firmly controlled and the choosing committee dominated by the most senior members of the party and the floor leader, there was little hope of replacing Arends with a younger man. Arends' almost impregnable position in the party was later to be made patently clear to the "young Turks."

With the top posts—leader, Policy Committee chairman, and whip—inaccessible, the only remaining elective leadership position was that of chairman of the House Republican Conference, a job held since 1959 by Charles Hoeven of Iowa. This post was considered largely symbolic, since the conference met so seldom and Hoeven had used the conference in accord with the wishes of Minority Leader Halleck. Even so, replacing Hoeven

[5] Class clubs organized to reflect the Congress in which a member entered the House (such as the Eighty-eighth Club, Eighty-ninth Club) have been formed both by Republicans and Democrats. The Republicans, however, have shown a greater tendency to activate and maintain them. Class clubs provide members with access to information about House affairs, sources for contacts that can help in influencing legislation, and social outlets.

with a younger member seemed well suited to obtaining the insurgents' objectives. It would bring into prominence a young House Republican and at the same time clearly demonstrate to the leadership that the younger members wanted a greater role in party affairs. At the same time, they did not think that it would permanently harm or split the party. Avoiding a serious intraparty rift was considered essential.

All involved believed that this was an undertaking they could ill afford to lose, lest each one's personal career in the House be hurt, or lest the whole movement to improve the party's operations be set back several years. One Republican who joined Goodell and Griffin in the initial discussions summed up the reason Hoeven was chosen as a target:

> There was talk of putting new life in the whip organization. But the whip is chosen by the Committee on Committees, so that was out. So we decided to replace Charlie Hoeven because, frankly, we had the best chance there.

Between the Wednesday when Goodell and Griffin had first initiated discussions of improving party operations and the following Friday, the group had gradually increased in size—first to six and then to approximately twelve. Participants were selected with care, lest word of what was happening be prematurely leaked to the leadership. In maintaining secrecy about their actions, the group was helped by the facts that many members had not yet come back to Washington for the start of the new session and that others were still in the process of settling their homes and offices. One of the early planners in the movement said that these circumstances were very helpful because:

> Ordinarily news and rumors fly fast around here. You say anything and it goes straight to the leadership. Well, this time the members were just getting back— settling their families and taking care of the things that had piled up since December. The normal communications system was not set up yet.

The leaders of the group had carefully sounded out other members to determine how much support they could expect. They were not disappointed.

By Friday, the group had determined that Gerald Ford should be their candidate, though it had considered three other members as well. Ford's credentials made him a strong candidate. He was good looking and vigorous (a former All-American football player), an effective and forceful debater, and he was respected by his colleagues and liked by the Washington press corps. One New England Republican enthusiastically described Ford:

> Gerry Ford looks and acts a lot younger than he is . . . a former All-American in addition to his intellectual ability. He's a fair man. You can trust him. . . . He has tremendous capacity for leadership. I really think he has the qualities to be President and certainly a vice-presidential candidate. . . . He works hard.

> I really think a lot of Gerry Ford. . . . I'm not one of his close friends either, though I have gotten to know him much better this session. I allowed my name to be used publicly in this movement. Lots of the boys were afraid to because they knew the leaders wouldn't like it. I even put it in my newsletter. Hell, I was proud of being in on it.

Ford was vice-chairman of the conference at the time. This enabled the insurgents to argue that the party should promote younger men who had done a good job and that the jobs of leadership should be moved around.

The Campaign:
The Use of Internal Sources of Influence

Ford did not actively seek the office. Indeed, he was not informed of the plans of the insurgents until Friday, January 4— only three days before the election. Goodell and Griffin explained their plans to Ford and asked if he would agree to have his name put in nomination. They could offer no assurance of success. Ford agreed to run if, after a weekend of sounding out their colleagues, Goodell and Griffin decided to go ahead with the project.

Griffin and Goodell then made tentative plans for a reception for freshmen Republicans elected in 1962 that would be sponsored by the last three classes of Republicans elected in 1956, 1958, and 1960. They reserved a reception room at the Congressional Hotel, near the Capitol, for Monday afternoon. In addition to this group, Goodell and Griffin were counting heavily on a favorable response from the thirty-one-member freshmen class.

On January 5 the leaders of the insurgents continued to talk to their colleagues in the hope of obtaining support. Although they had a good idea which Republicans would be sympathetic and which hostile to their efforts, they generally asked probing questions before requesting support. All was done in confidence, because there was fear that if word of what was happening leaked out prematurely, the leadership would be able to win a large number of votes just by sowing doubt about the movement's success. Since the burden of proof was on the insurgents, they had to act with caution until they had their votes counted and secure.

In gaining support for their cause, the insurgents relied entirely on personal contacts. The members of the group talked to their friends, fellow committee members, state delegation members, and to anyone whom they thought would give them a fair hearing. They made effective use of the Republican social clubs. (The Republicans have a series of social clubs of limited size, the Marching and Chowder Club, the S.O.S Club, and the Acorns. Membership is by invitation and when vacancies occur attempts are made to select club members so as to get a broad geographic and ideological representation. These clubs meet regularly to discuss legislative matters over refreshments. The Democrats have no comparable groups.) The insurgents had representatives in the social clubs and used these friendships to enlist support for Ford's election. Club members were urged to assist in building support for Ford. Friends within the state delegations were similarly used.

This was an example of the utilization of *inside* sources of influence in the House with no reliance on mobilizing support outside Congress to influence the GOP membership. The insurgents had no time to develop such a campaign and, furthermore, they thought that this was a matter for members themselves to decide and that outside influence would have been resented.[6]

Over the weekend the insurgents had trouble getting in touch with the Republican members of the House. Many were still traveling to Washington from their districts or were still at home. Reaching these people required spending many hours making calls throughout the country. Some of those who were in

[6] For an excellent analysis of the use of internal and external sources of influence in a battle for position of Majority Leader in 1962, see Nelson W. Polsby, "Two Strategies of Influence: Choosing a Majority Leader, 1962," in Nelson W. Polsby and Robert L. Peabody (eds.), *New Perspectives on the House of Representatives* (Chicago: Rand McNally, 1963), pp. 237-270.

Washington had not yet come to their Capitol Hill offices and were at their Washington residences. Many had unlisted telephone numbers. To reach such persons, it was necessary first to call their staff assistants to get the unlisted phone numbers.

On Sunday night Representative and Mrs. Goodell held a buffet for new freshmen Republicans at a Washington restaurant called "The Place Where Louie Dwells." In addition to the freshmen, some of the insurgent leaders were invited, along with some of the older Republican members. This welcoming reception had been planned by the Goodells long before the Congressman thought about reforming the House GOP in 1963. The timing of the buffet, however, proved fortuitous because it gave the insurgents an opportunity to talk to the freshmen. No specific plea was made at the buffet, but the insurgents did talk to the freshmen in a guarded way. Ironically, during the buffet, Halleck recommended Goodell to the freshmen as an excellent example to follow if they wanted to succeed in the House in a short time.

On Monday, the day before the meeting of the conference, twenty-three of the insurgents met and agreed to go ahead with the campaign to elect Ford and expand the voting membership of the Policy Committee. Though still not certain of victory, they were encouraged by the reception they had received. One member of the group said: "We thought that we'd have support mainly in the 86th and 87th classes, but as we talked to people we found that there were quite a few who had been here ten or twelve years or longer who wanted to be a part of it." Some who had been active in the move to oust Joseph Martin in 1959 supported the Griffin-Goodell group. They were also assisted by the neutrality of Representatives Bob Wilson (Cal.), chairman of the Congressional Campaign Committee, and John Byrnes of the Policy Committee.

Goodell and Griffin informed Ford of their decision to push ahead with the campaign. Ford, who had not been active up to this point, then attempted to solicit support in the twenty-four hours remaining before the conference meeting.

Goodell and Griffin then went to Halleck and told him of their objectives and plans. They considered this a matter of honor and thought that the leadership was entitled to know what they were doing. Further, they hoped to head off a fight in the conference meeting on Tuesday by presenting their proposals to the leadership in advance. The leadership was willing to see the Policy Committee expanded, but offered resistance to Ford's chairmanship. A member of the leadership said afterward, "When they said that they wanted to enlarge the Committee, we were glad to go along because it would give a little more balance to the group." One of the early activists in the movement has summarized why the leadership did not contest changing the Policy Committee:

> It [enlarging the Policy Committee] was eminently fair and they [the leadership] recognized that. It made the party more democratically organized in accordance with our principals and traditions. Furthermore, we had the votes on this one. It was fair. All we were really asking for was half a loaf—not even a whole loaf. It was an extremely reasonable request.

A resolution embodying the request of the insurgents to increase the voting membership of the Policy Committee was drawn up by the Policy Committee staff for presentation at the conference.

On Monday afternoon, approximately sixty to seventy persons attended the previously planned coffee hour for the freshmen at the Congressional Hotel. At this meeting the leaders of the insurgents informed the freshmen of their intentions and stressed that in large part the record of the Republican Party in the House would be decided at the conference meeting, at which the leadership would be chosen. In spite of their attempts to win needed freshmen votes, the extent of support among the freshmen remained in doubt until the end. Many of the freshmen were frankly confused and completely uninformed about the problems discussed by the insurgents. The freshmen were also reluctant to be a part of anything that might offend the leadership and older members on the Committee on Committees at the time when decisions were being made on their committee assignments—decisions that would profoundly affect their congressional careers. They did not want to offend the wrong people. As a result, it was extremely difficult to get a firm commitment from them. At least one freshman purposely stayed away from the Congressional Hotel gathering even though he later voted for Ford. After the meeting, Griffin and Goodell met the press (who had been alerted that an important story would break that afternoon) and told them of their plans. Following the meeting, the group, which had met earlier in the day, continued last-minute efforts to enlist support from colleagues.

An indication of how successful the insurgents had been in keeping their actions quiet until the last minute was the fact that Charles Hoeven did not learn of the plans to contest his office until Monday noon at a luncheon meeting of the Iowa Republican delegation. While at the delegation meeting, he received a call from Halleck telling him of the insurgents' plans. Hoeven mounted a campaign of telephone calls and personal contacts in an effort to gain re-election. In this he was assisted by Halleck and Arends, who let it be known that they were supporting Hoeven. This stand by Halleck and Arends caused wavering among some members who had earlier indicated that they would support Ford.

The work of the insurgents continued long into the night before the conference meeting, as Goodell, Griffin, and Ford, assisted by Goodell's staff, prepared letters to be distributed to the Republican membership early Tuesday morning. A letter written and signed by Goodell and Griffin formally advised House Republicans of the plans that had been evolved. Goodell's staff took care of duplicating the letter. Gerald Ford also desired to send a letter to all House Republicans telling them of his candidacy. He thought that the correct and proper thing for him to do was to advise all members personally of his candidacy, instead of their being informed by various third parties. By the time the coffee hour at the Congressional Hotel had concluded, however, Ford's office staff had gone home for the day and there was no one there to assist him in getting out the letters. The responsibility for duplicating Ford's letter therefore also fell to Goodell's staff, after Ford had secured for them a supply of his personal stationery. Goodell's staff worked until two o'clock in the morning, running off the letter, addressing envelopes, and assisting in telephoning.

On Tuesday morning Ford came to his office early and signed the letters that had been prepared in Goodell's office the night before. The letters were then hand delivered by staff assistants in time to reach members' desks early that morning.

Since a number of the freshmen had still not had an opportunity to meet Ford, Griffin and Goodell invited all those they could reach to a hastily called reception to meet Ford in the Education and Labor Committee room. Approximately a dozen freshmen attended.

Several of the state Republican delegations held meetings that morning prior to the meeting of the conference. The insurgents attempted to have a spokesman at all such meetings. Generally, these meetings were not considered instrumental to the election of Ford, because the deans of the state delegations were normally very senior members supporting Hoeven. The strategy at these meetings was essentially defensive: to make certain that the insurgent case was presented and that no ground was lost.

The result of the election remained in doubt until the actual vote. With the conference slated for 2:00 P.M., as late as 12:15 Goodell and Griffin were still in doubt about nominating Ford. They consulted with Ford and told him that some of the people they had counted on were wavering as it became known that the leadership was supporting Hoeven. Ford, however, stated that he thought that there was no turning back at that late date.

The House Republican Conference

When the conference convened, Hoeven assumed the chair and then refused to entertain a motion for a secret ballot on the position of a temporary chairman. Halleck and Clarence Brown (Ohio), the ranking Republican on the Rules Committee and a powerful figure on the Committee on Committees, intervened and worked out a compromise that guaranteed there would be a secret ballot on the leadership positions, if none were demanded on the issue of choosing a temporary chairman. The insurgents agreed and Hoeven was chosen temporary chairman. His ruling on the issue of a secret ballot for temporary chairman, however, was thought to have somewhat damaged his position.

When the nominations for conference chairman were opened, Representative J. Arthur Younger (Cal.) nominated Hoeven. In his speech he compared the ratings given Ford and Hoeven by the highly conservative group, Americans for Constitutional Action (ACA), and stressed that Hoeven was more conservative than Ford. This speech, critical of Ford, is thought by the insurgents in fact to have helped put over their cause. One commented:

> The events of the meeting were living proof of the very thing [need for younger spokesmen and an improved image] we were talking about. Younger nominated Hoeven. It was a bad speech—he kept saying that Gerry

> Ford is a good congressman; he must have said it 13
> times. But it was like Mark Anthony's speech about
> Brutus. There was living proof of what we were talking
> about. I think that it helped us a great deal.

Elford Cederberg of Michigan, a member of the House since 1953,
nominated Ford. In his speech Cederberg was careful not to
criticize Hoeven, but rather stressed Ford's record in the House
and his ability to meet the press well. The contrast between the
two nominating speeches was summed up by a Ford backer as
follows:

> [Cederberg's speech] was a pro-Ford speech and not an
> anti-Hoeven speech. We had nothing against Charlie
> Hoeven personally. He is a fine gentleman. . . . On the
> other hand, Younger gave a speech that was anti-Ford
> and not pro-Hoeven. I think that his speech helped us
> a great deal.

The remarks of Clarence Brown were also thought to have
helped the Ford cause. Brown told the insurgents, in effect, that
after they had been in the House for a while they would understand things.

When the vote was taken, Ford won by a vote of eighty-
six to seventy-eight. The ballot was secret, a procedure that helped
the insurgents because it permitted members to vote against the
older leadership without fear. The resolution increasing the voting
membership of the Policy Committee and giving increased representation to the last five classes was adopted without controversy.
Following the meeting, Ford and Halleck met the press jointly;
they expressed mutual respect and esteem and indicated that the
new leadership group expected to work effectively and coopera-
tively.

A Symbolic Victory: The Discontent Lingers

Charles Hoeven, bitter about his defeat, predicted that
this was the first act of a still unfolding drama: "I was picked as
the lamb for the slaughter. This should serve as notice to Mr.
Arends and Mr. Halleck that something is brewing." Ford and
the other insurgents disagreed. Rather, one of the "young Turks"
said, "What we tried to do was to strengthen Charlie's [Halleck]

position and at the same time shake the foundation under his feet." [7] Hoeven, however, proved to be right.

Ford's election to the conference chairmanship was largely a symbolic victory. The results were not far-reaching. For example, the conference did meet more frequently to discuss party action on the Civil Rights Bill of 1964 and the test ban treaty than it had under Hoeven. In addition, Ford appointed special study committees—this had never been done before—concerned with the problems of minority staffing, nuclear testing, NATO unity, space and astronautics, and the budget. A committee was also set up to study the operations of the conference. The conference was not, however, an active institution for the making of party policy, and Ford's responsibilities as the ranking minority member of the Defense Appropriations Subcommittee meant that the time he could devote to conference matters was limited.

Many close observers believed that as a result of the 1963 uprising Halleck was more responsive to the wishes of the younger members and more willing to share the spotlight with them in making public statements of the party's position on crucial issues. [8] Unrest among the more junior members, however, lingered, because there had been no remedy for the basic complaints behind the 1963 uprising. The party's image, they believed, had not been improved. The "Ev and Charlie show" was still running and still taking top billing among the performances of Capitol Hill Republicans. The junior members did not feel they were yet playing a sufficiently important role in party decisions, even though the Policy Committee had been reorganized and the conference was slightly more active. Nor did they believe the party was coming forward with positive and attractive alternatives to proposals of the Democratic Administration.

Halleck's own popularity was not enhanced during the long Eighty-eighth Congress (1963-1964). He was unable to satisfy either the liberal or the conservative wings of his party. For example, eighty-six House Republicans (forty percent of the GOP membership) in a meeting presided over by Representative Durward G. Hall (Mo.) criticized Halleck for promising GOP support for what eventually became the Civil Rights Act of 1964 without first

[7] Quoted by Lawrence Stern, *The Washington Post*, January 10, 1963, p. A4.
[8] Paul Duke, "GOP Leader Halleck Acts to Mollify Young Republicans in the House," *The Wall Street Journal*, February 19, 1963, pp. 1, 6.

consulting the Policy Committee. One senior House Republican complained:

> Kennedy's going to get whatever credit there is for passing a bill, so why should we get him off the hook? This will cost us 10 to 15 new members from the South, split the coalition, and prevent us from getting any benefit from Northern white reaction against civil rights.[9]

There was also unrest on the left. During the Eighty-eighth Congress an informal liberal GOP organization, called the Wednesday Club, was formed. The name was derived from its regular meeting day. By the second session of the Eighty-eighth Congress this group had a membership of fifteen moderate-to-liberal Republicans who were unhappy about what they considered the conservative and negative tone of the House Republican leadership. While this group, informally led by John V. Lindsay (N.Y.), was not large and certainly not powerful, its very existence was symptomatic of the unrest within the party.[10]

The underlying unrest was crystallized by the 1964 election disaster. The GOP lost forty-eight seats to the Democrats while gaining ten seats previously held by Democrats: a net loss of thirty-eight seats. When the Eighty-ninth Congress met in January 1965, the ranks of the Republicans contained 140 members—the lowest total in twenty-eight years.

The 1964 election dealt most harshly with those members who could be expected to be firm supporters of Halleck, the more senior and conservative Republicans. Following the election, the relatively junior nature of the House Republican membership was even more pronounced than it had been in 1963. At that time, the unusually high percentage of members whose service had started after 1956 had been one of the factors contributing to Ford's victory over Hoeven. Table 7 demonstrates the manner in which the 1964 election depleted the senior GOP ranks and gave numerical dominance to the more junior members. Twenty-four GOP rep-

---

[9] Quoted by Richard L. Lyons, *The Washington Post*, October 31, 1963, p. A21.
[10] See Paul Duke and Stanley Meisler, "Republicans After the Debacle: The Frustrated Moderates," *The Reporter*, February 11, 1965, pp. 26-28; Rowland Evans and Robert Novak, "Inside Report: The Wednesday Club," *New York Herald Tribune*, August 19, 1964, p. 24.

TABLE 7   HOUSE REPUBLICAN MEMBERSHIP GROUPED ON BASIS OF
LENGTH OF SERVICE IN THE HOUSE, JANUARY 1965

Year of election	Number, 1965	Percent of total GOP membership	Number, 1963	Net loss after 1964 election
1964 (89th Club)	18	12.9	—	—
1962 (88th Club)	24	17.1	31	−7
1960 (87th Club)	25	17.9	31	−6
1958 (86th Club)	16	11.4	21	−5
1956 (85th Club)	12	8.6	14	−2
1954 (84th Club)	4	2.8	9	−5
1952 (83rd Club)	16	11.4	21	−5
Prior to 1952	25	17.9	49	−24
Total	140	100.0	176	54

resentatives elected prior to 1952 were retired. Members elected since 1958 (with only six years of House service) now constituted a firm majority, 59.3 percent of the House Republican membership. Defeated were powerful senior leaders, firm supporters of Halleck such as Mrs. Katherine St. George (N.Y.), a member of the Rules Committee and a powerful figure on the Committee on Committees; Ben Jensen (Iowa), the ranking minority member of the Appropriations Committee; Walt Horan (Wash.), the second ranking GOP member of the Appropriations Committee; and Walter Riehlman (N.Y.), ranking Republican on Government Operations.

Halleck's base of support among his colleagues was also weakened by the fact that the number of staunchly conservative Republicans was also greatly reduced by the Johnson landslide. The *Congressional Quarterly* listed thirty-one of the most conservative Republicans who were beaten. By contrast, the moderates or liberals came through the election with only a minor reduction in their strength.[11]

The 1964 election disaster (for which Halleck could hardly be held responsible) gave increased salience to the rank-and-file discontent that had been building up since Halleck assumed the

[11] Only four of thirty-four Republicans endorsed by the Committee to Support Moderate Republicans were defeated. They were Abner Sibal (Conn.), Fred Schwengel (Iowa), Frank Osmers (N.J.), and James Weaver (Pa.). *Congressional Quarterly Weekly Report*, XXII (November 6, 1964), p. 2643.

leadership in 1959. The election thus weakened the position of the self-styled "gut fighter" from Indiana.

The Revolt: Part II (1965)

Following the 1964 election, the press was filled with speculation regarding the possibility of either procedural or personnel changes within the House Republican leadership. These journalistic comments were the public manifestations of the informal discussions being conducted in Washington by activist Republican congressmen as they returned from their districts and surveyed the congressional scene in the light of the 1964 elections.

The concern of these men for the future of their party was reflected in an open letter written by Thomas Curtis to all his GOP colleagues on November 18, 1964. Curtis, a hard-working and respected figure in the House, called for a party caucus in December that would give the party an opportunity to prepare adequately for the legislative battles ahead in 1965. His letter also noted the concern of many members about the need for a leadership change. It said in part:

> I am a little tired of behind the scenes maneuvering when it comes to establishing party machinery and policies which deeply concern our entire party. . . . I received a note from Gerry Ford with Charlie Halleck's blessing that, on Jan. 4, 1965, we will meet in Republican caucus. Well, that is entirely too late to get moving, unless again it is the plan of a few self appointed members of our waning group to make the decision for the rest of us ahead of time in the hopes that they can get the majority of us to go along. Let's get our leadership established on one basic premise, if no other, that major decisions on party organization and policy matters be made on as broad a base as possible. . . . In order to do this, I suggest that we have a party caucus within the next two or three weeks.[12]

Curtis's suggestion for an early conference was picked up by some of the younger activists, including Goodell and Griffin, who had successfully managed Ford's campaign against Hoeven. They persuaded Ford, who as conference chairman had the power

[12] This portion of the letter was reprinted in *Congressional Quarterly Weekly Report*, XXII (December 4, 1964), pp. 2766, 2789.

to call such a meeting, to call a conference meeting for December 16, 1964. Ford said the purpose of the meeting would be to "discuss and develop a program with reference to our Republican organization structure in the House, possible changes in House rules and strategy on development and presentation of Republican legislative programs." [13] While on the surface the GOP meeting was to be a high-level, issue-oriented affair, underneath there was the undercurrent of speculation about possible changes in leadership personnel. The day before the meeting, Mary McGrory of Washington's *Evening Star* noted that a substantial number of people would have their "long knives out for House Leader Charles Halleck." [14] One insurgent commented: "Nobody is going to get up and say 'Let's get rid of Charlie Halleck. . . .' But after we get through discussing the system as it has been operating, a lot of people will be thinking he ought to go." [15] In addition to pointing up some of the problems of the existing leadership structure, the meeting also provided the activists with an opportunity to discuss the matter with some of the twenty-one freshmen elected in 1964. If a move were to be made against Halleck, freshman support would be important, just as it had been in 1963.

The widely publicized conference meeting on December 16 did not live up to its billing. There was no talk of ousting anyone. Rather, the session was confined to a discussion of party rules changes and changes in the House rules. After the conference, the consensus of the Washington press corps was that Halleck would probably hold his job, especially since no opponent had yet come forward and declared himself.

The December 16 conference was only one of the meetings to discuss changes. A more private gathering took place in the office of Charles Goodell. Attending were eleven anti-Halleck, activist, and younger House Republicans. On the basis of what they observed at the conference and their conversations with their colleagues, they had come to the conclusion that Halleck had to go. Their choice for his successor was Gerald Ford.

Ford himself was reluctant to make the race against Halleck, just as he had been the reluctant candidate of the insurgents in

[13] Quoted by Richard L. Lyons, *The Washington Post,* December 3, 1964, p. Al.
[14] *The Evening Star* (Washington), December 15, 1964, p. Al.
[15] Mary McGrory, *The Evening Star* (Washington), December 18, 1964, p. Al.

1963. Many of the same men who had persuaded him to run in 1963—including Griffin and Goodell—again pressed him to run for the leadership. Others active in urging him to run were Donald Rumsfeld (Ill.), Albert Quie (Minn.), and Silvio Conte (Mass.). After discussing the matter with his family, he agreed on Friday, December 18, to have his name placed in nomination for leader at the January 4 organizational conference. The following day he appeared before TV cameras at a news conference to announce his candidacy. His announcement reflected the nature of the insurgents' discontent with the Halleck regime. Ford said:

> We have within our Republican ranks a great wealth of talent, energy, and dedication. . . . When properly channeled and utilized to the fullest this talent will promote and communicate the image of a fighting, forward-looking party seeking responsible and constructive solutions to our national problems.
>
> By finding ways to better utilize this impressive talent through new techniques and bold leadership, by a willingness to try new ideas, by leading rather than simply reacting, we can and must develop the strength, and the support of the American people.[16]

Halleck immediately interrupted a Florida vacation to mount his campaign and confidently predicted victory. He said that he would run on his six-year record as leader. During that time, the GOP had compiled an "impressive record" of unity, he said, which would be even more important with the Republican minority at its lowest ebb in twenty-eight years. He immediately began phoning his colleagues to line up support. The Ford supporters did not underestimate Halleck. His reputation as a shrewd political "gut-fighter" was well deserved. One Ford backer summarized Halleck's advantages: "Charlie has a lot of strength. He has done a lot of things for a lot of people. He's given them committee assignments. He's spoken for them in their districts. And he's their leader." [17] Ford, too, had advantages. The discontent among the younger members, who now constituted a majority, was strongly felt. Halleck, though respected, was not popular. He had made his share of enemies through the years. Ford, the diligent

---

[16] *The New York Times,* December 20, 1964, p. 28.
[17] Quoted by Richard L. Lyons, *The Washington Post,* December 20, 1964, p. A1.

Republican defense appropriations spokesman, was respected as well as popular. Aside from the 1963 battle against Hoeven, he was relatively unscarred by intraparty squabbles. Ford also benefited from the fact that the contest for minority leader was never structured as an ideological battle pitting the conservatives against the liberals and moderates. The voting records of Ford and Halleck were quite similar. Both were considered conservatives. The issue was a matter of who could best convey a favorable image of the party. In such a struggle, the blond, ruggedly handsome (looking younger than his fifty-one years), and articulate Ford had a definite advantage over Halleck, the sixty-four-year-old veteran of numerous congressional wars, presidential nominating fracases, and the rough politics of the Hoosier state.

Once again, the fact that the actual decision would be made by a secret ballot was also to Ford's advantage, for congressmen would not have to fear reprisal for voting against the leadership. This had been recognized in 1959 when Halleck was an insurgent seeking to oust Joseph Martin. Halleck and his backers changed the GOP conference rules to require secrecy in balloting for officers. Ironically, what had helped Halleck in 1959 could help defeat him in 1965.

The campaign over the Christmas-New Year holiday season was an intense one, as both sides relied upon informal persuasion to bring people into their camp. It was clear throughout that the outcome would be close, and both sides predicted a narrow victory. The closeness and the tenseness of the situation can be seen by the fact that one day before the conference, Ford's supporters could count only sixty-seven "sure" votes—with seventy-one needed to elect.[18]

On January 4 the conference met in a mood of anticipation. In a preliminary contest for the conference chairmanship (the post being vacated by Ford), Melvin Laird (Wis.) defeated Peter Frelinghuysen (N.J.) seventy-five to sixty-two in a surprisingly close race. Early in his House career, Laird, like Ford, had been tapped for an important role by being assigned to the prestigious Appropriations Committee, where he had specialized in health and welfare matters and defense. He had also served as a member of the Congressional Campaign Committee, and as vice chairman

[18] See Robert L. Peabody, *The Ford-Halleck Minority Leadership Contest, 1965* (New York: McGraw-Hill, 1966), p. 30.

of the Republican Platform Committee of 1960, chairman of the Joint Committee on Republican Principles in 1962, and chairman of the Platform Committee in 1964. In his last post he had alienated many moderates and liberals, because the platform written by his committee was quite satisfactory to the Goldwater wing. Frelinghuysen was the moderates' candidate against Laird. He was the ranking Republican on Education and Labor and the second ranking member of the Foreign Affairs Committee. His candidacy was a last-minute effort, organized when it appeared that Laird would have no meaningful opposition. That he did as well as he did was thought to be in part a reflection of the continuing resentment at Laird's role at the San Francisco Convention.

With the preliminary event over, the contest for leader was on. Elford Cederberg again nominated Ford, declaring that he would give the party "new energy and a forceful fresh image." Halleck's Indiana colleague, Ross Adair, nominated Halleck and cited his long experience and record of effectiveness. Then came the vote—a seventy-three to sixty-seven decision for Ford. Halleck took the result gracefully. He promised support and loyalty to Ford and moved to make the election unanimous.

Afterward, in response to the questions of the press, Ford said that he did not consider his victory a repudiation of Goldwaterites. "This is not a repudiation or endorsement of any wing of the Republican party," he said. Rather, he spoke of "expanding the efforts to present positive alternatives" and promised that "We're going to use everybody. Every Republican will be a first-team player, a 60-minute ball player." [19]

The Trials of Leadership

Robert Griffin, Ford's campaign coordinator, said in the flush of victory that "a new chapter in the Republican party has begun." But leading a band of relatively independent political entrepreneurs such as those found in the House of Representatives was not to prove easy for the new GOP leader. Indeed, he was hardly accorded even a brief honeymoon before the reality of the congressional party's decentralized character and the leader's meager sources of influence were made apparent.

In an attempt to further infuse the leadership with new

[19] *Congressional Quarterly Weekly Report,* XXIII (January 8, 1965), p. 34.

faces, younger men, and a broader base of support, Ford, in one of his first acts as leader, sought to have Peter Frelinghuysen elected Republican whip. The whip is an assistant leader whose job is to act as a communication link between the leadership and the rank and file, making certain that the rank and file know the leadership position on crucial issues and that they are present on the floor for important votes. In this he is assisted by regional whips who have responsibility for contacting the GOP members from their respective geographic areas.

Leslie Arends, the whip since 1944, had amassed a large following in the House on both sides of the aisle since coming to the chamber in 1934. It was a following based not on his being an ideological leader (he is generally considered to be right of center and was a preconvention backer of Barry Goldwater for President), but on his "virtually unfailing friendliness and good humor," [20] important qualities for a whip, whose basic tool of leadership is a friendly persuasion.[21] In addition, he had provided wise counsel to younger members and dispensed favors from his office. Also of importance to his role was the fact that the tall, slender, silver-haired midwesterner looked at least ten years younger than his sixty-nine years.

Frelinghuysen was a sharp contrast to Arends. An Ivy League-educated descendant of an old and illustrious eastern family, Frelinghuysen had not established great popularity for himself in the House. Some of his colleagues, occasionally offended by his rather abrasive manner, had dubbed him "petulant Peter."

Nonetheless, Arends, with Halleck's support, campaigned hard to retain his job. He utilized the informal communications network he had developed through the years as whip. Until just before the conference meeting he was on the phone, attempting to solidify his position, arguing that there was no need to replace him, since he worked for the leader no matter who he might be. He stressed his loyalty to all past leaders. "I was loyal to Joe Martin and I was loyal to Charlie Halleck. I would be just as loyal to Gerry, and I have told him so."

When the conference met a second time on January 14, Arends was the victor by a vote of seventy to fifty-nine over Ford's

---

[20] *The New York Times*, January 15, 1965, p. 16.
[21] Ironically, on the wall of Arends' office just off the House chamber hangs a long, black bull whip, a symbol of his office.

personal choice, Frelinghuysen. Arends renewed his pledge of loyalty to Ford, while Ford said that he did not view the vote as a repudiation of his leadership. Arends and Frelinghuysen agreed, but most observers thought it indicated that Ford's life as leader would indeed be a trying one.

Ford suffered additional rebuffs in trying to reward Charles Goodell's work for him. First, his choice of Goodell to fill a vacancy on the powerful Ways and Means Committee was rejected by the Committee on Committees. The seat was given instead to James Battin (Mont.), who had seconded Arends' nomination as whip. The Committee on Committees, which handles GOP committee assignments, is dominated by the senior representatives from states having large Republican delegations: California, Illinois, Pennsylvania, Ohio, and New York.

Secondly, Ford chose Goodell to fill a vacancy in the chairmanship of the Policy Committee. A 1965 change in the GOP rules that forbids an elected leader from also holding a position as the senior Republican on a standing committee, resulted in the vacancy. John Byrnes, who had held the job since 1959, resigned in order to retain his position as ranking Republican on the Ways and Means Committee. Despite Ford's preference for Goodell, John Rhodes (Ariz.), an able young member who had been an early and strong supporter of Goldwater for President, quickly announced his own candidacy for the chairmanship. To avoid further intraparty strife, Ford changed his mind and appointed Goodell to head up a new Planning and Research Committee. The function of the new committee was to develop GOP alternatives to Johnson Administration proposals. He was given staff assistance through the designation of William Prendergast, the research director of the Republican National Committee prior to Goldwater's nomination, as minority sergeant-at-arms. Despite his official post, Prendergast's duties were to work with Goodell as a research aide. Goodell's appointment removed the planning and research functions from the Policy Committee, which would now concern itself with the more immediate questions of what GOP policy should be on measures about to come before the House for a vote.

Rhodes was later elected Policy Committee Chairman without opposition. But at the same meeting, a motion by Ford backers to elect Goodell to a slot on the committee was rejected. Goodell, however, was later appointed under a provision in the new GOP rules authorizing the leader to appoint seven members.

After these initial organization conflicts, the new leadership team did attempt to carry through its aims of creating a new image of the party and of presenting alternatives to the Johnson Administration's proposals. Task forces were set up to study issue areas, such as the Vietnam war, the Administration's budget, agricultural policy, education, and NATO. The party also developed its own alternatives to Administration bills in the areas of voting rights for Negroes, aid to education, medicare, and the "war on poverty."

Conclusion

Congressional decisions are of many types, but there are few where the stakes are as high as in contests for party leadership positions. With a leadership post goes power and prestige. By dispensing committee assignments, sharing political information, giving campaign assistance, securing passage of legislation, and other aid, a party leader can have a strong influence on whether or not a member of Congress achieves his objectives. By being on the winning team, a member can greatly enhance his standing in the House, while being on the losing side can cause a withdrawal of the leadership's favors. The intensity of the battles waged within the GOP in 1963 and 1965 testify to the members' awareness that their political futures were involved.

It is unusual for a congressional party to unseat its incumbent leaders. Yet the House Republicans did this in three out of four Congresses between 1959 and 1965. That the coups were staged only within the GOP is probably attributable to the natural dissatisfaction and frustration that wells up in ambitious men when they find themselves continually the *minority* party and therefore deprived of the power and privileges that accompany *majority* status. Adverse elections, such as those of 1958, 1962, and 1964 for the House GOP, act as catalytic agents to push men toward some action that they hope may change their circumstances.

In the case of the Republicans, the adverse elections only underscored basic grievances shared by a substantial number of party members about party operation in the House. These grievances were a result of concern for the party's image and of the discontent stemming from feeling left out of party decisions or at being underutilized.

Frustration is always present, however, in any large organization because it is impossible for all or any to fully achieve their goals. But why was it possible for a band of restless and aggressive junior members to manage successfully a series of revolts in a body like the House of Representatives, that venerates experience and seniority? After all, as Richard Fenno has pointed out, one of the guiding norms of House behavior is "the seniority-protégé-apprenticeship system." [22] This system permits the domination of a few senior members, who bring into leadership circles younger protégés who have been tested in lesser roles during a lengthy apprenticeship period. The key to the success of the 1963 and 1965 uprisings was an unusually large number of junior Republican members. This brought the inherent conflict between junior and senior members into the open and permitted a breach in the system.

These leadership struggles illustrate the endless ferment that exists among the relatively independent politicians who make up the United States Congress. Ambitious younger men seek power and influence. They chafe under the informal rules that dictate that junior members must serve quiet periods of apprenticeship. More senior members also seek to enhance their positions and maintain their influence and prerogatives. Below the surface there are thus always the ingredients of conflict—intraparty conflict—that are not necessarily ideological battles.

Successful *intraparty* struggles are not waged the way most important legislative conflicts are portrayed in the popular press or in novels. In none of the insurgent movements that have been discussed were lobbyists and administrative officials actively engaged in button-holing members and in "twisting arms." Rather, these were "family" affairs, in which the most successful technique of influence was the direct personal appeal to a fellow member of the House. Members of Congress are, then, much more than proverbial billiard balls who react when struck—pressured—by some exterior force.

[22] See "Internal Distribution of Influence: The House," in David B. Truman (ed.), *The Congress and America's Future* (Englewood Cliffs, N.J.: Prentice-Hall, 1965), pp. 71-73.

The group life of the legislative body is also an important determinant of legislative behavior. For, although debates examined here concerning the Republican leadership centered around the question of who would give dynamic leadership and create a better party image, the congressional party remained after the elections a decentralized institution. The limitations that the party system imposes on the powers of any congressional party leader immediately made themselves felt.

THE DEMOCRATIC EIGHTY-NINTH ORGANIZES FOR BUSINESS

By most outward indicators, the first session of the Eighty-ninth Congress was unique in modern legislative history. Some observers, including the AFL-CIO, stated that it was "the most productive congressional session ever held." With overwhelming Democratic majorities in both houses and astute leadership from the White House, Congress dealt vigorously with many public policy concerns: voting rights; medical care for the aged; a Cabinet Department of Housing and Urban Development; new housing legislation; new aid programs for education, the arts, depressed areas, and high-speed interurban transportation; and a Constitutional amendment on presidential succession.

The deluge left Republican legislators frustrated as they watched their amendments and alternative bills summarily voted down. For their part, conservative editorial writers were soon urging Congress to adjourn so that the public, as well as the members, could get a rest. Senate Majority Leader Mike Mansfield, returning to Washington from a short visit to his home state of Montana, reported that his constituents were a little dizzy from all the activity. "They like it," he remarked, "but we've passed so many bills that their impression of what we've done is getting a little blurred."

The Democrats had controlled both houses of Congress for a decade, but never had the liberal "presidential" wing of the party held such a clear congressional majority with which to enact the shopping list of social-welfare legislation that had accumulated during the post-World War II years. During the Eisenhower era the Democratic leadership performed a holding action, playing a role of "responsible opposition" in the face of the more modest legislative goals of the Administration. The Kennedy Administration produced action on a number of proposals, but always under the threat of a Republican-conservative Democratic coalition which could swing a majority of votes on particularly controversial issues.

Liberal discontent came to a head during the seeming legislative stalemate of 1963, when liberal columnist Walter Lippmann was questioning "what kind of a legislative body is it that will not or cannot legislate." The situation had changed little by November 22, 1963, when the New Frontier was deprived of its articulate young leader. Opinion surveys taken before and after President Kennedy's assassination showed mounting public restiveness with congressional performance. Yet by the time the Eighty-eighth Congress collapsed in fatigue on October 3, 1964, many of its former critics were singing its praises.

The aftermath of the assassination, and the accession of a "consensus" President knowledgeable in the ways of Capitol Hill, had served to unblock significant remnants of the New Frontier program. The 1964 elections produced such preponderant Democratic majorities that the old conservative coalition on Capitol Hill was at least temporarily immobilized. Thirty-eight new Democratic congressmen were sent to Washington, bringing the party's House majority to 295. In the Senate the already substantial majority was increased by two, to sixty-eight. As a group these young Democrats (some of whom had defeated senior conservative Republicans) were among the Administration's staunchest supporters.

It was in this atmosphere that the Eighty-ninth Congress convened in January 1965. The unique aspects of this Congress can best be ascertained through the eyes of the liberal Democrats, who are the major actors in our narrative. To understand their viewpoint, it will be necessary to sketch the outlines of their battles against the stubbornly conservative traditions of Congress during the preceding decade. Viewed in the perspective of historical continuity, it will be clear that the Eighty-ninth Congress did not just "happen." Nor did the temporarily outsized Democratic majorities suspend the "laws" of legislative politics. Unique as it was, therefore, the Eighty-ninth Congress was useful for viewing the internal life of the congressional Democratic parties.

The Senate: End of an Era?

When Senator Joseph S. Clark first arrived in the Senate in January 1957, he and the five other freshman Democrats were treated to a luncheon by then Majority Leader Lyndon B. Johnson. As the newcomers sat down to their steaks, they found in front of them copies of *Citadel: The Story of the U.S. Senate*, by journalist William S. White.[23] The books were inscribed "with all good wishes" not only by the author, but also by Johnson. The Majority Leader urged the newcomers "to consider Mr. White's book as a sort of *McGuffey's Reader* from which [they] could learn much about 'the greatest deliberative body in the world.' " He also counseled them to "mold" themselves into the Senate's "way of life." [24]

White's volume propagated the thesis that a shadowy "inner club" ran the Senate according to a set of tacit bylaws that approximated Speaker Rayburn's maxim that members who want to "get along" must learn to "go along." Highly laudatory of Johnson's "consensus leadership," White intimated that the conservative "inner club" kept the Senate on an even keel by bridling the enthusiasms of the "young Turk" liberals.

Some observers disputed the existence of White's "inner club." The Senate, according to White's own testimony, was tolerant of diversity; and any roster of its "leaders" revealed many diverse personality types, leadership styles, and policy preferences. A few Senators, such as Abraham Ribicoff (see Chapter 2), were able to use their prior prestige to exert extraordinary influence very early in their Senate careers. And while many young Senators chose to serve out their apprenticeships gracefully and docilely, others explicitly selected the role of an "outsider," appealing over the heads of the Senate leadership to external public opinion.

In choosing this latter course, Clark followed the example of Senator Paul H. Douglas (see Chapter 6) and other well-known dissenters. And like most Senate outsiders, Clark soon became a disgruntled believer in White's thesis. For example, he anticipated that the election of a number of young liberals in 1958 would alter the Senate's power structure. But largely through manipula-

[23] New York: Harper & Row, 1957.
[24] Related in Clark's *Congress: The Sapless Branch* (New York: Harper & Row, 1964), p. 5.

tion of committee assignments, the "club" retained its influence virtually intact. The climax of Clark's rebellion came in February 1963, when he took the Senate floor to denounce the "Senate establishment" in a series of widely publicized (if poorly attended) speeches.[25] There were still unbelievers when Clark finished, but there could be little question that the notion of a tight, conservative ruling clique had become an obsession with liberals who perceived themselves on the outside looking in.

The Committee Assignment Imbroglio   Clark's immediate target was an intricate series of maneuvers over committee assignments that occurred at the beginning of the Eighty-eighth Congress. Liberal Democrats contended that the increase in Democratic seats from the 1962 elections should be reflected in a readjustment of party ratios in committees. Rather than unseating low-ranking Republicans, they proposed to expand three key committees: Finance (from seventeen to twenty-one), Appropriations (twenty-seven to twenty-nine), and Foreign Relations (seventeen to twenty-one). By appointing Democrats to the new vacancies, a change in party ratio could be effected without unseating any Republicans. The makeup of Finance was of special concern, for this committee was to consider President Kennedy's tax reform bill, high on the Administration's legislative shopping list.

The fifteen-member Senate Democratic Steering Committee, which draws up committee assignments, was safely in conservative hands. Five of the seven southerners on the group were committee chairmen; two nonsouthern chairmen were also members. Only six members, including Clark, could be considered consistently liberal. Yet Clark estimated that only twenty-seven of the sixty-seven Democratic senators could be classed as "conservatives." He charged that the Steering Committee failed to represent the increasingly liberal Senate Democratic contingent. In 1961, and again in 1963, he noted, the Democratic Conference (caucus) had approved a resolution that the Steering Committee should reflect the geographic and ideological views of all Senate Democrats.

Liberals also suspected that senators who had voted for a liberalized cloture rule early in 1963 were passed over for favorable committee assignments. (It was believed, and later charged publicly, that the then secretary to the Majority Leader, Bobby Baker, actually falsified requests for committee assignments. When the

[25] Reprinted as *The Senate Establishment* (New York: Hill & Wang, 1963).

Steering Committee meets, a large chart is prepared listing all committee vacancies and the names of senators desiring new assignments and their first, second, and subsequent choices. Since Baker prepared the charts, he was in a position to omit key requests made by certain senators.) During his "establishment" speech Clark produced a chart showing that of the eight nonfreshman Democrats who voted against easing the cloture rule and had also requested new committee assignments, seven received new assignments and six were given their first choice. But of the fourteen nonfreshmen who favored easing cloture and asked for new assignments, only five were granted them. And only one, Majority Leader Mansfield, received his first choice. Clark neglected to mention, however, that the seven (out of nine) freshman Democrats who voted with the liberals appeared to have received the major committee posts they had wanted. This was the result of an informal policy of assuring each new Democratic senator at least one major committee assignment—the so-called "Johnson rule," initiated by Majority Leader Lyndon B. Johnson in 1963.

On February 13, 1963, the Steering Committee rejected a Mansfield motion to enlarge the Finance Committee from seventeen to nineteen (adding two Democrats and retaining the six Republicans). The Majority Leader said the vote against the proposal was "very substantial" (ten to five, apparently), and declared that the plan had been his own and not the President's—as had been rumored. One observer called the Steering Committee's action the product of a "privately arranged political double-play between the conservative Republicans and the southern Democrats." [26] Reportedly, Minority Leader Everett Dirksen (Ill.) decided to put in for the one vacant Republican seat on Finance (caused by the retirement of Senator John M. Butler [Md.]) and so informed Mansfield and the southerners. Paradoxically, the Steering Committee did agree to change the ratio on Appropriations from seventeen-ten to eighteen-nine. This had the effect of bumping from the committee Senator Jacob K. Javits (N.Y.), the lowest-ranking Republican and a liberal.

When Clark condemned this power play on the Senate floor, Mansfield replied with unusual tartness. "It is all very well," he said, "for Senators to immerse themselves in household management. But I think it is about time for someone to remind the

[26] Rowland Evans, Jr., in *Washington Post*, February 16, 1963, p. A2.

Senate of its higher responsibilities under the Constitution." The Senate finally rejected by a sixty-eight to seventeen vote Clark's amendment to expand the Finance Committee from seventeen to twenty-one members (fourteen Democrats and seven Republicans); and by a seventy to twelve vote it rejected a similar bid to expand Appropriations from twenty-seven to twenty-nine members. Clark withdrew his amendment to reconstitute Foreign Relations—a committee assignment he himself desired. Then a resolution (S. Res. 90) setting the size of all other standing committees was passed by a voice vote. The committee-assignment controversy had ended in a temporary defeat for the liberal forces.

Conflict over Cloture   The Senate's biennial battle over Rule XXII, which governs limitation of debate, began on January 14, 1963, when Senator Clinton P. Anderson (D. N.M.) introduced a resolution (S. Res. 9) to lower the majority needed to invoke cloture from two-thirds to three-fifths of those Senators present and voting. The Senate prides itself on its "unlimited debate." Under the present Rule XXII, debate may be closed by an elaborate procedure. A petition must be signed by sixteen senators, and the question of cloture is brought up two days later. Two-thirds of the senators present and voting must agree to the motion, after which each senator still has up to one hour of remarks on the issue at hand.

Proposals for changing Senate rules at the beginning of a session face a thorny procedural dilemma: "Do the rules of a previous Congress automatically govern proposals to change the rules at the outset of a new Congress . . . ? If not, then a filibuster could be stopped by a majority vote, and the substantive proposals for changes in the rules voted on." [27] The question turns on whether the Senate is a "continuing body." Since the House has a totally "new" membership with each new Congress, it must re-enact its rules every two years. But because two-thirds of the Senators are incumbent at the start of each Congress, it is debatable whether the Senate must re-enact its rules. It has traditionally chosen not to do so. But if it followed the alternative course, "unlimited debate" would not be in effect until the rules were enacted, and debate could be cut off by the normal parliamentary method of majority vote.

The liberals sought from the presiding officer, Vice Presi-

[27] *Congressional Quarterly Weekly Report* (January 18, 1963), p. 73.

dent Lyndon Johnson, a ruling that a majority could shut off debate on a rules change. Johnson handed the question back to the Senate—a decision made many times before by Senate presiding officers. Johnson declared:

> It is a matter for the Senators. The Vice President cannot tell Senators how to make up their minds. He cannot make rules for the Senate that the Senate has not made for itself. Nothing in the Constitution gives the Vice President the power to determine when he thinks the Senators have talked enough.

After three weeks of debate, the liberals failed by ten votes to invoke cloture and end the conservative filibuster over the rules change. It was this vote that Clark charged had been used against procloture senators in committee assignments.

In the Eighty-ninth Congress the liberals again pressed for amendment of Rule XXII, with substantially the same result. The effort was largely an exercise in frustration, although one bizarre incident deserves recounting. The liberals hoped that by delaying their request for a ruling from the Chair until after the Inauguration, they could induce Hubert Humphrey, the new Vice President and a former colleague, to rule in favor of simple majority cloture on rules amendments. Needless to say, there was no assurance that Humphrey would do this. After Johnson's ruling in 1963 Humphrey was quoted as saying that he was not certain he wanted to give the Vice President the power to shut off debate. "I should like the Senate itself to face the responsibility," he stated.

On January 6 Anderson introduced his resolution (S. Res. 6) to reduce to three-fifths the majority needed for cloture. Senator Dirksen objected to "immediate consideration" of Anderson's amendment. This meant that unless action could be completed during the so-called "morning hour" the following day, the proposal would be placed on the calendar and further delays would ensue.

As soon as routine business had been transacted the next day, Dirksen moved to send Anderson's resolution to the Committee on Rules and Administration. The Republican leader announced that his purpose was to see S. Res. 6 "buried in the deepest, deepest grave with enough earth over it so that we will never see its ugly face again." Anderson countered with an amendment to Dirksen's motion directing the Rules Committee to report the resolution by January 25—after the Inauguration. The amendment further stipulated that when the committee reported, "all rights in existence at the opening of Congress shall be deemed preserved." Senator Richard B. Russell (D. Ga.), one of the Senate's masters of parliamentary procedure, inquired whether this amendment was not out of order. The eighty-seven-year-old President Pro Tem, Carl Hayden (D. Ariz.), who was in the Chair, answered inaudibly. Hayden then declared the "morning hour" to be closed, and Anderson's resolution was placed on the calendar.

A few moments later Senator Paul H. Douglas (D. Ill.) claimed to have heard a rumor that Hayden had ruled Anderson's amendment out of order. Since the transcript was not yet ready, Majority Leader Mansfield called a brief recess. Douglas rushed to the Senate Reporters' room and found that Hayden had indeed ruled against the Anderson amendment. As the session resumed, Douglas asked for permission to question the reporter and journal clerk—an unheard-of procedure. Tempers flared, and Mansfield moved for a second recess. The dispute was finally resolved when it was agreed to send the Anderson resolution, along with S. Res. 8 (which would lower to a simple majority the vote needed for cloture) to the Rules Committee. Two months later, both resolutions were reported adversely by the committee and no further action was taken.

Though the rule itself proved unshakable, cloture was successfully invoked three times in the early 1960s. In 1962 an unusual liberal filibuster over the communications satellite bill was terminated under Rule XXII by a bipartisan coalition. After a two-and-one-half month southern stand against the Civil Rights Act of 1964, cloture was again successfully invoked. And on May 25, 1965, a seventy-thirty cloture vote shut off extended debate on the Voting Rights Act of 1965. As long as the present cloture rule is in effect, liberals themselves have not been hesitant to resort to filibusters. As Clark explained, "Why should I tie both my hands behind my back? I'm in favor of changing the rule, but until they change it I'm going to play the game according to the rules."

"Disestablishment" in the Senate   While actual modifications of Senate rules and procedures were not spectacular, the complexion of the body changed markedly in the years following publication of White's book. Whether or not the "Senate establishment" ever existed as an identifiable group is a difficult question

to resolve. But of this much one can be certain. At some point in the mid-1960s the old rules of the game were modified, and the "old guard" Senators lost much of their earlier influence.

A portion of the change was generational, as the seniority system worked its inevitable way and "young Turks" became "old Turks." In the Eighty-ninth Congress, for example, several veteran liberals found themselves in choice committee seats previously denied them. Senators Clark and Claiborne Pell (D. R.I.) were appointed to Foreign Relations; two years earlier they had lost out when a vacancy on that committee was pre-empted by Senator George A. Smathers (D. Fla.). In 1965 Senator Quentin N. Burdick (D. N.D.) was given a seat on Judiciary, and Senator Ralph W. Yarborough (D. Tex.) was assigned to Appropriations. Even earlier Senator William Proxmire (D. Wis.) had won a coveted place on Appropriations.

Meanwhile, the 1962 and 1964 elections brought to the Senate "a group of brainy young liberal newcomers unimpressed with the old rules about the sanctity of seniority." [28] These included such Democrats as Edward M. Kennedy (Mass.), Joseph Tydings and Daniel B. Brewster (Md.), Birch Bayh (Ind.), Robert F. Kennedy (N.Y.), and Daniel K. Inouye (Hawaii). These freshmen did not hesitate to assert their strength when the occasion presented itself. "We don't feel there's time to waste on that old seen-and-not-be-heard business," one of them explained. "After all, if a man manages to get to the Senate, he must have something to contribute."

The rise to prominence of the young liberals, assisted by the "Johnson rule" on committee assignments, was accompanied by the aging of many of the conservative leaders. The southern filibuster on the Voting Rights Act of 1965 was disorganized and almost half-hearted; and the chief southern strategist, Senator Russell, was ill and participated very little in the debate. As a staff aide to one southern leader commented, "They're tired. . . . Many of them have been sick. And the civil rights fight [of 1964] really took the heart out of most of them."

Other developments made easier the prospects for younger senators wishing to make a reputation for themselves. Within the Democratic party, Majority Leader Mansfield wielded much looser

---

[28] Several quotes in this section are drawn from: Dan Cordtz, "The Senate Revolution," *Wall Street Journal,* August 6, 1965, p. 8.

reins than had his predecessor, Johnson. "We've had a dispersal of responsibility," Mansfield conceded. "I'm not the leader, really. They don't do what I tell them. I do what they tell me." [29] In addition, a number of issues that gained prominence in the 1960s were those demanding a sharp, inquisitive mind rather than an expertise derived from extended committee tenure. As Senator Thomas H. Kuchel (Calif.), the Republican whip, observed, "Now we have things like reapportionment and voting rights—a new man can get his teeth into those [issues] right away."

With this changed atmosphere, it was understandable that most of the younger Democratic senators failed to become enthusiastic for wholesale procedural revisions. The breakdown of the filibuster in civil rights legislation, for example, shunted the cloture issue into the background. As one observer explained, the younger senators have "discovered what mostly was lacking was votes— and now they have them." For the older generation of liberals, Douglas, Clark, Anderson, Morse, and others, the Eighty-ninth Congress was a kind of long-awaited "new deal." Clark himself was led to conclude: "The old times have changed. The Senate establishment is gone. Democracy is now pretty much the rule in the Senate." [30]

The House: Revising the Rules

On January 5, 1965, just minutes after the members of the House of Representatives had received the oath of office, Majority Leader Carl Albert of Oklahoma offered House Resolution 8, which provided for adoption of the rules and procedures of the preceding Congress with three significant amendments. The changes were: reinstatement of the so-called "twenty-one-day rule" to foreclose delays by the Committee on Rules; a procedure permitting bills to be sent to House-Senate conferences without action by the Rules Committee; and removal of the dilatory tactic of demanding an engrossed copy of a bill before passage.

After a brief floor debate, Speaker John W. McCormack of

---

[29] Quoted in *New York Times*, July 17, 1961, p. 11. Under recurrent attack for his leadership, Mansfield delivered a fascinating reply in *Congressional Record*, CIX (Eighty-eighth Congress, 1st session; November 27, 1963), pp. 22857-22866.

[30] *Congressional Record* (Eighty-ninth Congress, 1st session; September 13, 1965, daily edition), p. 22636.

Massachusetts stepped down from the dais and addressed his colleagues. In his unmistakable South Boston accent, he gave his imprimatur to the rules changes. A few minutes later, the House approved H. Res. 8 by a 224 to 201 roll-call vote. By this simple act, the House of Representatives was exercising its prerogative under the Constitutional guarantee that "each House may determine the rules of its proceedings." [31]

Liberal Democrats, who were veterans of the battle against the inherent conservatism of their institution, looked upon H. Res. 8 as a long-awaited reward for years of frustration. The victory, once it arrived, was almost casual; but those who had planned for it believed it was a major step in the institutional reconstruction of Congress.

The Liberals Bide Their Time   The reforms enacted by the Eighty-ninth Congress can be understood only in the light of the liberal discontent of the 1950s and early 1960s. For one thing, most committee chairmanships have for many years been controlled by conservative elders whose one-party districts assured them of long tenure. In the Democratic Eighty-eighth Congress, for example, twelve of the twenty committee chairmen were southerners. Though chairmen range from ineffectual to dictatorial, considerable formal powers accompany seniority positions. Most committee chairmen assume responsibility for assigning bills to subcommittees, selecting subcommittee chairmen, scheduling consideration of bills, supervising preparation of reports on bills, and finally transmitting reports to the Rules Committee. There are enough detours in the legislative process so that the chairman of a substantive committee may tie up important items of legislation for extended periods of time.

The House Committee on Rules was another irritant. Dominated since the late 1930s by a conservative coalition, this committee stands between the substantive committees and the House floor—since important bills reported by a substantive committee must be granted a "rule" specifying the terms of the floor debate. Under the skillful direction of Judge Howard W. Smith (D. Va.), the Committee consisted of a deceptive eight-four Democratic majority during Democratic Congresses from 1955 to 1961. Two of the Democrats, Smith and second-ranking William

[31] Article I, Section 5.

M. Colmer of Mississippi, often sided with the four conservative Republicans to create a deadlock on liberal measures.

Procedural devices to release measures from the Rules Committee are extremely hazardous and have been rarely employed. A "twenty-one-day rule" adopted by the Democratic Eighty-first Congress in 1949 permitted the chairman of a legislative committee that had reported a bill favorably to call it up for floor debate if the Rules Committee had failed to grant a rule within twenty-one days. The 1950 elections depleted the liberal forces sufficiently to produce a deletion of the rule when the Eighty-second Congress adopted its rules in January 1951. During the two years it was in effect, the rule was invoked on eight different occasions; but its mere existence no doubt induced Rules to release other measures it might otherwise have delayed. House liberals considered the revocation of the rule a severe setback.

A third source of frustration for liberal congressmen arose when the Senate—already more sensitive to urban interests than the House—witnessed an influx of young liberals in the late 1950s and early 1960s. This new generation of senators encountered its own difficulties with the "Senate establishment," as we have seen. But the increasingly liberal complexion of the Senate also produced strains in interhouse comity, since agreement by House-Senate conferees on different versions of bills passed by the two houses became more difficult to achieve. When compromises were reached, the House had its way more often than not; liberals in both bodies had frequently to decide whether a diluted bill was better than no bill at all. And in the House, motions for interhouse conferences had to revert to the Rules Committee for scheduling in the absence of unanimous consent. This gave the Rules Committee added dilatory powers, especially during the crowded closing weeks of each session.

The 1960 election and its aftermath focused the attention of liberal Democrats on the problem of party responsibility. Four Mississippi Democrats—Colmer, John Bell Williams, Arthur Winstead, and Jamie Whitten—supported an unpledged slate of presidential electors in that state. And Louisiana's fiery foe of foreign aid, Otto Passman, refused to back the Presidential candidate, although he refrained from announcing support for Republican nominee Richard Nixon. The southerners' refusal to endorse the

Democratic nominee was particularly irksome to liberal supporters of John Kennedy, for there were no immediate local pressures on the five to back Nixon (who was little more acceptable than Kennedy to most voters in the deep South).

Kennedy's narrow victory was accompanied by a loss of twenty Democratic seats in the House. When House liberals sat down shortly afterward with Speaker Sam Rayburn to discuss ways of dealing with the Rules Committee, they suggested that the party caucus punish the five "turncoats" by stripping them of seniority and choice committee seats. This would have the desired effect of ousting Colmer from the Rules Committee. If he were replaced by a moderate, the committee deadlock would be broken. But Rayburn was firm in arguing that this alternative should be avoided because of its *ex post facto* character. The liberals relented, and the more direct course of expanding the Rules Committee was settled upon. Although a floor fight was involved, this move was chosen because, as Rayburn said, it was the most "painless" procedure. The Speaker explained that expansion was "a way to embarrass no one unless they want to be embarrassed." After a personal appeal by Rayburn on the House floor, expansion was approved by a 217 to 212 margin. The resulting eight-seven split was exceedingly tenuous, for the defection of a single "liberal" could serve to reinstate the stalemate. But the liberals who had urged caucus discipline of the party defectors had learned from Rayburn's example, and they bided their time.

The Democratic Study Group   A series of small, informal meetings in the fall of 1956 laid the groundwork for the organization that by 1965 was perhaps the most influential group in the House of Representatives. This organization was to become the "Democratic Study Group," which was largely responsible for the rules changes of the Eighty-ninth Congress.

In December 1956, shortly before the Eighty-fifth Congress convened, Representative Eugene J. McCarthy (Minn.) circulated among a group of his friends a statement of aims that became known as the "Liberal Manifesto." By January 8, 1957, the document had twenty-eight signers; and when Representative Frank Thompson Jr. (N.J.) inserted the program in the *Congressional Record* three weeks later, the list of signers had grown to eighty.[32]

[32] *Congressional Record*, CIII (Eighty-fifth Congress, 1st session; January 30, 1957), pp. 1324-1326.

These liberal Democrats, many from urban areas, welcomed the opportunity to articulate their own ideas on the sort of measures they thought Congress should be considering. A rudimentary and informal whip system was soon installed to implement these goals, and on June 1 the group ("McCarthy's Mavericks," as they were called) acquired a staff assistant. In 1958, with McCarthy deeply involved in his senatorial campaign, Representatives Thompson and Lee Metcalf (Mont.) assumed the reins of leadership. Bolstered by an influx of young liberals known as the "Class of '58," Representatives Chet Holifield (Calif.) and John A. Blatnik (Minn.) met with Speaker Rayburn early in 1959 to urge that action be taken against the Rules Committee. Rayburn agreed to do what he could; but nothing came of the effort, partly because the overthrow of Republican Minority Leader Joseph W. Martin Jr. (Mass.) by "gut-fighter" Charles A. Halleck (Ind.) ended the long-standing comity between Rayburn and the GOP leadership (see the preceding section of this chapter). The first session of the Eighty-sixth Congress thus saw no lessening of the liberals' frustrations.

Toward the close of the session the liberal organization began to take shape. William G. Phillips, an aide to Representative George M. Rhodes (Pa.), was loaned part time and then hired (in May 1960) as full-time staff director, a post he held until the end of 1965. On September 12, 1959, the Democratic Study Group was formally launched with Metcalf as chairman. The following year Metcalf followed McCarthy to the Senate, and Holifield became chairman. The formal House Democratic leaders at first feared that the new group might turn into an unfriendly rival. Nevertheless, as one student remarked, "the attitudes of the House leadership toward the group which became the DSG might best be described . . . as benevolent neutrality that grew into tacit approval." [33]

Thus matters stood until the 1960 election, when the negotiations with Rayburn took place. While yielding to the Speaker on the tactics for dealing with the Rules Committee, DSG leaders nonetheless expected that expansion of the committee would lead to other rules changes. A prerequisite was the acquisition of new

[33] Kenneth Kofmehl, "The Institutionalization of a Voting Bloc," *Western Political Quarterly*, XVII (June 1964), p. 272. Much of this account of DSG's early history is drawn from Kofmehl's article.

recruits for the liberal ranks. The 1960 election had seen a loss of twenty Democratic seats, with a number of casualties among the liberal "Class of '58." During the 1962 campaign, therefore, the DSG supplied campaign materials and other assistance to liberal Democratic candidates. Though the party lost four more House seats that year, more than one hundred members were affiliated with the DSG at the beginning of the Eighty-eighth Congress (a formal membership list has never been published).

Blatnik was elected DSG chairman in the spring of 1963. He and other DSG leaders were sensitive to the public and press criticisms of congressional inaction that persisted into the summer and fall of that year. Even when the impasse ended following Kennedy's death, the liberals remained convinced that changes were needed in congressional procedures. After all, a change in mood or the shift of a few seats might reinstate the old deadlock on Capitol Hill. Yet the liberals still lacked the necessary votes to control the House Democratic caucus, and the 1964 elections were the key. The electoral windfall that followed placed the DSG in the center of the House Democratic party.

Mobilizing the DSG Majority   The same day that saw Lyndon Johnson receive his unprecedented victory from the American electorate also witnessed a dramatic (and not unrelated) change in the Democratic congressional party. The Democratic majority in the House was the largest since 1938. The liberals now had an undeniable majority in the party caucus and enough votes on the floor to neutralize the old Republican-conservative Democratic coalition.

The DSG's campaign committee, headed by Representative Richard Bolling (Mo.), had put more than $70,000 at the disposal of 105 House candidates. Of the thirty-nine incumbents receiving DSG aid, all but one were re-elected; and more importantly, of the sixty-six nonincumbents who were helped, forty were sent by the voters to Washington. The DSG effort involved more than financial support. Many types of campaign materials were provided: sets of information cards on issues; "Lip from the Hip," an eighty-page document containing the full texts of Republican campaign arguments and sample rebuttals; and a booklet entitled "Goldwater, Either/Or," described as "a careful compilation and analysis of the Republican candidate's controversial and contradictory statements in 16 major public policy areas." In giving aid, the

DSG worked closely with the Democratic National Committee, the Democratic Senatorial and Congressional Campaign Committees, and the National Committee for an Effective Congress (a citizens' group that supports liberal candidates of both parties).

While the campaign was getting under way, an important step was taken on Capitol Hill. DSG leaders decided to arrange a caucus on party loyalty just before the members adjourned for the campaign, but the swift pace of end-of-the-session business scuttled this idea. Upon Bolling's initiative, however, a statement was drafted expressing the DSG's intent to purge disloyal Democratic Congressmen at the January caucus. The day before adjournment (October 2), the statement, which had previously been mailed to all Democratic House candidates, was inserted in the *Congressional Record* by DSG Chairman Blatnik. Signed by ten liberals, all members of DSG's Executive Committee, the declaration read in part:

> All of us are aware that, in past campaigns, some Members of the Democratic caucus have openly supported presidential candidates of other political parties or independent electors in their states. This they have every right to do. We do not feel, however, that such Members should be welcomed back into the Democratic fold and be entitled to committee assignments on an equal basis with those Members who supported our national candidates and platform. . . .
>
> We are, therefore, taking this means to serve notice of our firm intention to oppose the seating, in the January 1965 Democratic caucus, of any present Member or candidate elected to the House . . . on the Democratic ticket who supported, campaigned for, or otherwise advocated the election of a President or Vice President other than the candidates nominated by the Democratic Party. . . . Similar action will be directed toward any Member or candidate who supported so-called unpledged or independent slates of electors. . . .[34]

This statement was intended to follow the late Speaker Rayburn's injunction that a purge required prior warning. The liberals hoped to neutralize pressures on possible defectors, and to set up those who did defect for discipline by the caucus. "We really thought

[34] *Congressional Record* (Eighty-eighth Congress, 2d session; October 2, 1964, daily edition), p. 22926.

we'd catch quite a bag-full," remarked one DSG member, noting the strong pressures on southern Democrats to support Goldwater.

But beyond the immediate desire to "clip the wings of the turncoats" lay the long-range objective of creating a new sense of party loyalty among congressional Democrats. "It was a wise, new, fresh precedent," one liberal commented. "We wanted to make the Democratic Party count for more."

The DSG's challenge was soon taken up. Three days after Blatnik's announcement, Albert W. Watson, a freshman Democrat from South Carolina, announced support of Goldwater in a locally televised speech. Then Democratic Representative John Bell Williams of Mississippi made a similar statement amid considerable fanfare. As a freshman congressman, Watson had little to lose in the way of seniority; but Williams was an eighteen-year veteran who, as ranking Democrat on the Commerce Committee, was next in line for the chairmanship.

A complicating factor was the possibility of presidential intervention. After his landslide victory, President Johnson's thoughts naturally turned to the problem of reconciliation to gain future southern support. DSG leaders realized that White House intercession on behalf of the defectors would destroy all hopes for a purge. Publicly, Thompson expressed hope that the President would remain neutral: "I doubt that he would interject himself into this matter," he said. "Those of us who signed [the pre-election notice] are determined to implement it." Though rumors persisted, there was no communication either to or from the White House.

The election outcome renewed interest in all types of reform. A draft list of reform proposals had been circulated among DSG members as early as September, but the end of the session and the campaign had suspended discussion. On December 3, however, the DSG Executive Committee held an important meeting in Chairman Blatnik's office. On the agenda prepared by Staff Director Phillips were about twenty topics, including suggested caucus actions and House rules changes.

The two-hour meeting produced unanimous agreement on eight proposals. The following day DSG Secretary Thompson sent to all DSG members and congressmen-elect a letter describing the package. Exclusive of the Williams-Watson purge, the proposals were as follows:

1. Return to the pre-1951 procedure of having the full caucus meet a second time to approve, amend, or reject the committee assignment recommendations of the Democratic Committee on Committees (which consists of the Democratic members of the Committee on Ways and Means).

2. Adjustment of party ratios on House committees to reflect the more than two to one Democratic margin—including seventeen Democrats on the twenty-five-man Ways and Means Committee, and thirty-four of fifty on Appropriations.

3. Establishment of a Democratic Policy (or Steering) Committee, similar to that of the Republicans.

4. Enactment of a modified twenty-one-day rule to unbottle the Rules Committee. Unlike the old rule, the proposal would give discretionary power to the Speaker to recognize any member of the committee desiring to bypass Rules.

5. Creation of a Joint Committee on Congressional Organization, modeled after the 1945 LaFollette-Monroney committee.

6. A rule permitting the Speaker to recognize committee chairmen to offer privileged motions to send to conference by majority vote a bill passed by both houses.

7. A liberalized discharge petition, requiring only 175 signatures for "major measures which are a part of the majority party's legislative program," with the standard 218 signatures for other bills.

Although some of the changes would require approval by the full House, the crucial target was the opening Democratic caucus scheduled for the afternoon of January 2. A meeting of the entire DSG was therefore called for the morning before the Democratic caucus.

DSG strategists knew that the elected party leadership, and especially Speaker McCormack, must be kept informed. "There's no use trying to do things behind the Speaker's back," one observer commented. "He'll find out anyway." The first formal approach to the leadership came on December 15, when two DSG Executive Committee members had lunch with a key southern advisor to the Speaker. They hoped to soften his expected objection to parts of the reform package. The liberals were somewhat surprised, therefore, when toward the close of their discussion they realized that he had indicated support for seven of the eight proposals—expressing apprehension only about changing the party ratio on Ways and Means. The southerner reasoned that the votes to pass medicare were already assured, and that if necessary a discharge petition could blast the bill out of the committee. More importantly, being "hard-nosed" about committee ratios might set an unfortunate precedent: if the Democrats were again in the minority, the Republicans might well reciprocate with a vengeance. What most struck the liberals was the southerner's acceptance of the Williams-Watson purge and his readiness to allow caucus approval of committee assignments. As for the purge, he explained that many southerners who had "stuck their necks out" to support President Johnson would be more than happy to see the defectors punished. A secret ballot in the caucus, he felt, would enhance the chances for success.

The DSG members were also advised on tactics. First, the DSG should designate a "safe" congressman such as Blatnik as their leader in the caucus, keeping the "ultraliberal" types in the background. Secondly, the Speaker should be consulted in person and assured that the proposed changes would strengthen his own position, and that the DSG had the needed caucus votes.

Holifield and Blatnik, who had served as go-betweens before and had earned the Speaker's confidence, were dispatched to negotiate with McCormack. They met on three successive days between Christmas and New Year's for lengthy discussions on each of the proposals. The second and third days, McCormack brought in House Parliamentarian Lewis Deschler to refine the DSG's preliminary drafts of the rules changes. "When Deschler showed up, we knew we were making progress," one DSG man said.

McCormack needed little encouragement on reinstatement of the twenty-one-day rule. At first he balked at the proposed discretionary feature, but he yielded to Blatnik's and Holifield's vigorous arguments in favor of strengthening the Speaker's powers. McCormack also endorsed the change in the conference report procedure, along with a provision that would "deprive any Member of the privilege of demanding a fully engrossed copy of a bill." Not a part of the liberals' package, this latter proposal was added at the insistence of Representative Neal Smith (D. Iowa), a DSG member who lobbied personally with the Speaker to obtain it. Smith wanted to prevent the dilatory tactic of requesting an engrossed copy of a bill in order to hold up final passage for twenty-four hours. McCormack was agreeable, and he ordered the change incorporated into the resolution.

The Speaker pledged neutrality in the Williams-Watson affair, though he maintained that stripping the two of seniority on their committees would be sufficient punishment. He argued that refusing caucus seating would be more controversial and would only serve to make martyrs of the two men. DSG leaders had arrived at the same conclusion. As one of them reasoned, "We bought neutrality from the leadership by agreeing to go for seniority rather than caucus seating. We weren't really after those two ineffectual clowns."

McCormack was cool toward the steering committee idea, if the group were to be given decision-making powers (he had opposed the proposal two years earlier). He was also reluctant to endorse the discharge petition change, since it would give him added discretion in designating "major measures" eligible for a reduced number of signatures. The DSG representatives raised the possibility of applying a liberalized discharge petition solely to the District of Columbia Committee, since District home rule was the only outstanding liberal measure expected to encounter committee opposition. Deschler contended, however, that no rule should be drawn to apply to a single committee.

McCormack agreed, however, to work out new committee ratios with the Republican leadership, and he promised to call a second Democratic caucus to ratify the report of the Committee on Committees. He said that he interpreted the caucus rules to provide for review of committee assignments, even though the practice had been unused since 1951. He therefore requested that no motion for a second caucus be offered. Many DSG leaders viewed review of committee assignments as the most important item of the reform package. Two objectives were embedded in this seemingly innocent proposal: First, it would assure that the Committee on Committees followed caucus instructions on the Williams-Watson assignments; secondly, it would re-establish a precedent for future party control of committee assignments.

Thus the groundwork was laid for a liberal victory in the

caucus and on the House floor. No explicit "treaties" had been signed with the leadership, but the bargains had nonetheless been struck—in the subtle, roundabout manner so familiar to Congress. The Speaker and the DSG knew each other's strength and worked to preserve comity. On New Year's Day the DSG sponsored a reception at the National Capitol Democratic Club in honor of the newly elected Democratic congressmen and their wives. To everyone's surprise, the Speaker was one of the first guests to arrive. His presence was symbolic. An air of confident anticipation prevailed, for the final DSG strategy session and the caucus were to be held the next day.

The Changes Are Enacted   At 10:00 A.M. on January 2, the newly enlarged DSG gathered in Room 1302 of the Longworth House Office Building. More than 150 congressmen were present—enough to control that afternoon's Democratic caucus. DSG Chairman Blatnik opened the meeting by reviewing the reform proposals and outlining the available stratagems.

One by one the proposals were discussed. The matter of party ratios on the committees need not be pressed because the Speaker had assured it would be taken care of through negotiations with GOP leaders. Also deleted was the request for a second party caucus to review committee assignments, since the Speaker had promised to call the caucus himself.

The proposal to reduce to 175 the number of signatures needed for certain discharge petitions was then debated. Some members thought a liberalized rule would allow many undesirable measures to reach the House floor. Others quibbled over the number of signatures: some favored 190, others 175. Opinions were so divided that the proposal was dropped from the package. One DSG leader confessed afterward that this was a wise tactical move. "As it turned out," he said, "the package had all it could carry. Pressing for the discharge change might well have cost us the whole package." Another reason for shelving the proposal was knowledge of the Speaker's antipathy toward it.

On the other proposals there was unanimous approval. If accepted by the caucus, the rules changes would be presented as a resolution at Monday's opening session of the entire House. The Williams-Watson purge would also be pressed at the caucus. No immediate action was required on the two final items: The Joint

Committee on the Organization of the Congress would be created through normal legislative action (S. Con. Res. 2), and the Democratic Steering Committee idea would have to be explored informally.

The Democratic caucus met in the House chamber at 2:30 that afternoon. A secret ballot yielded a 157 to 115 vote in favor of stripping Williams and Watson of their seniority. Representative Harley O. Staggers of West Virginia would replace the unpopular Williams as second-ranking Democrat on the Commerce Committee. When it was learned the following summer that Chairman Oren Harris planned to retire after twenty-five years in the House, one DSG member quipped, "Oren should really be grateful to us."

The caucus also agreed by a 189 to 71 vote to submit the rules changes, the twenty-one-day rule and the conference report rule, to the House. The next task was to obtain favorable House action on the changes.

If the opening day of the new Congress seemed routine, it was only deceptively so. After the clerk called the House to order and the chaplain offered the prayer, the roll of representatives-elect was called by states. The next order of business was the election of a Speaker from the candidates nominated by the two party caucuses. On a straight party-line teller vote, and to no one's surprise, McCormack was duly re-elected. Minority Leader Gerald R. Ford of Michigan then gracefully introduced McCormack, who took the oath of office administered by the dean of the House, Emanuel Celler (D. N.Y.).

Shortly thereafter, Majority Leader Albert rose to present the resolution embodying the rules changes. Judge Smith then launched a defense of his Rules Committee, questioning the need for a new rule. "The 21-day rule I am opposed to," he said. "We had it once, we used it for one Congress, then it was abandoned as not workable." Then the late Clarence J. Brown (Ohio), ranking Republican on the Rules Committee, argued that the change would give the Speaker inordinate power. When McCormack stepped down from the dais to defend the change, calling the new discretionary power "a reasonable provision," Brown replied that "We gave that power to 'Uncle Joe' Cannon and Tom Reed, as the gentleman recalls. We gave them too much power." After several minutes of debate, the yeas and nays were ordered and the clerk called the roll. By a vote of 224 to 201, H. Res. 8 passed and the liberals had won an important victory.[35]

New party ratios for all committees were fixed at a conference of both parties' leaders the next day: Ways and Means went from fifteen-ten to seventeen-eight, and Appropriations from thirty-twenty to thirty-four-sixteen. In a few weeks a new Democratic Steering Committee was created. Chaired by Representative Ray J. Madden (Ind.), the group consisted of six *ex officio* voting members (speaker, majority leader, whip, chairman and secretary of the Caucus, and chairman of the Campaign Committee) and eighteen regional representatives, generally the deans of the geographic areas. One DSG leader predicted that the group would collapse; but another expressed the belief that, while the group was "not all it could be, it's not a fiasco either." The President held monthly meetings with the Steering Committee during 1965 to give members a full view of the legislative program. In late August the House quietly authorized a full-time staff member for the Steering Committee (as well as one for the House Republican Policy Committee). Only time would determine, however, whether the group could assume real authority.

In late January, the Speaker called a special caucus to ratify committee assignments made by the Committee on Committees. After carefully weighing the alternatives, DSG leaders decided not to challenge any of the recommendations. It was felt that the mere precedent of having the second caucus was sufficient for the time being. The review caucus could conceivably be employed in the future to challenge certain assignments on a selective basis. "We'll pick a target, amend a committee list, and set still another precedent," a DSG leader predicted.

The package of procedural changes enacted in 1965 was the product of varying motives and pressures. One DSG member observed that two schools of thought had emerged within the liberal camp. "There are the caucus reformers, and the rules reformers," he said. "This time we went down both roads at once." Some liberals, including Wisconsin's Henry S. Reuss (D.), favored formal rules changes as the best method for speeding up the legislative process. The twenty-one-day rule was such a change,

[35] *Congressional Record* (Eighty-ninth Congress, 1st session; January 4, 1965, daily edition), pp. 14-23.

as were the modifications in the conference report and engrossed copy procedures. Others in the liberal camp—including Richard Bolling (D. Mo.), Morris K. Udall (D. Ariz.), and James G. O'Hara (D. Mich.)—leaned toward strengthening party responsibility through the caucus. From their point of view, the precedents established in the caucus, if retained, were a potentially more significant development than the more spectacular rules changes. The "caucus reformers" may have greater opportunity to work their will in the future; for, while the Republicans can recover their strength in the House, the chances are good that, as one member put it, "the liberals will control the Democratic caucus for as long as we can see." Viewing the events of January 1965, two well-known Washington columnists concluded that "The subject of congressional reform—along with the DSG—is being approached with new respect on Capitol Hill." [36]

Conclusions

The liberal Democrats have provided the focus for this narrative, not out of any ideological preferences of the authors, but because the liberals' point of view is the most useful one for analyzing the Democratic party's organizational problems in the 1960s. All stable institutions are by definition conservative, and Congress is no exception. For a number of reasons, the sweeping changes of post-World War II America were reflected only imperfectly in the structure of Congress. To the increasing numbers of urban-minded members, it seemed as though Congress was dominated by a senior coalition which spoke the language of another era. The perspectives of a Harry F. Byrd, Sr. (of Berryville, Va.), a Richard Russell (of Winder, Ga.), a John McMillan (of Florence, S.C.), or a Howard W. Smith (of Broad Run, Va.) seemed to their younger colleagues strangely inappropriate, not because these men were untalented (as they were not), but simply because they were considered out of touch.

The clash of perspectives is amusingly illustrated by a minor incident that took place in Judge Smith's Rules Committee in mid-1965. Representative George Miller (D. Calif.), chairman of the Committee on Science and Astronautics, was appearing to

[36] Rowland Evans and Robert Novak, "The Liberal House," *Washington Post*, January 6, 1965, p. A 17.

defend his committee's recommendation for a study contemplating adoption of the metric system of measurement in this country. Miller painted a vivid picture of the advantages of the metric system. To this, Judge Smith replied that he had been educated in a one-room schoolhouse and that he didn't know anything about the metric system.

In the wake of the 1964 election, the atmosphere was subtly but significantly altered. In structural terms, of course, very little was actually changed. In the Senate the old cloture rule remained, though hardly an issue after it had been successfully invoked twice on major civil rights legislation. (Extended debate was invoked on other issues, however, including reapportionment and repeal of the Taft-Hartley Labor-Management Relations Act's provision permitting state "right to work" laws.) But gradually the build-up of liberal strength began to be felt in committee assignments, in floor encounters that would have been considered presumptuous a few years before, and perhaps most of all in the erosion of the old Senate "folkways."

In the House, of course, the DSG was able to push a notable package of procedural reforms. These innovations served to ratify the liberals' new majority position, and to make the "Great Society" legislative proposals less vulnerable to conservative opposition. The twenty-one-day rule, the most immediately important of the changes, was invoked by the Democratic leadership in 1965 on no less than six measures, five of which were eventually passed by the House. Even so, Judge Smith dutifully reported out a number of bills that were abhorrent to him, no doubt hoping to demonstrate that the new rule was unnecessary.

Behind the procedural innovations, of course, lay the temporary redistribution of power within Congress. This did not mean that the liberals were given a totally free hand in processing legislation. They were still constrained to compromise, to strike bargains, to forego certain legislative goals, and even to confront defeat. Legislative coalitions (in the American definition) can be pushed just so far and no further.

There was no assurance that the liberal hegemony would be permanent. The gain of thirty-eight Democratic House seats in the 1964 elections was closely related to the immense popularity of President Johnson at the polls (or conversely, to the unpopularity of his opponent). As we have seen in our discussion of campaigns, local candidates are never unaware of the voters' assessments of their party's national candidates. This is especially true in closely contested districts, where sufficient numbers of voters may be pulled by the presidential tide to influence the Congressional races.[37] About fifteen percent of the voters in a Presidential election, moreover, do not vote in "off-year" congressional elections. Such voters tend to be less involved politically, less intense in their party loyalties, and therefore more apt to swing with presidential tides. These factors account for the apparent influence of the presidential race on local contests, and the frequent loss of legislative seats by the presidential party in off-year elections.

The pull of the presidential race was especially strong in 1964. In his unprecedented landslide, President Johnson carried 375 congressional districts; in 274 of these, he ran ahead of the Democratic congressional candidate—an unusual feat for modern Democratic Presidents. The clear expectation throughout the campaign that Johnson would win handily undoubtedly encouraged many voters to cast straight Democratic ballots and it certainly encouraged the party's congressional aspirants to identify themselves closely with the national ticket. Once elected, the seventy-one freshman Democrats in the Eighty-ninth Congress gave conspicuous support to President Johnson's "Great Society" programs. Taken together, they supported the Administration eighty-nine percent of the time on twelve key votes, and eighty-three percent on sixty-six votes on which the President had taken a position.[38]

These were the political facts of life underlying the unique position of the congressional Democratic party in the Eighty-ninth Congress. Precisely because the party had "won big" in 1964, it faced the possibility of an unusual loss of seats with a "normal" mid-term vote in 1966. For their part, Democratic liberals realized that 1965 presented a fleeting opportunity for significant revisions in congressional rules or procedures. The outsized majorities could not be expected to continue forever; hence future liberal reform would have to depend upon the internal character of the congressional Democratic party itself.

[37] See, for example, Charles Press, "Presidential Coattails and Party Cohesion," *Midwest Journal of Political Science*, VII (November 1963), pp. 320-335.
[38] Figures through August 4, 1965. See *Congressional Quarterly Weekly Report*, XXXV (August 27, 1965), pp. 1746-1747.

THE CONGRESSIONAL COMMITTEE 5

Congress is an illustration of what Robert A. Dahl has called the "coalition of chieftains" leadership pattern: individuals, each with significant political resources, accommodate each other despite their various competing interests, in order to achieve integration of policy through negotiation and bargaining.[1] Foremost among the congressional "chieftains" are the chairmen of the standing committees (twenty in the House and sixteen in the Senate, plus the Joint Committee on Atomic Energy). With varying styles of leadership and degrees of control, they preside over the congressional subunits that, while technically only creatures of Congress, in reality dominate its decisions. The final decisions made on the floor of the House and Senate are usually ratifications, perhaps with minor modifications, of previous judgments made in the standing committees.

These powerful subsystems of Congress all function differently. Some, such as the House Appropriations Committee,

[1] *Who Governs? Democracy and Power in an American City* (New Haven: Yale University Press, 1961), pp. 186-187.

operate with a minimum of internal conflict and effectively serve as institutions for the resolution of conflict.[2] Other committees, for example, the House Education and Labor Committee, work in a highly charged atmosphere of partisanship and ideological conflict.[3]

While congressional committees exhibit a wide range of behavior patterns, the functioning of all committees is influenced by a number of common factors including the chairman and his style of leadership; the subcommittee organization; the staff; the committee's recruitment patterns; the degree of member interest in committee work; the members' work orientation; the degree of committee integration; and the configuration of issues and agencies with which the committee deals. These factors have affected the operations of the Senate Committee on Banking and Currency. In the analysis of this committee that follows, particular attention is directed to the manner in which these factors have limited the committee's oversight activities.

An Overview of the Committee

The Banking and Currency Committee has jurisdiction over a wide range of legislation and agencies having a far-reaching impact on the economy. The committee handles all banking legislation, encompassing the operations of national banks, the Federal Reserve System, the Federal Deposit Insurance Corporation, the Comptroller of the Currency, the Home Loan Bank Board (the federal regulatory agency for savings and loan associations), credit unions, the Federal Savings and Loan Insurance Corporation, and the Export-Import Bank. Matters pertaining to the Securities and Exchange Commission and the regulation of the sale of securities also fall within its purview. The committee handles the almost annual omnibus housing bills that provide for FHA mortgage insurance, urban renewal, public housing, veterans' housing, public-works assistance to small and medium-sized cities, housing for senior citizens, military housing, college housing, farm

---

[2] Richard F. Fenno, Jr., "The House Appropriations Committee as a Political System; The Problem of Integration," *American Political Science Review,* LVI (June 1962), pp. 310-324.
[3] Frank Munger and Richard F. Fenno, Jr., *National Politics and Federal Aid to Education* (Syracuse: Syracuse University Press, 1962), pp. 106-136.

housing, and secondary mortgage market stability (the last through the actions of the Federal National Mortgage Association). The Small Business Administration (SBA) programs of assistance to small businessmen and the depressed-areas programs of the Commerce Department are under jurisdiction of the committee, as is legislation concerned with consumer credit, price and rent control, export control, defense production, and the striking of commemorative medals.

The political salience of Banking and Currency's subject matter has fluctuated with the economic and political conditions at a particular time and with the character of the forces controlling the committee. During World War II and postwar years, its activities regarding price and rent controls, government reconversion policy, and the Employment Act of 1946—a landmark in terms of government's commitment to sustain a prosperous economy—made the committee a center of intense conflicts over the future of the American economy. Also attracting widespread attention were the postwar housing bills that were (and continue to be) important measures, both in terms of assisting the housing-construction industry and in performing broad social welfare functions. Consideration of such issues as these, plus the important question of the nature of defense production policy in meeting the challenges of the Cold War, made the committee until the mid-1950s a much sought-after assignment. More recently, however, Banking and Currency issues have been less prominent and it has not therefore been considered as attractive a committee assignment as in the past. The following sections dramatize the impact that this change in attractiveness has had on the committee's operations.

The diminished desirability of the Banking and Currency assignment is reflected by the fact that in 1965 its size was reduced from fifteen to fourteen members, while other coveted committee assignments, Commerce, Foreign Relations, and Judiciary, were expanded.

The ratio of Democrats to Republicans through the years has reflected fluctuations in party strength within the Senate itself. Since the Eighty-third Congress, party ratios on Banking and Currency have been as shown in Table 8.

The Committee has a full complement of subcommittees whose respective jurisdictions cover the range of its activities. In

1961-1962, for example, there were five subcommittees: Housing, International Finance, Production and Stabilization, Securities, and Small Business. In 1963 a sixth, Financial Institutions, was

TABLE 8   PARTY RATIOS ON THE SENATE BANKING
AND CURRENCY COMMITTEE, 1953-1966

Congresses	Party ratios Democratic	Republican
83rd (1953-1954)	7	8
84th (1955-1956)	8	7
85th (1957-1958)	10	5
86th (1958-1960)	10	5
87th (1961-1962	10	5
88th (1963-1964)	10	5
89th (1965-1966)	10	4

added. Subcommittee chairmanships are awarded on the basis of seniority and interest among majority party members. Thus in 1961-1964 the committee's six senior Democrats each chaired a subcommittee.

The Chairmanship

Most commentaries on Congress emphasize the tremendous power of committee chairmen because they can call meetings and set their agendas, appoint subcommittees and fix their party ratios, appoint staff members, refer bills to subcommittees, control committee funds, act as floor manager of committee bills, and make recommendations on appointments to conference committees. Although these powers must be used within the limits a committee majority will tolerate, challenges to the prerogatives of a chairman are rare and made reluctantly. The leadership styles of chairmen are varied, but they dramatically affect the capacity of committees to perform legislative functions such as oversight, as may be seen by a comparison of the operation of the Senate Banking and Currency Committee under its chairman from 1955 to 1959, J. William Fulbright (D. Ark), with its operation under Senator A. Willis Robertson (D. Va.) from 1959 to 1966.

A *"Service Chairman"*   When the Democrats regained control of the Senate in 1955, Fulbright assumed the chairmanship of Banking and Currency from Senator Homer Capehart (R.

Ind.). During his brief tenure (1953-1954), Capehart had demon-strated a consuming interest in committee work and had run the committee in a highly centralized manner. Subcommittees existed on paper, but in reality had little power, since major legislative proposals (housing, defense production) were handled in the full committee, where Capehart was personally in charge. Capehart also personally supervised much of the work of the committee staff.

By contrast, Fulbright's main interests were not with the Banking and Currency Committee, but rather with the work of the Foreign Relations Committee where he was the second rank-ing Democrat. His method of running Banking and Currency re-flected this preoccupation. He was a "service chairman"; that is, he permitted his committee colleagues relatively free rein and would normally assist them wherever possible. For example, under Fulbright each Democratic senator was given a subcommittee chairmanship. Instead of handling major bills in full committee, he permitted each subcommittee chairman an opportunity to as-sert leadership in shaping legislative proposals within the sphere of his jurisdiction. Thus, Senator Douglas (D. Ill.) used his Pro-duction and Stabilization Subcommittee as a forum to develop support for his depressed-areas bills (proposals for which Fulbright demonstrated no enthusiasm; see Chapter 6); Senator Robertson, the Banking Subcommittee chairman, embarked on a massive study of federal banking laws preparatory to introducing the Financial Institutions Act of 1957, the first attempt at codification and up-dating of all federal banking laws since the 1930s.

A further indication of Fulbright's assumption of the serv-ice chairman role may be seen in his treatment of the Subcom-mittee on International Finance. Fulbright himself initially served as its chairman; when, however, Senator Mike Monroney (D. Okla.) conceived of the need for an International Development Association as an affiliate of the World Bank, Fulbright surren-dered his subcommittee chairmanship to Monroney, who was not even a member of the subcommittee. Monroney was allowed to take the initiative in the matter and was given assistance by Fulbright, including the services of a staff man assigned to the subcommittee. In the housing field, Fulbright was quite willing to have the Housing Subcommittee under Senator John Sparkman (D. Ala.) assume the massive burden of handling the almost annual omnibus bills. He delegated this authority even though most participants in committee activities believed that housing was the most important and politically rewarding phase of their work since it benefited such a wide array of interests, including the National Association of Home Builders, the National Association of Real Estate Boards, the Mortgage Bankers Association, the U. S. Conference of Mayors, the American Municipal Association, the Americans for Democratic Action (ADA), and AFL-CIO, to name only a few.

Fulbright's decentralized and permissive style of leadership meant that his committee colleagues, particularly the subcommittee chairmen, were able to engage in oversight activities if they wished. It was during this time, for example, that Sparkman's Housing Subcommittee became extremely active in studying the performance of the Housing and Home Finance Agency (HHFA) and in pointing out problem areas in the housing field. In spite of his essentially favorable attitude toward the Federal Reserve Board (FRB) and its policies, Fulbright also showed more willingness than his successor, Senator Robertson, to permit committee members the opportunity to publicly criticize its actions. For example, because there was dissatisfaction within the committee regarding FRB policies in 1958, the chairman authorized a public hearing for the purpose of critically reviewing FRB monetary policies. At this hearing the FRB and its chairman, William McChesney Martin, were subjected to hostile questioning by members of the committee. Following the hearing, Fulbright commissioned an economist from the Library of Congress to study further the FRB's recent credit policies. The ensuing report was extremely critical and was believed by close observers to have been disturbing to the FRB.[4]

Fulbright further facilitated the activities of the membership by making funds available for hearings (including field hearings held outside Washington, such as in Senator Douglas's hearings designed to mobilize support for a depressed-areas bill) and for travel (for example, for a member to go abroad and study foreign-lending operations of the government agencies). In addition, he both maintained the committee's tradition of employing a

[4] U.S. Senate, Committee on Banking and Currency, *Federal Reserve and Economic Stability, 1951-57* (Eighty-fifth Congress, 2d Session, 1958, S. Rep. 2500 [prepared by Asher Achinstein]).

well-qualified and able staff and permitted senior committee members, Capehart, Sparkman, and Douglas, to appoint staff members who would work primarily for them. Fulbright was anxious to keep the staff abreast of administrative developments. He therefore readily accepted the suggestion of his chief of staff that the FRB staff annually present to the committee the same report it gave the Federal Reserve's Open Market Committee on the projected outlook for the economy.

Since Fulbright's main interests were not with the committee and he operated as described, he was not considered an aggressive leader. He and his committee, however, could be extremely forceful when his interest was aroused. In 1955 he became concerned about the potential dangers of rising stock-market prices and the policies of government regulatory agencies in this situation. After having careful preparations made by the committee staff, Fulbright launched the Stock Market Study of 1955, which thoroughly and aggressively examined and criticized the agencies charged with regulation of the stock exchanges.[5] Following the hearings, the FRB raised its margin requirements (tightened the credit terms under which stocks can be purchased). Within the committee it was thought that the critical hearings had a direct influence on this FRB decision.

This was, however, an exception. Mainly, Fulbright was a service chairman who kept the facilities of his committee open to the membership, permitting initiative to pass to the other members and staff. A member of the committee summarized his chairmanship: "I always thought that Fulbright's main interests were in Foreign Relations. While he was chairman, the committee pretty much ran itself."

A *"Minority and Restraining Chairman"* Senator Robertson, by contrast, can be characterized as a "minority and restraining chairman"; that is, his policy preferences put him in a minority position within his committee, and he uses his prerogatives as a quiet and subtle restraint on its activities. His reputation is that of a mild-mannered man; he has been described by columnists Rowland Evans and Robert Novak: "As oligarchs go, Robertson is relatively benign. Though unmistakably a foe of the New Frontier, he has never been as ruthless as some of his fellow

[5] U.S. Senate, Committee on Banking and Currency, *Hearings, Stock Market Study* (Eighty-fourth Congress, 1st Session, 1955).

Southerners in blocking liberal legislation" [6]; and by a staff assistant to a liberal committee member: "He is an amiable and benevolent chairman who doesn't believe in using his power in an unfair or abusive manner. He's not an obstructionist so much as a drag. He won't obstruct, but he won't help." Because Robertson has used his powers and prerogatives as chairman to restrain the committee in quiet and seemingly innocuous ways, the members have not thought his actions worth the cost of challenging and possibly alienating him. Senator Joseph Clark (D. Pa.) has explained that in 1964 he did not press for adoption of a change in the rules of the committee that would have limited the powers of the chairman because Robertson took the proposal as a personal affront. Clark did not want to work in an atmosphere of personal antagonism within the committee and so he withdrew the proposed rules changes.

Robertson's restraining influence has left a clear mark on the operation of the subcommittees. Robertson retained the eight subcommittees that he inherited from his predecessor, Fulbright, until 1961 when there was a substantial turnover of committee membership and Senator J. Allen Frear (D. Del.), chairman of the Federal Reserve Subcommittee, was defeated for re-election. In the 1961 organizational meeting of the committee, Robertson announced that the subcommittees on Banking and Federal Reserve were being eliminated and that their work would henceforth be handled in the full committee. The reason given for this action was that these were subjects of general interest to the membership, and that therefore, even if they were first considered in subcommittee, the full committee would want to take them up. Thus the committee's work would be expedited if the first step were eliminated. Most observers, however, placed a different interpretation on the decision. It was known that Senators Clark and William Proxmire (D. Wis.) desired the chairmanship of the Federal Reserve Subcommittee and that they would undoubtedly have used it as a forum for vigorous criticism of the FRB. Abolition of the subcommittee kept the Federal Reserve sheltered from such criticism and brought Federal Reserve and banking matters under the tight control of Chairman Robertson, a firm supporter and friend of the FRB and its policies.

[6] "Inside Report: Mr. Robertson's Summer," *The Washington Post*, July 23, 1963.

Although it is a commonplace on Capitol Hill that committees carefully guard their jurisdictions, Robertson has not zealously protected the Senate Banking and Currency Committee's area of control. For example, for twelve years following enactment of the Legislative Reorganization Act of 1946, the committee had exercised jurisdiction over foreign lending institutions by means of an informal agreement with the Foreign Relations Committee (which technically had been given the jurisdiction by the 1946 Act). When Fulbright resigned as Banking and Currency chairman in 1959 to assume the chairmanship of Foreign Relations, however, jurisdiction over foreign lending was quietly returned to Foreign Relations. This came as a surprise to certain members, including a senior Republican, and was regretted by the chairman of the International Finance Subcommittee, since it left his subcommittee with no meaningful jurisdiction. None of the members felt that this matter was worth objecting to, however, since foreign lending had traditionally been Fulbright's domain.[7] Nevertheless, the result has been restraint of the committee's power.

Similarly, as chairman, Robertson has taken pride in his efforts to reduce the cost of government, and his frugality with committee funds has had a restrictive impact on the committee. Until finally outvoted in 1963, for example, he successfully prevented expenditure of committee funds for field hearings designed to build support for Douglas's Truth-In-Lending bill. (Compare this with Fulbright's record.) This measure, which Robertson has vigorously opposed, would require lenders to disclose full interest rates in any transaction. He has also shown reluctance to print staff studies that he thought might be used as supporting evidence in pleas for expanded government housing programs. Similarly, the committee staff has been kept small, with the result that few staffmen are available for oversight or legislative work.

Such restraints as these have severely limited the capacity

[7] Robertson also failed to assert the committee's claim to jurisdiction over nominations to the Office of Emergency Planning other than to write a perfunctory letter to Chairman Richard Russell (D. Ga.) of the Armed Services Committee that successfully claimed jurisdiction. As with the question of jurisdiction over foreign lending institutions, most members did not feel strongly enough about the matter to challenge the chairman. The exchange of letters between Robertson and Russell is reprinted in U.S. Senate, Committee on Banking and Currency, *Hearings, Defense Production Act Inventories* (Eighty-eighth Congress, 2d Session, 1964), pp. 42-44.

of the committee to engage in oversight activities. This is acceptable to the chairman, however, since his concept of the proper function of a committee places little emphasis on oversight. The purpose of committees is to legislate. A colleague summarized the chairman's attitude by saying that Robertson felt that committees should "not be poking around the agencies and stirring things up." This attitude is illustrated by the following incident. At the organizational meeting of the committee in 1962, one member suggested that the committee attempt to influence the SBA to correct its administration of an existing program. Robertson replied that if the senator desired to change administrative policy he should introduce a bill. With that, the matter was removed from consideration.

Comparison of committee operations under Senators Fulbright and Robertson gives further substantiation to the Capitol Hill dictum that committee functioning depends heavily on the chairman's style of leadership. Through his loose control of the committee, Fulbright, the "service chairman," provided an atmosphere conducive to legislative innovation and oversight activities by others; the leadership of Senator Robertson, a "minority and restraining chairman," has had exactly the opposite effect.

Subcommittees

The different treatment accorded subcommittees by Senators Fulbright and Robertson underscores the finding of George Goodwin that, like its parent committee, subcommittee organization reflects "to a great degree the nature of the chairman—his personality, his political ideology, and his concept of his role" and that "a conservative chairman will not generally want to see much development of subcommittees." [8] The Banking and Currency experience also indicates that when subcommittees are given a prominent role in policy-making and permitted to operate relatively free of restraints from the chairman, they can be extremely active legislative and oversight units. This has certainly been true of the Housing Subcommittee, which both Fulbright and Robertson allowed to become virtually the personal domain of Sparkman. Fulbright, the "service chairman," had little interest in housing

[8] George Goodwin, Jr., "Subcommittees: The Miniature Legislatures of Congress," *American Political Science Review*, LVI (September 1962), p. 598.

matters and tended to follow Sparkman's leadership (he frequently left his proxy with the Alabama Senator). Robertson, though opposed to the liberal omnibus housing bills emanating from the subcommittee, has not tried in a significant way to limit its activities. Close ties exist between Sparkman and Robertson, and Sparkman (who normally supports the Chair on procedural issues within the committee) has been accorded considerably more freedom than any other subcommittee chairman. A committee majority in favor of housing legislation of a more liberal nature than Robertson prefers also buttresses Sparkman's position.

The autonomy of the Housing Subcommittee is also strengthened by the fact that it has had more money available than any of the other subcommittees. Financed by special annual resolutions to which there has ceased to be significant opposition, its greater resources have enabled it to build up a larger and more specialized staff than any of the others.[9]

The Housing Subcommittee became an active overseer of the HHFA, particularly during the later years of the Eisenhower Administration when most of the subcommittee Democrats thought the HHFA was being unduly restrictive in its administrative practices. It had an aggressive chairman who justified the existence of the subcommittee because of its oversight responsibilities, a majority of its membership firmly committed to expansion of housing programs, a moderate-sized staff, and adequate financing. The subcommittee engaged in studies designed to review agency performance and to point out areas calling for HHFA action. As the 1960 election approached, it also barraged the public with criticism of HHFA policy. At a lower policy level, the subcommittee staff carried a heavy case work load as it checked complaints regarding HHFA actions—ranging from individual home owners' complaints about shoddy construction in FHA-approved homes to criticisms coming from large housing interest groups such as the National Home Builders and the National Association of Housing and Redevelopment Officials.

The other subcommittees of Banking and Currency have never been accorded the autonomy of the Housing Subcom-

---

[9] During the Eighty-seventh and Eighty-eighth Congresses, the subcommittee had a staff of seven persons, whereas the remaining subcommittees had no more than two staff assistants who normally devoted only part of their time to subcommittee work.

mittee and have never approximated it in extent of oversight activity. All have operated under limitations of budget and staff. In addition, unlike Senator Sparkman, the other subcommittee chairmen have seldom used their positions to develop their subcommittees into active oversight units. Senator Clark, former chairman of the International Finance Subcommittee, for example, did not do so because the bulk of his subcommittee's jurisdiction was lost to the Foreign Relations Committee when Fulbright resigned as Banking and Currency chairman, and also because he had no regularly assigned staff assistance. His, therefore, was a virtually meaningless subcommittee. Senator Douglas does not view the function of his Production and Stabilization Subcommittee as being one of oversight. Instead, he considers it a forum useful in agitating for and producing new legislation. In spite of the prominent role he played in the enactment of the depressed-areas bill of 1961, therefore, Douglas failed to offer any guidelines to the Area Redevelopment Administration (ARA) on how the act should be administered. When pointedly asked by his staff whether he wished them to keep a careful eye on the ARA's activities, he replied in the negative.

The Committee Staff

When a committee has recruited a sizeable and competent staff, and when a chairman directs the staff to scrutinize carefully agency activities, even to the extent of knowing more about agency operation than the agency's own staff, the staff can become a valued information source for committee members. With committee support, it can also actively interject itself in agency policy deliberations, as the Joint Committee on Atomic Energy has done in Atomic Energy Commission decisions. The Banking and Currency staff, however, has not operated under such a mandate. Staff members were not made to understand that surveillance of agency behavior was expected of them, but felt their prime function to be assisting the processing of legislation.

The impact of the committee's staffing practices on its performance of the oversight function may be seen by comparing the functioning of the Housing Subcommittee staff with that of the full committee staff. The Housing Subcommittee has more available staff assistance than does any other Banking and Currency subcommittee. The subcommittee staffmen constitute the center of Senate expertise in housing matters and are the only committee staff personnel instructed to oversee actively the agencies under the committee's jurisdiction. As a result, the HHFA has been subjected to greater surveillance than other Banking and Currency agencies.[10] Studies prepared by the staff have been used to prod the agency into adopting policies favorable to a majority of the subcommittee. The staff assisted in preparing for hearings that were highly critical of the Eisenhower Administration's handling of housing programs. It also acted as a communications link between the HHFA and members of the committee. During the Eisenhower years HHFA officials operated under the assumption that the staff had such excellent information sources within the agency that there was little the subcommittee did not know about HHFA activities. The staff continued to be an important information conduit during the Kennedy Administration. For example, HHFA took pains to explain its actions and proposals to the staff and relied heavily on the staff to explain the agency's actions to committee members.

Nevertheless, although the Housing Subcommittee staff has continued to engage in more oversight activity than any other committee staff personnel, it has not been as active since 1961 as it was during the Eisenhower years. Since 1961 initiative for developing and pressing for adoption of new programs has shifted from the subcommittee to the HHFA. In addition, the staff is smaller (with some key people having moved to administrative jobs), and Chairman Sparkman has assumed greater responsibilities for the work of the Foreign Relations Committee. This leaves him less time to devote to Housing Subcommittee work.

There is no other specialized staff within the Banking and Currency Committee available to oversee the work of the non-housing agencies under the committee's jurisdiction. As a result, committee review of these agencies has been severely restricted. For example, Senator Proxmire, the chairman of the Small Business Subcommittee, attempted to oversee the Small Business Ad-

---

[10] Even after the advent of the Kennedy Administration, when it was assumed that the new HHFA administrators would be sympathetic to the objectives espoused by a majority of the subcommittee, Sparkman warned the staff to maintain an arm's length relationship with agency personnel and to remember that the staff's first responsibility was to the subcommittee and not the HHFA.

ministration carefully; but because he had only minimal staff assistance, his activities were limited in both scope and effectiveness.

Although the general orientation of the committee has been against staff activity in overseeing administrative agencies, the full committee staff has acknowledged a responsibility to "keep up to date" with administrative developments. Staff members believe they should maintain a high level of professional competence in the subject matter and at the same time be alert for new developments, so that committee senators will not be embarrassingly surprised. They also profess a desire to "cover themselves," namely to have sufficient information at their fingertips to answer senators' questions on short notice. Staff members also hope to be able to demonstrate that they have taken appropriate action on any matter likely to cause controversy, so that neither they nor the committee will be accused of administrative mismanagement. Appropriate action, however, has frequently merely meant obtaining an agency explanation for any criticism lodged against the staff by such an organization as the General Accounting Office.

The principal sources of staff information on agency performance are informal contacts within the agencies and complaints received from pressure groups and the constituents of subcommittee members. If there are no complaints about an agency, the staff feels there can be little seriously wrong with its performance.

Despite its desire to "keep up" and "cover itself," the small size of the Banking and Currency staff, and the extensive number of agencies under the committee's jurisdiction, have forced the staff to concentrate on those few agencies in which the committee members (especially those who control staff appointments) demonstrate an interest, particularly the HHFA and to a much lesser extent the SBA.

Committee Recruitment Pattern

A committee's behavior is, of course, affected by the quality of the legislators it can attract to membership. For example, the tendency of the House Education and Labor Committee to attract Republican and Democratic congressmen with strong and frequently conflicting ideological commitments has made consensus-building extremely difficult. Similarly, the recruitment pattern of the Senate Banking and Currency Committee has influenced its capacity to perform legislative oversight. The committee's work is held back strongly by the fact that Banking and Currency is not considered an attractive assignment. Indeed, it is difficult to get members to serve on the committee. Senator Clark, a member of the Democratic Steering Committee, which makes party committee assignments, has commented: "When we came to the Steering Committee this year [1963], we couldn't get anybody to volunteer to go on Banking and Currency—it was a vacancy—we had to shanghai young Tom McIntyre (D. N.H.) and put him there. He wouldn't volunteer." [11] Republicans, too, did not view the committee as a good assignment. A senior GOP member has said: "When I came to the Senate, I didn't know much about the committee system and seniority. My whole life was in business. So I asked for Finance and Banking and Currency. . . . I often wonder why I stay on this Committee, but now that I'm here, I guess I'll stay. I'd hate to lose my seniority."

A more objective measure of the relative lack of appeal of the Banking and Currency assignment is provided in Table 9, which records the number of times since 1947 (when the Legislative Reorganization Act took effect) that senators have switched committee assignments to join Banking and Currency or to leave it for some other committee. A record of which committees have had the greatest gains in membership from other committees provides an index of the committees that senators consider the most attractive assignments. Table 9 indicates that Banking and Currency had a net-membership gain from only three committees.

A basic reason for the committee's low appeal is its subject matter. Though the actions of agencies under its jurisdiction (such as the HHFA, the FRB, the Export-Import Bank, the Federal Deposit Insurance Corporation, the Home Loan Bank Board) are far-reaching, the committee is not considered on a par with Appropriations, Armed Services, and Finance in terms of power. Nor has it the prestige and publicity value of a Foreign Relations assignment.

The composition of Banking and Currency also affects its attractiveness. Liberal Democrats believe that the committee will not be active so long as Senator Robertson is chairman, and try to avoid it, even though Senator Douglas has urged junior Demo-

[11] *Congressional Record* CIX (Eighty-eighth Congress, 1st Session), p. 17852.

TABLE 9   NET MEMBERSHIP GAINS AND LOSSES OF SENATE BANKING
AND CURRENCY COMMITTEE (1947-1965)*

Committees showing a net gain of members from the Banking and Currency Committee			
Appropriations	+3	Judiciary	+3
Armed Services	+3	Commerce	+2
Foreign Relations	+3	Finance	+1

Committees showing a net loss of members to the Banking and Currency Committee			
Post Office and Civil Service	−2	Rules and Administration	−2
District of Columbia	−2		

* Source: Appropriate volumes of the *Congressional Directory*.

cratic colleagues to request the assignment. Instead, the committee tends to be composed of first-term senators receiving their first assignment. Seventy-four percent of the members appointed from 1947 to 1962 held such initial appointments. As Table 10 indicates, the number of initial appointees to Banking and Currency was substantially higher than for the Commerce and Finance Committees, the other two Senate committees dealing with commercial, financial, and monetary matters. In terms of average length of service in the Senate prior to appointment to these committees, members of Banking and Currency had shorter average prior service than did senators on the other two committees, although not significantly less than Commerce Committee members (see Table 10).

In addition to a membership with low seniority and therefore little experience in the Senate, the committee has also tended to recruit a substantial number of persons without prior experience in major elective office. Half the committee members during the Eighty-seventh Congress were in this category, compared with less than one-third for the Senate as a whole or for the Senate exclusive of its Banking and Currency members (see Table 11).

Because of the recruitment pattern described above, at the beginning of each new congress the committee has had a number of members without training in the work of the committee, the folkways of the Senate, or the work load of a high elective official. The number of members prepared and available for demanding

TABLE 10   COMPARISON OF LENGTH OF SENATE SERVICE PRIOR TO
APPOINTMENT TO COMMITTEES ON BANKING AND CUR-
RENCY, COMMERCE, AND FINANCE (1947-1962)*

	Banking and Currency	Commerce	Finance
Size	15	17	15
Total membership	43	47	38
Average length of service prior to appointment (in years)	1.4	1.5	3.5
Number of initial appointees	32	21	7
Percent of initial appointees	74.4	44.7	18
Number of initial appointees, 1962 membership	14	9	3
Percent of initial appointees, 1962 membership	93.3	52.9	20
Average length of service prior to appointment, 1962 membership (in years)	15	1.1	4.2

* Source: Appropriate volumes of the *Congressional Directory*.

committee oversight work has therefore been severely restricted. Of the four senators appointed to Banking and Currency during the Eighty-seventh Congress, for example, none was sufficiently interested or prepared to utilize committee resources for oversight work.

Member Interest in Committee Work

The job of a legislator is much more complex than merely deciding how he will vote. More importantly, he must decide how and where to allocate his scarce and precious resources: time, money, staff, information, good will. Ideally, these resources are expended so as to maximize the opportunities to secure the goals a senator has set for himself in the legislative process. As an institution of decentralized authority, the Senate permits each member to choose from a variety of roles and gives each considerable freedom in deciding when and how to use his resources. Hence a

TABLE 11   COMPARISON OF THE POLITICAL EXPERIENCE OF BANKING AND CURRENCY MEMBERS AND THE U.S. SENATE AS A WHOLE, EIGHTY-SEVENTH CONGRESS, 1961-1962*

	Prior service in House		Prior service in major state or local elective office		Held major elective office	
	Number	Percent	Number	Percent	Number	Percent
Banking and Currency Committee (16 members)	5	31.3	4	25	8	50
U.S Senate (105 members)	44	41.9	31	29.5	73	69.5
U.S. Senate, exclusive of Banking and Currency members (89 members)	39	43.8	27	30.3	65	73.03

* Data taken from *Congressional Directory*; *Current Biography*; *Congressional Quarterly Weekly Report*, XX (June 2, 1961), p. 934; XX (January 12, 1962), p. 53. Percentages in the Banking and Currency Committee and U.S. Senate categories do not add up to 100 because senators are listed both as having served in the House and as having held major state or local office.

senator's interests, or his "time-choice pattern," become extremely important in explaining his behavior and that of the committees on which he serves.

A senator must automatically accept membership on standing committees, but how interested or involved he becomes depends primarily on his own interpretations of the senatorial role. Most committees have their "formal" members, who remain essentially passive toward committee work, and their active and "efficient" members, who do the real work of the committee.[12] Because Banking and Currency is not considered a good assignment, a substantial number of its members remain essentially formal rather than efficient members. Some have stayed on the committee only until a more desirable assignment opened up for them. Between 1947 and 1962 thirty-three percent of the members of Banking and Currency transferred to other committees, while only fourteen percent and thirteen percent, respectively, left the Commerce and Finance Committees. Of particular interest is the fact that two members, Senators Fulbright and Charles Tobey (R. N.H.), voluntarily resigned from the committee to accept other assignments after having amassed sufficient seniority to have served as chairman of the committee.[13]

Interviews with members and their staffs indicated that for most members the work of the committee has not been a matter of overriding importance. This has contributed to the general lack of oversight activity. The committee has tended to become intensely interested in the activities of agencies under its jurisdiction only in special circumstances, such as a major scandal (for example, the investigations into the work of the bank regulatory agencies following the disclosures of the Orville Hodge banking scandals in Illinois), or such as administrative developments that result in a controversy about which the agency receives complaints. (An example of such a situation was the lengthy study of the Export-Import Bank in 1953-1954 that the committee made after it had received complaints that an administrative reorganization of the agency had resulted in a cutback in the loans made by the Bank.)

[12] Holbert Carroll, *The House of Representatives and Foreign Affairs* (Pittsburgh: University of Pittsburgh Press, 1959), p. 28.
[13] Tobey served as Chairman in the 80th Congress before transferring to Foreign Relations; Fulbright left the committee after having served as chairman during the 85th and 86th Congresses to become a member of Finance.

Most members, however, feel that investment of their valuable time, staff, and good will to oversee agencies under the committee's jurisdiction is not worthwhile. Note the following comments from Democratic senators:

> I suppose we should do more in this area [legislative oversight]. But I have so many other irons in the fire that I don't do it. To do anything would probably just be frustrating and would be apt to involve a fight in the Committee. I'd prefer not to have that.

> It's hard to expect that people will get very interested in the work of agencies that regulate the economy. It is technical, complicated and dry. . . . Unless a person has background in the field or a special interest, it is not likely he will give it much attention. There are too many other demands on a person's attention—such as sub-committees that are very active—to let a person really get into this field.

Senior members of Banking and Currency, those in the best position to make the committee active in oversight, often yield to alternative demands on their time. These members have important and compelling noncommittee duties. Senator Robertson, for example, is an active member of the Appropriations Committee, having served as acting chairman of the time-consuming Subcommittee on the Department of Defense and as chairman of the Treasury, Post Office and Executive Office Subcommittee. Senator Sparkman, the second ranking Democrat, is also the second-ranking majority member of the prestigious Foreign Relations Committee. In addition, he has been chairman of the Select Committee on Small Business and a member of the Joint Economic Committee and the Joint Committee on Defense Production. Such non-Banking and Currency responsibilities, in conjunction with lack of compelling interest in committee business on the part of the senior members, have restricted the committee as an oversight unit.

Work Orientation of the Members

Committee performance of oversight has also been affected by the manner in which members view their committee responsibilities. The members and staff tend to have a legislative orientation: they view the function of the committee primarily in terms of processing legislation. This has been the attitude of Senator Robertson and of most of the subcommittee chairmen. Accordingly, when asked to describe their duties, staff members have spoken primarily in terms of preparing for hearings on bills, making digests of bills, drafting reports, and perhaps suggesting amendments and strategy.

Changes in the laws affecting an agency are certainly one method (and probably the most effective ultimate method) of bringing about changes in administration policy; and exercising some scrutiny of agency operations is usually required before acting upon agency legislation. Indeed, some long-time observers of the committee believe that the major stimuli for interest in agency operations comes from agency requests for new legislative powers or renewals of existing authority. Members and staff have frequently asserted that oversight is most frequently practiced, and certainly most regularized, at hearings on the legislative requests of the agencies.

Because of this legislative orientation and the periodic need of agencies to seek new legislative authority, members do not necessarily have continuing interest in the workings of existing or newly enacted programs. For example, the committee's 1962 approval of extension of the Defense Production Act was criticized on the grounds that past performance under the Act had not been examined with sufficient care. Though Chairman Robertson agreed that committee consideration had been less thorough than was desirable, he offered as an explanation the failure of the Administration to send Congress its proposals for renewal of the Act until shortly before it was scheduled to expire.[14] The need to renew an agency periodically had thus failed to stimulate continuing interest in its activity.

Committee Integration

Like every social system, committees must solve the problem of making their various components achieve a minimum degree of integration. They must control conflict and so organize that the members will reach a substantial number of their objectives by participation in committee work. Committees character-

[14] *Congressional Record* CVIII (Eighty-seventh Congress, 2d Session, 1962), p. 11707.

ized by a high degree of integration, it has been shown, are effective in gaining support for their policy preferences both when legislation reported from the committee is being considered on the floor (as in the case of the House Appropriations Committee),[15] and when dealing with administrative agencies under their jurisdiction (note, for example, the decisive influence that the Joint Committee on Atomic Energy has exerted over the AEC).[16] Integration is, then, an important ingredient of committee influence.

Committee integration is encouraged by attracting to membership legislators who will readily fit into the committee group and who will view the assignment as desirable. Such members are apt to remain on the committee for a long period, thereby giving the committee stability and the opportunity to develop informal behavioral norms that will encourage relatively smooth operation. Members recruited under such circumstances are also likely to have an intense interest in the work of the committee.[17] The nature of a committee's subject matter also affects its capacity to meet the problem of integration. For example, a committee dealing with matters of national security is not apt to be wrenched by serious splits because of general agreement on the necessity of maintaining a strong defense posture. Also, the integration problem of the appropriations committees is somewhat easier than that of subject-matter committees, in part because they deal with specific dollar amounts to be spent by the government and not directly with the substance of policy. Hence it is possible to work out compromises by splitting budgetary differences mathematically.[18]

Informal behavioral norms within a committee may also work toward or against committee integration. For example, the House Appropriations Committee has a norm of minimal partisanship under which members are expected to keep their party-motivated behavior to a minimum. The sheer size of the appropriations job, encompassing, as it does, virtually all the government agencies, encourages specialization by subcommittees. This is one means of resolving conflict. The committee also has an informal

[15] Fenno, "The House Appropriations Committee," pp. 313-315.
[16] See Harold P. Green and Alan Rosenthal, *Government and the Atom: The Integration of Powers* (New York: Atherton Press, 1963).
[17] Fenno, "The House Appropriations Committee," pp. 313-315.
[18] Fenno, "The House Appropriations Committee," pp. 312-313.

rule requiring that subcommittees present a unified front when reporting bills to the full committee. The committee is then expected to respect the decisions of its subcommittees. Once the full committee has made its decision on a bill, there is a further expectation that committee members will not file minority reports dissenting from the action. Integration is also facilitated because committee members specialize in the work of their own subcommittees and do not interfere with the work of others.

Integration-producing conditions have not been present in the Senate Banking and Currency Committee. We have shown that the committee is not a highly desirable assignment, that its membership is unstable and characterized by a high rate of turnover, and that it is not a consuming interest for most of its membership. Furthermore, there has been no conscientious attempt to recruit members whose style would be readily adaptable to the group. Indeed, in recent years it has had among its members such maverick senators as William Proxmire, Paul Douglas, Joseph Clark, and Jacob Javits (R. N.Y.).

Nor is the subject matter such that it stimulates committee unity and compromise. The committee must decide thorny issues: whether there will be an expansion or even a continuation of public housing; how the costs of urban renewal will be shared; whether there should be federal rent subsidies for persons whose incomes are too high for them to gain admittance to public housing; whether there should be federal assistance for depressed areas and for mass-transit facilities in metropolitan areas; whether creditors must state to customers the full interest rate being charged. These are issues that do not readily lend themselves to compromise by a device such as splitting budgetary differences. Nor are they the types of issues that are relieved of their controversial impact by falling under the protective banner of national security. Instead, Banking and Currency is responsible for a field in which traditional divisions on domestic policy can easily assert themselves with intensity.

The norm of minimal partisanship is not practiced in the committee; on the contrary, partisanship is frequently strong. In the late 1950s Banking and Currency was the battleground for a major partisan conflict: the committee's Democratic majority twice attempted to override a presidential veto of the 1959 housing bill before finally compromising with the Eisenhower Administration on a third bill; and in 1958 and 1959, it passed a "Democratic" depressed-areas bill, actually courting a presidential veto.

The committee also lacks the norm of strict specialization in subcommittee work and the willingness to accept readily the decisions of its subcommittees. The committee does have its specialists, such as Robertson in Banking and Sparkman in housing, but virtually all members maintain an interest outside the domains of their particular subcommittees. For example, practically all take part in deliberations on housing legislation, and the decisions of the Housing Subcommittee are given careful scrutiny in the full committee. At times, important bills have been considered in full committee without having been referred to subcommittee.

Dealing with issues that are controversial and operating in an environment devoid of norms encouraging integration, the Banking and Currency Committee contains well-defined blocs that are normally aligned against one another on issues coming before the committee. This was brought out by interviews conducted in 1962 with committee members, staff, and other close observers. The interviewees were asked with whom they most often worked and which members most frequently worked and voted together in committee. The results are diagrammed in Figure 3, which shows the existence of two blocs—called liberal and conservative— that can normally be found in opposition to each other. The four senators designated as being in the liberal fringe were considered by the persons interviewed to be less liberal than the members of the liberal bloc and apt from time to time to side with the Republicans and Chairman Robertson. They were thought, however, to give the committee a liberal majority on most issues, though that majority was never certain. Republicans Capehart, Beall, and Bush constituted a category whose members displayed considerable independence and whose votes were frequently in doubt, though they had a tendency to vote with the conservatives. Although the committee is a small group, ease of communication is often lacking among its members; some are reluctant even to call one another on the phone. Instead, communication is often more indirect, with committee and office staff acting as conduits for information or as probes into another member's feelings.

Senator Sparkman was consistently identified as the middle-man of the committee, the person who could bridge the gaps and

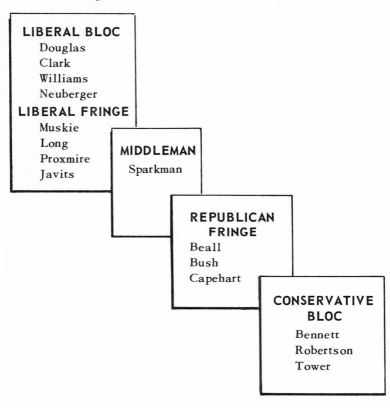

FIGURE 3

Internal Structure of the Senate Committee on Banking and Currency, 1961-1962

frequently bring differing individuals together. Neither doctrinaire nor dogmatic, he is skilled in building majorities and muting conflicts. A staff assistant described Sparkman's guidance of housing legislation in committee executive sessions in this way:

> I've watched him in executive sessions and he will be there quietly presiding. You almost think he is asleep at times. People will begin to argue and be getting nowhere and be about to take unalterable stands. Then he will start to move. He has the benefit of long experience in the work of the Committee and has been through similar arguments before. He will discuss past

problems on this issue and possible solutions and then
he will suggest a little for both sides and the matter will
be settled. He is very effective—a real statesman.

Sparkman was acknowledged to be a man having considerable
influence over his colleagues. Republicans, Democrats, HHFA
officials, and many lobbyists believed that in order to win in the
Banking and Currency Committee, it was always best to have
Sparkman on one's side.

Figure 3 also indicates that in their intracommittee behavior neither Democrats nor Republicans were a particularly
stable group in 1962. Neither was considered to have strong leadership: Chairman Robertson was not in a position to lead his more
liberal Democratic colleagues; Senator Capehart, the senior Republican, though an energetic man, was not able to act as a strong
leader of his party. Senator Javits could not be counted upon to
vote with the Republicans, and during the later years of the Eisenhower Administration, Capehart himself was at odds with the
Administration on housing matters and worked actively to override the President's vetoes of two housing bills in 1959.

Banking and Currency has thus lacked the conditions
that might make it a well-integrated committee. Its recruitment
pattern, subject matter, and lack of integrating norms have frequently split it. Unable to present a united front to either the
Senate or the administrative agencies it sought to influence, when
it did engage in oversight activities, its power has been limited.
This, in turn, has contributed to its general passivity toward this
function.

Conclusion

Although the standing committees of Congress are generally thought to be active and aggressive, our analysis has shown
that they can exhibit a quite different behavior pattern of inac-
tivity and passivity.

This is a finding worthy of more than passing interest, because most discussions of the modern Congress stress that legislative oversight has become the most important function of Congress. Other committees, of course, may have very different relationships with the agencies under respective jurisdictions; and in

the future Banking and Currency-agency relationships may also change, particularly with the defeat of Senator Robertson in the Virginia Democratic primary in July 1966.

Whatever the differences, we have indicated something of the wide range of behavior patterns open to congressional committees. The particular pattern of Banking and Currency is but a part of the spectrum of committee operations. Its experience, however, indicates that the following variables have strong impact on how a committee will function: committee chairmen and their style of leadership, subcommittee operation, staff, recruitment patterns, member interest in committee work, work orientations of members, committee integration, and the structure of the issues and agencies with which the committee must deal.

THE POWER OF THE RULES | 6

An omnipresent feature of the legislator's environment is the complicated set of rules and procedures under which he must operate. Congress is no different from any other complex organization in its need for regularized procedures, and the Constitution clearly provides that "each House may determine the rules of its proceedings." [1] In a legislative body, rules and procedures are intimately related to the political conflicts among individuals and interests. That is, the rules are not neutral but rather work to encourage certain types of actions and discourage others. Mastery of the rules can give a member a formidable resource in the "legislative struggle," and constitutes a part of the mystique of a Sam Rayburn, a Richard B. Russell, or a Howard W. Smith.

Some of the differences between the House and the Senate are reflected in the development of their rules. Both houses derive their procedures from three sources: *Jefferson's Manual* of parliamentary laws, the rules of each house, and precedents derived from rulings of the chair in each house. The House of Representatives has forty-three complicated rules, supplemented by *Hinds' and*

---

[1] Article I, Section 5.

Cannon's Precedents, an eleven-volume compendium of interpretations by various speakers and chairmen of the "Committee of the Whole House." For the average congressman, the 500-page synopsis, *Cannon's Procedure in the House of Representatives,* is sufficient for daily needs. The operation of the House is necessarily more complex than that of the Senate, because of the former's size. It has therefore evolved a tight system of procedures that leaves little room for dilatory tactics. Yet, during debate on most bills flexibility is obtained by resolving the House into the Committee of the Whole House. Under this device, debate is actually regulated by agreement between the managers of the bill and the chief opponents. This procedure will be discussed more fully below.

In the smaller and more leisurely Senate, the rules are simpler and more lenient. The last general revision of the forty rules was done in 1884. Debate is typically fixed by unanimous consent, and, as in the House, the standard practice is to divide and control time between proponents and opponents of the bill by prior agreement. The Senate cherishes its privilege of free and unfettered debate. A recent attempt to alter the cloture rules has been described in Chapter 4. More recently, the Senate adopted a "rule of germaneness," which directed that debate after the "morning hour" (the daily period prior to consideration of pending legislation) must be relevant to the business at hand. Attempts at compliance have met with confusion and anguish, and the rule has not so far altered the pace of senatorial business.

Detailed description of congressional rules would be a tedious and, for the most part, pointless endeavor. (Fortunately for most members and their legislative aides, a call to the parliamentarian will clarify most entanglements with the rules.) The role of procedures in legislative politics can be illustrated by the case history of the Area Redevelopment Act of 1961. During the six years prior to its passage, this measure encountered most of the procedural hurdles common to social-welfare legislation of the 1950s and 1960s. In this sense, the story of the Area Redevelopment Act serves as a concrete illustration of the frustrations of congressional liberals that led to the rules changes described in Chapter 4. The following account is not the *whole* story of the enactment of Public Law 87-27; it is a synopsis of its legislative history, focusing on congressional rules and procedures as the principal variables.

Committee Referral

The original depressed areas legislation was hastily introduced in the summer of 1955 by Senator Paul H. Douglas (D. Ill.) and was designed to implement the policy dictum of the 1946 Employment Act: "It is the continuing policy and responsibility of the Federal Government to use all practicable means . . . to promote maximum employment, production, and purchasing power." In spite of general postwar prosperity, it soon became apparent that long-term unemployment in certain declining industries and localities was creating persistent "pockets of poverty." This hard-core unemployment was especially visible during periods of economic slack, and with the 1954-1955 recession depressed-areas legislators began prodding the Eisenhower Administration to devise a solution for the problem. Concerned over the plight of southern Illinois' depressed coal regions, Douglas introduced a $390-million package-proposal for financial and technical aid— including preferential treatment in government contracts, technical assistance, vocational retraining, and loans and grants to help communities lure new industry.

Six months later, the Eisenhower Administration sponsored a modest $50-million bill. Republican leaders continued to give lukewarm support to the Administration's proposal, but the focal point of discussion during the next six years remained "the Douglas bill," in its various and evolving forms.

A combative liberal with a mercurial temperament, Douglas typified the Senate "outsider." [2] His theory was that he would have influence on Congress later, if not *in* it now; and his heroes (their pictures adorned his office walls) were such legislators as George W. Norris and Robert M. LaFollette, Sr. He was used to having the rules used against him; and when the Area Redevelopment Act became law in 1961, it was the first law to bear his name in his twelve years as a senator.

Yet Douglas was strategically positioned to lead the **fight**

[2] For an explanation of the conflicts between "outsiders" and the "Senate establishment," see Chapter 4.

for his legislation: in addition to being rotating chairman of the Joint Economic Committee (which does not handle legislation), he held a seat on two Senate committees: Banking and Currency and Labor and Public Welfare. As it turned out, the former committee had the best claim for considering the measure, but for several reasons the bill, S. 2663, was referred to Labor and Public Welfare. In the Labor Committee Douglas chaired his own subcommittee, and committee Chairman Lister Hill (D. Ala.) allowed him free rein. Liberal majorities in both the subcommittee and full committee were favorable and ultimately passed the Douglas bill over to the floor with only minor changes. The other claimant for jurisdiction over the measure, the Senate Banking and Currency Committee, presented no such bright prospect. Douglas did not have a subcommittee there, and the committee's membership seemed less favorable to such "welfare" measures as S. 2663.

Thus, it seemed merely good politics when Douglas requested, and was granted, referral of his bill to Labor and Public Welfare. On jurisdictional grounds, however, referral to Labor and Public Welfare was questionable. On the other side of Capitol Hill, the House Banking and Currency Committee had taken charge of the legislation. Senate Rule XXV seemed to confirm this decision: Banking and Currency shall have jurisdiction over "financial aid to commerce and industry, other than matters relating to such aid which are specifically assigned to other committees. . . ." It was not long before this rule began to raise trouble for Douglas.

On January 5, 1956, Banking and Currency Chairman J. William Fulbright (D. Ark.) wrote Chairman Hill and warned that his committee would be "compelled to reserve the privilege of requesting an opportunity to consider the bill." The letter apparently went unanswered, and Fulbright refrained from playing his hand until June 28, the day after Hill's committee reported S. 2663. At that time Fulbright wrote Majority Leader Lyndon Johnson (D. Tex.) that he intended to ask that the bill be referred to Banking and Currency. At such a late date in the session, this action could only kill the bill. "I felt that it was necessary . . . to raise this question," Fulbright explained later, "because I believe it is my duty to protect the jurisdiction of that committee under the rules." Fulbright's real motives, however, lay deeper: as a southerner, he regarded the area redevelopment bill as an effort to preserve "old and worn-out" industrial regions at the expense of such expanding areas as his own state of Arkansas. A jurisdictional dispute could serve as a lever to halt the Douglas bill, or at least to force its revision. (Contrast this move with Fulbright's usual attitude toward his committee, as described in Chapter 5.)

Fulbright's move caught the Douglas forces at an inopportune moment. Douglas had just resigned from Labor and Public Welfare to take a long-coveted seat on Finance, and Douglas' old subcommittee was no longer active. Moreover, there was no way to sidestep Fulbright's impeccable parliamentary position so late in the congressional session. Majority Leader Johnson and Chairman Hill therefore arranged for Senator John F. Kennedy (D. Mass.), now ranking member of Douglas' old subcommittee, to bargain with Fulbright. At a series of meetings, staff aides hammered out a series of three amendments favoring rural areas of unemployment and designed to render the bill more acceptable to southern senators. Accepted "reluctantly" by Kennedy during the brief floor debate, the amendments were Fulbright's "price" for dropping his jurisdictional objections. In addition, Fulbright received assurances that his committee would assume jurisdiction over the bill in the future. The deal having been consummated, S. 2663 passed the Senate easily, by a vote of sixty to thirty.

This incident illustrates the importance of "the politics of referral and jurisdiction." [3] In most cases referral is routine and thus removed from the legislative struggle. But complex or "borderline" bills may straddle several committees, making the matter of referral an important tactical consideration. A miscalculation, as in this case, may have costly consequences.

The End-of-the-Session Squeeze

While Fulbright was exacting his concessions in the Senate, the bill's advocates in the House were waging a hopeless battle against time. At the center of the controversy was the House Rules Committee, which, through exercise of its broad scheduling powers, stands between the legislative committees and the House

---

[3] Another example of referral politics, involving the accelerated public works bill, is discussed in Chapter 5.

floor.[4] For controversial measures that cannot be disposed of by more automatic parliamentary devices, the Rules Committee must grant a "rule" under which the bill is considered on the House floor. When a rule is requested by the legislative committee, Rules must first decide whether to hold hearings; if this is granted, it may then vote on whether to grant the rule.[5] As will be seen, a negative action by Rules (refusal to schedule hearings, or a negative vote on granting a rule) usually serves to kill the bill, because the methods of circumventing the Rules Committee are cumbersome and time-consuming. Under the time limitations accompanying the end of the legislative session, alternative procedures become even more difficult to apply.

As early as June 29, the depressed-areas bill had been reported by Banking and Currency, but the Rules Committee, working through the end-of-session log jam, showed no inclination to clear the bill for floor debate. To further complicate the situation, the bill was caught in the crossfire of a feud between Rules and Banking and Currency over housing legislation. At the insistence of the Democratic leadership and friendly Rules members, a hearing was finally held on July 21—six days before adjournment! The committee merely voted to defer action on granting a rule, apparently killing the bill for the Eighty-fourth Congress.[6]

One last chance remained for House passage that session. With adjournment imminent, the House was operating under an agreement whereby the Speaker would recognize members to move passage of bills under suspension of the rules (such a motion requires a two-thirds vote). According to precedent, the Speaker will recognize a member to move the suspension of the rules only with the consent of both majority and minority floor leaders. Speaker Rayburn and Majority Leader John McCormack (D. Mass.) agreed to allow the depressed-areas bill to be called up; but Minor-

---

[4] For a thorough analysis of the operations of the Rules Committee, see James A. Robinson, *The House Rules Committee* (Indianapolis: Bobbs-Merrill, 1963).

[5] The type of rule granted may also have important consequences for the bill's fate on the floor. "Open rules" permit floor amendments; "closed rules" either prohibit them or allow only specialized types of amendments. Some rules waive points of order against bills where there may be some parliamentary objection. In addition, rules typically specify a time limit for debate.

[6] Votes in the Rules Committee are seldom recorded. It appeared that, had a final vote been recorded, the bill would have lost by a six to five vote.

ity Leader Joseph Martin (R. Mass.) said he would have to consult with Administration officials "downtown."

The Senate sent S. 2663 to the House early on the afternoon of July 26. The devious process of extracting a definitive answer from the Administration occupied the remainder of that day, and most of the next. Finally, Representatives Ivor Fenton and James Van Zandt, Pennsylvania Republicans who had authored depressed-areas bills of their own, were enlisted to obtain the Administration's approval. It soon became apparent that the White House was leaving the decision to the Commerce Department. Secretary Sinclair Weeks, who was known to be skeptical about the legislation, dispatched Assistant Secretary Frederick H. Mueller to the Capitol to negotiate with Fenton and Van Zandt. After two hours of discussion, during which congressional supporters even offered to substitute the Eisenhower bill, the two Pennsylvanians emerged to inform their colleagues that the Administration was opposed to having any bill whatsoever brought to the floor. In view of the Administration's position, there was no hope for last-minute passage of the bill.

This story was repeated publicly by Democrats throughout the 1956 presidential campaign. For their part, Administration spokesmen never bothered to deny the incident. Running on the slogan of "peace and prosperity," they were content to let the issue ride. Administration officials argued privately, however, that they had been victimized by a trap play: had they consented to House passage of the President's bill, the Douglas forces would have used the House-Senate conference as leverage to restore the provisions of the original S. 2663—thus driving the Administration into an even more awkward position. Needless to say, their suspicions were not without foundation. The lesson of this incident was that the end of the session places a premium on time, if the niceties of the rules are to be observed. If the rules are to be sidestepped, there must often exist an interparty comity not obtainable where controversial legislation is involved. Thus a special challenge faces legislative tacticians.

Power Play in Committee

Early in 1957, Douglas reintroduced the depressed-areas bill as S. 964. This time it was referred to Fulbright's Banking and

Currency Committee and Douglas' newly-acquired Production and Stabilization Subcommittee. For more than a year, the bill was stalled, confirming the sponsors' original fears about Banking and Currency.[7] (The alignment on the committee is shown in Table 12.) Douglas charged that his subcommittee was "stacked" against

TABLE 12   THE BANKING AND CURRENCY COMMITTEE
ON THE DOUGLAS BILL, 1957-1958

	AGAINST	FOR	DOUBTFUL
Subcommittee	Fulbright (D)	Douglas (D)	
	Frear (D)	Sparkman (D)	
	Capehart (R)		
	Bricker (R)		
	Bush (R)		
Total	5	2	0
Full Committee	Robertson (D)	Monroney (D)	Payne (R)
	Bennett (R)	Clark (D)	Beall (R)
		Proxmire (D)	Case (R)
Total	7	5	3

him, while Fulbright insisted that nothing of the kind had been intended. The only hope lay in bringing the bill to the full committee, and this could be done either through an informal agreement with Fulbright or a formal vote of the full committee.

For a time, Douglas failed to perceive the solution to his dilemma, preferring futile negotiations with Fulbright on dislodging the bill from the subcommittee. These negotiations were perfunctory, for the two men had never been close associates. For his part, Fulbright was still suspicious that the bill would disadvantage the new industrial areas, which depended on low wages to lure industries from the older, heavily unionized areas. Moreover, he was not generally disposed to favor federal intervention in such problems.

The impasse broke in early 1958 when Senator Frederick Payne (R. Me.) let it be known that he was available for a compromise. Payne faced a tough re-election fight that fall in a state in which hard-core unemployment in the Saco-Biddeford-Sanford textile region was a major issue. Douglas and Payne quickly reached

[7] For a comprehensive analysis of the Senate Banking and Currency Committee, see chapter 5.

an accord: Payne would introduce a new bill, which would be substituted in full committee for the Douglas bill. Senators Clifford Case (R. N.J.) and J. Glenn Beall (R. Md.) would go along to make the eight-seven majority.

On March 11 Payne introduced his bill, S. 3447, in what he called "a sincere effort to compromise the differences between the Douglas and Administration bills. . . ." Beall and Case were cosponsors, along with Senator Margaret Chase Smith (R. Me.). The bill was, of course, referred to Banking and Currency; and Payne asked Fulbright to schedule S. 3447 for early action by the full committee.

The step of placing Payne's bill on the full committee's agenda was accomplished a week later, when hearings opened on Fulbright's own antirecession measure, the ill-fated community facilities bill (S. 3497). According to plan, as soon as Fulbright called the meeting to order Payne moved that the committee go into executive session. Fulbright refused to bring the motion to a vote, and for thirty minutes witnesses waiting to testify were treated to a rare display of verbal fireworks.[8] Payne led off by observing that, in view of the speedy consideration accorded Fulbright's own bill, the depressed-areas proposal ought to be considered promptly. Fulbright countered by reminding the committee that Douglas was chairman of the subcommittee and "in no way inhibited from holding a meeting of his subcommittee at any time he wants to, and submitting the matter to a vote." Instead, he asserted—glaring at Douglas—"you only talk about it."

To this Douglas retorted that he had not dared bring the issue to a vote "in view of the membership . . . selected for that subcommittee by the Senator from Arkansas." Moreover, he had been trying to negotiate with Fulbright; but the latter's "unyielding determination to kill the bill" had forestalled agreement. Fulbright elaborately denied both charges.

An acrimonious free-for-all ensued. Douglas called Fulbright a "deep-freeze artist," and the latter replied that Douglas was "derelict in his duty." Soon the entire committee was hopelessly

---

[8] Transcripts of hearings, as well as floor debates, are "revised" by Members and their staffs before publication—ostensibly to clear up grammatical errors, but often for more extensive alterations. Even the "sanitized" version of this incident makes zesty reading, however. See U.S. Senate, Committee on Banking and Currency, *Community Facilities Act of 1958* (Washington: 1958), pp. 1-13.

entangled in parliamentary procedure. Then Payne inquired whether his own bill, S. 3447, had been referred to a subcommittee. It was discovered that it had not; that is, the bill was still technically before the full committee. Douglas then moved that the bill be declared the "pending order of business" of the full committee. After some further haggling Douglas' motion was adopted, by a vote of eight to five.[9]

Having forged a winning coalition in the committee, Douglas and Payne had employed a power play to breach their bill's major obstacle in the Senate. The "clean bill" (a new bill embodying the original bill and the proposed alterations)—so favorable to Douglas' goals that he refused to call it a compromise—soon cleared the full committee. The unhappy incident in the committee illustrated that a chairman's prerogatives may border on the arbitrary, and that to control the exercise of these prerogatives may require a determined majority willing to risk the costs of forcing a confrontation. Fulbright could not have been expected to make concessions until Douglas had enough votes in full committee to pass the bill. Once his bipartisan coalition had been fashioned, Douglas could force Fulbright to back down, either through informal agreement or a committee showdown. The fact that the latter course was followed was probably a function of the somewhat tenuous relationship between the two men.

Judge Smith Enters

Once out of the Senate Banking and Currency Committee, the Douglas-Payne compromise readily passed the Senate by a forty-

---

[9] Senator Bennett (R. Utah), who would have voted with the minority, was absent. Senator Frear (D. Del.) was subject to cross-pressures and voted "present." The following colloquy illustrated his dilemma:

FREAR: "I am in favor of following the rules of the committee. I am in favor of having the chairman . . . exercise the rules. I have no objection, personally, to having the full committee act on the bill of the Senator from Maine but I do not desire to place myself in the position of voting against what the chairman has the authority to do. Nor do I want to vote against the Senator from Illinois (Douglas), because I think he has a right to ask that. I therefore ask I be excused from voting."

ROBERTSON: "With all due deference, I do not think the gentleman is correct. I was in the same position. I did not want to go against the chairman, and had no personal feeling, but I voted and I think you should too. You have no personal reason except a little embarrassment."

six to thirty-six vote. The House Banking and Currency Committee trimmed the bill somewhat and reported it on July 1, 1958. This shifted the arena to the often troublesome House Rules Committee. And as in 1956, the end-of-the-session problem began to loom ahead.

With an eye to the fall congressional elections, House Democratic leaders let it be known that they wanted the Douglas-Payne bill brought to the floor. They reasoned that President Eisenhower might be induced to sign the bill as a "bipartisan" solution to the depressed-areas problem. If he vetoed the bill, Democrats would have a ready-made campaign issue. A midyear economic recession added urgency to the situation.

After some delay, Rules Chairman Howard W. Smith (D. Va.) scheduled a hearing, during which his committee forced the bill's sponsors to agree to offer a floor amendment eliminating a direct Treasury borrowing ("backdoor financing") provision. (Strongly favored by Douglas and the liberal advocates of the bill, this feature would have allowed the agency to draw authorized funds directly from the Treasury, rather than submitting expenditures to the annual appropriations process. Liberals argue that this device permits agencies to make long-range financial commitments, while many legislators—especially in the House—view it as a threat to the prerogatives of the appropriations committees.) The Rules Committee forced the deletion of backdoor financing and then cleared the bill by a six-five vote on August 7, nearly six weeks after Banking and Currency had reported it.[10] By this time it was late in the session; and under pressure of time Judge Smith's prerogatives might be sufficient to prevent debate. Following the vote, Smith told reporters that "a rule was ordered reported on the depressed-areas bill." Smith had three legislative days in which to file his report; then, seven more legislative days might elapse before the rule was called up on the floor. If the Judge did neither of these things within the prescribed time, further delays would ensue. Any of these could be fatal to the bill in the closing days, and even hours, of the session.

[10] The "usual" liberal-conservative division on the Rules Committee at this time was six-six, with Chairman Smith and Representative William Colmer (D. Miss.) voting with the four Republicans. However, on this bill Representative Hugh Scott (R. Pa.), running for the Senate, provided the pivotal vote by voting for a rule. Another "liberal," Judge James Trimble (D. Ark.), was absent.

Since adjournment was set for Labor Day, Representative Daniel Flood (D. Pa.) led a delegation of congressmen to Judge Smith's Alexandria, Virginia, home. By agreeing to delete a section of the bill providing subsistence allowances for unemployed workers while they were being retrained, the group was able to get Judge Smith to promise he would report the rule by August 12. Smith was as good as his word, and the Douglas-Payne bill—complete with the amendments Smith had extracted—passed by a standing vote. On the eve of adjournment, the revised bill was sent to the White House.

Even when operating within the confines of the rules, such holders of institutionalized power as Judge Smith have considerable latitude of action. These prerogatives may be enhanced by time shortages at the close of each session. As we have seen, costs may have to be incurred in such cases to assure that the rules are meticulously observed.

Calendar Wednesday

President Eisenhower vetoed the Douglas-Payne bill—a move that some commentators held partially responsible for Republican losses in the congressional elections that fall. (Senator Payne himself was defeated for re-election.) Both the Administration and the Douglas camp introduced new bills as the Eighty-sixth Congress convened, and by the end of March the Senate had passed the Douglas version (S. 722). Two months later, the House Banking and Currency Committee reported the bill. This brought the measure again into the hands of the Rules Committee, where it languished for a full year.

The "depressed-areas congressmen," now bolstered by the newly formed liberal Democratic Study Group,[11] attempted to enlist Speaker Rayburn's help in dislodging the bill from Rules. Faced with a troublesome Rules Committee, Rayburn had to exercise caution by not expending credit on hopeless legislative ventures. The task of the depressed-areas coalition was to convince the Speaker that the bill was needed in their districts, that it would have favorable consequences for the Democratic party, and—perhaps most important—that it had enough votes to pass on the House floor. The late Clem Miller (D. Calif.), then a freshman

[11] The Democratic Study Group (DSG) is discussed in detail in chapter 4.

congressman and an active member of the Democratic Study Group, has provided an engaging account of the confrontation with Rayburn:

> Groups cluster in the big antechamber outside his "official" office just off the floor of the House. Six or eight of us crowd about, ushered into the half of a railway car by his quite correct and unassuming aides. The Speaker is very friendly. The mouth, so downcurved for public ceremony, turns up readily and warmly in private. We range ourselves on the edges of chairs and sofas. The conversation begins all brisk and rapid-fire, about this and that and the other. The Speaker answers easily, and in good humor. His eye flicks over the group. He is a coachman for a poorly harnessed team. When will we begin? As I am the only freshman, he singles me out for special comment. This is simply delightful. Finally, a senior member of the group says, "Now, Mr. Speaker, about the Depressed Areas Bill."
>
> The joviality evaporates. But just as easily as before, the Speaker responds, "When are you boys going to do something about them upstairs?" He gestures towards the ceiling, above which the Rules Committee has its rooms.
>
> "That's what we came to see you about." The Speaker tries another tack. "With everything going well in the country . . . this bill . . . I don't see any great need for it." At once a chorus of anguish. We are ready for him on this. In rapid salvos everyone present, each experienced in the science of telling words, fires off bits —his reasons why this bill is needed now. There is even a scattering of shot—about aircraft shutdowns in Texas. We had received reports of the Speaker's doubts about the urgency of this bill, and to be forewarned is to be forearmed. So many problems of Congress are of such long standing that, many times, the basic issues get clouded with the passage of time. Everyone had presumed that the Speaker knew the facts about the depressed areas legislation. He had heard the story retold over so many years. Actually, his information was out-of-date.
>
> 'Round the room we went, each adding a fast reappraisal of the need for this legislation.
>
> The Speaker saw this was no group to go through the center with, so he tried his first move again. When were we going to do something with the Democratic members of the Rules Committee? And what could we do, we asked? We were asking the help of the Speaker

with the gentlemen upstairs. The ball remained in mid-
field. The interview limped to a close.

Had there been achievement? Perhaps. Perhaps
a fresh understanding by the Speaker of a perplexing national disgrace. Perhaps a word would go out "upstairs."
Perhaps he would not put in a fatal objection should
we try something on our own. The question, as always,
boiled down to an appraisal—did we have the votes?
Yes, the Speaker was interested in the currency of the
problem itself. He was interested in the connection between chronically depressed areas and the areas of auto-
mation and technological change. But—but, he asked,
could we produce the needed votes when and if we got
to the Floor?

To this, we had chorused assent. Yes, we had
the votes by a wide margin if we could only go to a
test.[12]

Rayburn promised help but seemed in no hurry: since
Eisenhower had already vetoed a bipartisan bill, there was no
reason to press the House for a more liberal measure until the
1960 presidential campaign was closer at hand. It was not until
March of 1960 that Rayburn induced Judge Smith to hold hearings; on April 21, the committee turned down the rule by a six-
six vote.[13] (When he had the necessary votes to withhold a rule,
Judge Smith was a particularly tenacious opponent.)

The leadership now had to settle on a means of circumventing the committee. Of the available alternatives, suspension of
the rules (see the section on The End-of-the-Session Squeeze,
above) was out of the question because the consent of the Minority
Leader, Charles Halleck (R. Ind.), could not be secured. A more
feasible method, the discharge petition, was considered but dis-
carded. Under the rules, any committee that refuses to report a
piece of legislation may be discharged of its responsibility by a
motion signed by a simple majority of the House (218 signatures).
If the petition is successful, the bill is printed on the Discharge
Calendar and taken up on the second and fourth Mondays of each
month. House norms discourage discharges, because they represent
a vote of "no confidence" in the committee system. Only two laws

---

[12] Clem Miller, *Member of the House*, John W. Baker, ed. (New York:
Scribner, 1962), pp. 90-91.
[13] Representative Hugh Scott (R. Pa.) had moved to the Senate in 1959, and
the conservative coalition of Smith, William Colmer (D. Miss.), and the four
Republicans remained firmly opposed to the bill.

in modern times have been enacted via the discharge route.[14] Seven days after the Rules vote, therefore, Majority Leader Mc-Cormack notified the House that S. 722 would be brought to the floor under a third procedure, Calendar Wednesday.[15]

In this procedure, the names of standing committees are called alphabetically by the clerk each Wednesday. The chairman of a committee desiring immediate action on one of its bills before Rules may call up the bill when his committee's name is reached. Action on such a bill must be completed by the end of the calender day, under a two-hour limit for general debate. This feature of the rule makes users of Calendar Wednesday vulnerable to delaying tactics by the opposition. Because of this hazard, the procedure is normally dispensed with by unanimous consent, and the most recent use had been ten years before, in 1950.

On Wednesday, May 4, an objection to dispensing with Calendar Wednesday by unanimous consent was to have launched the festivities. But, at 12:02 P.M., when the final "Amen" of the chaplain's invocation had hardly been uttered, one of the two "sentries" stationed on the floor by Republicans and southern Democrats opposed to the bill—John C. Davis (D. Ga.)—raised a point of no quorum and the quorum bells rang out. Twenty-one minutes were spent calling the roll, and 379 members were found present.[16] Then the Speaker moved that "further proceedings [rounding up all absentees] under the roll call be dispensed with" by unanimous consent. When the anticipated objection was heard from John Bell Williams (D. Miss.), McCormack moved to dispense with further proceedings and called a "previous question" on his motion. Davis countered by moving to table McCormack's motion of previous question and demanding a roll call. Davis' motion was defeated after a twenty-three-minute roll call. Similar

---

[14] The Wage and Hour Act of 1938 and the Federal Pay Raise Act of 1960.
[15] Another device for circumventing the Rules Committee, the so-called "21-day rule," was not operative during the period of this case study. First enacted by the Democratic 81st Congress in 1949, the rule provided that, if the Rules Committee had reported adversely on a bill, or if it had failed to report favorably within 21 days, the Speaker might recognize the chairman of the legislative committee to call up the bill for House consideration. The rule was repealed in 1951 but was reinstated in 1965 at the instigation of Speaker McCormack and a liberal coalition (see Chapter 4).
[16] A quorum of the House is a simple majority, or 218. For the Committee of the Whole, a quorum is only 100—one reason this device is so convenient for substantive debate.

roll calls to approve McCormack's two motions (previous question, then the main motion) took another half hour. By this time the House had consumed one hour and thirty-eight minutes in satisfying everyone that a quorum was present.

Rayburn now moved to dispense with reading of the journal —normally a routine means of facilitating business. On this afternoon, however, Davis insisted on a full reading. Members were heard to groan audibly as they disappeared for lunch. Four minutes later Davis, noting that the chamber was emptying, made a point of no quorum. Twenty-two minutes were required to reassemble a quorum, after which the round-robin of roll calls began again. Three roll calls were completed. Up to this point, the House had spent three hours and fifteen minutes on quorum calls.

The clerk resumed the reading of the journal while members drifted away once more. Twenty minutes later Williams looked around at the empty chairs and raised a point of no quorum. And so it went for most of the afternoon.

In the end Davis and Williams relented to allow the House to consider the bill. After the journal was approved, Speaker Rayburn ordered the call of the committees under the Calendar Wednesday procedure. When the clerk reached Banking and Currency, Chairman Brent Spence (D. Ky.) called up S. 722 for consideration. Minority Leader Charles Halleck (R. Ind.) ordered a test vote on the bill by demanding a roll call on whether the House wanted to consider it. The motion carried comfortably, 221 to 171. With this vote the House was automatically transformed into a "Committee of the Whole." This relatively informal procedure has the effect of easing the fight against dilatory tactics, since only 100 members are required for a quorum and time-consuming roll calls are prohibited. When substantive debate finally commenced at 5:08 p.m., the House had consumed almost four and one-half hours calling the roll twelve times.

Only two hours were devoted to general debate, but even then dilatory tactics were employed by the bill's opponents. When Chairman Spence offered an amendment to substitute a committee-approved $251-million measure for the Senate's $389.5-million bill (S. 722), Congressman James Haley (D. Fla.) forced a thirty-minute reading of the thirty-two-page substitute. When Representative William Widnall (R. N.J.) offered the Adminstration's $53-million version, it too had to be read verbatim. The committee substitute was accepted, but the Widnall version was rejected by a 152 to 77 standing vote. The decisive vote—on a motion to recommit the bill to committee—came at 9:30 p.m., and the margin was 223 to 162 against recommittal. The Committee of the Whole then dissolved and reported its decision to the full House so that the House could vote final passage of the bill.

The obstruction of the southern sentries, Davis and Williams, demonstrated the risky nature of Calendar Wednesday, since the rules specify that it may consume no more than a single day. The majority's victory in this case depended not entirely upon the exhaustion of the minority's dilatory weapons, but also on the minority's deliberate decision to relent. Since the depressed-areas bill obviously had the necessary votes, the southern Democratic opponents decided that the better part of wisdom was to avoid carrying their obstructionism to the extreme. No doubt they did not want to be responsible for depriving the Democratic party of a useful campaign issue, in light of the assumption that Eisenhower would veto the measure. Nevertheless, a price must be paid when extraordinary legislative channels are invoked. The price for passage of S. 722 under Calendar Wednesday was the bothersome and time-consuming series of roll calls.

Conference Committee Politics

As predicted, President Eisenhower vetoed the 1960 depressed-areas bill—thus presenting the Democrats with a prime campaign issue. Conveniently, a recession had set in during mid-1960 and the issue of unemployment was a salient one in the depressed areas of New England, Appalachia, and the Midwest. The new Democratic Administration, which assumed office in January, was committed to the passage of a Douglas-type bill for the relief of such areas. As a senator, Kennedy had been a cosponsor of area redevelopment legislation from its inception; and his campaign in the West Virginia primary of 1960 had left an indelible impression of the joblessness and poverty he found there.

The passage of a Douglas-type bill was thus a foregone conclusion. The six-year impasse between a Republican Administration and Democratic majorities on Capitol Hill was at an end. Negotiation now focused on several important details of administering the program. Douglas lost several of these skirmishes, the chief one being a fight over where the new agency would be located in the executive structure. Douglas favored creation of a new, independent Area Redevelopment Administration that would presumably be free of the "vested interests" embodied in the regular departments. He was especially suspicious of the Eisenhower Administration's insistence on placing the program in the Commerce Department, since he feared that its "business clientele" would sabotage the program. When the Kennedy Administration came out for this alternative, Douglas realized he was "surrounded" and accepted defeat.

A second major skirmish centered around the perennial issue of backdoor financing. Douglas had always favored Treasury financing over the customary annual appropriations process in order to permit the agency to make long-range financial commitments. It was not clear, however, what position the Administration would take. In fact, two depressed-areas bills introduced in 1961 could claim to have Administration "sponsorship." One was Douglas' own bill, which had been recommended by a pre-Inaugural "Task Force on Unemployment" appointed by President-elect Kennedy and chaired by Douglas. This bill had been awarded the honor of being numbered S. 1 and, in accordance with Douglas' thinking, included Treasury financing. The actual Administration bill (H.R. 4569), prepared downtown in February, was obligingly introduced by Chairman Spence under his own name. It called for financing by appropriations.

Douglas successfully steered the Treasury financing provision of S. 1 through the Senate. But the House, always more sensitive than the Senate toward the appropriations committees' prerogatives, accepted the Spence bill without even a test vote on the financing issue.

When the two chambers pass different versions of the same bill, a conference must be held to resolve the discrepancies before the measure can go to the President. Conference politics are as complex as any on Capitol Hill, and are undoubtedly least understood of all the aspects of congressional procedure. Conferences had been involved earlier in the history of depressed-areas legislation, in 1958 and 1960; but an ingenious twist in parliamentary maneuvering made the 1961 conference particularly noteworthy.

First, White House aides sent word to Chairman Spence that the Administration would prefer Treasury financing—an obvious gesture to appease Douglas. With ill-concealed feeling, Spence remarked to his fellow House conferees that he wished the White House would make up its mind. But Spence would remain loyal to the Administration's wishes, as would the rest of the House Democratic conferees: Wright Patman (Tex.), Albert Rains (Ala.), and Abraham Multer (N.Y.).

The problem then became how to induce the House to accept Treasury financing. As chairman of the conference, Douglas gave considerable thought to the question and came up with an adroit parliamentary maneuver. Since the House had acted upon the legislation most recently, it was the Senate's decision whether to ask for a conference.[17] The Senate did so, and the House acquiesced. The distinction was important, for if precedent were to be honored, "a conference report is made first to the house agreeing to the conference," in this case, the House of Representatives.[18] If the House were allowed to pass on the conference report first, it would undoubtedly decline to approve the backdoor-financing feature and send its conferees back to the bargaining table, probably with instructions not to "recede" on that issue.

But *Cleaves' Manual* governing conferences is based on precedent and not on rule. Accordingly, Douglas directed the Legislative Reference Service to prepare a lengthy memorandum outlining his rights as conference chairman and citing relevant precedents. Several precedents were turned up that were at variance with normal practice. Armed with this information, and with the consent of the House Democratic conferees, Douglas refused to turn over the conference papers (records) to the House conferees and instead delivered the report directly to the Senate floor, where it was approved.

The House was thus confronted with a take-it-or-leave-it choice: It had to accept the report with Treasury financing, or there would be no bill at all. It chose to pass the bill, 223 to 193; observers estimated that only about twenty-five votes were lost because of the financing provision. But the incident provoked an outburst from Appropriations Chairman Clarence Cannon (D. Mo.). "What a way to run a business—any business from a peanut stand to a bank," he exclaimed. "And yet that is the way we are

---

[17] "The request for a conference must always be made by the house in possession of the papers." *Cleaves' Manual*, section 3.
[18] *Cleaves' Manual*, section 35.

running the greatest government on earth. Let us close the back door."

Douglas was very proud of his victory. Like many liberals, he had long viewed the rules as silent partners of the conservative bloc. Now he felt the weight of the rules on his own side. With a mastery of the rules—and the connivance of relevant persons— much is possible on Capitol Hill. Without these resources, little can be accomplished.

Epilogue

In the end, Douglas' master tactical stroke was of doubtful value. In the final bill of the 1961 session, a supplemental appropriations bill, a piqued Clarence Cannon and his colleagues wiped out backdoor financing for the Area Redevelopment Administration simply by appropriating it $170.75 million for fiscal 1962. On September 27, the House debated the bill (P.L. 87-332), approved it, and then adjourned for the year.

Even as the House was acting, the Senate was debating the appropriations bill; and when the Senators discovered that the House had adjourned, they were enraged. Even such fiscal conservatives as Everett Dirksen (R. Ill.) and Karl Mundt (R. S.D.) decried this "affront to the Senate." "An outrage is being perpetrated on the Senate," Minority Leader Dirksen declared. "Are we a coordinate branch of the legislative establishment, or are we not?" Though the Senators sullenly approved the bill, they indicated that the interhouse dispute had not ended. This incident contributed substantially to the spectacular 1962 feud between the House and Senate appropriations committees.

On the other hand, observers noted that the House bill included all the funds ARA had requested. It was conceded that Douglas' earlier coup may have served the negative function of inducing Cannon to exercise caution in overruling the conferees' decision.

The lesson to be gleaned from this epilogue is that the arenas for legislative maneuvering are numerous and continuous, and that tactical defeats of the moment may be turned into victories in another arena and at another time. Or, as in this case, a tactical advantage may be nullified by subsequent action. In commonplace idiom, "He who laughs last, laughs best."

Conclusions: The Rules and Legislative Politics

The Area Redevelopment Act of 1961 (P.L. 87-27) was signed into law by President Kennedy on May 1, 1961—the first major legislative accomplishment of the "New Frontier." Thus ended a seven-year struggle for depressed-areas assistance on the part of an unwieldy coalition of liberal legislators, trade unionists, economists, city planners, and farm progressives. There are many "nooks and crannies" in the history of P.L. 87-27 that are of interest to students of politics. The foregoing account has not done justice to this history, since our purpose has been the narrower one of illustrating the role of rules and procedures in legislative politics.

In the light of this objective, several themes have recurred throughout this analysis:

1. "The rules" have influence over legislative outcomes. They are resources, and mastery of them is a form of power in Congress. Senator Douglas' absence from the Senate floor while southerners speedily referred the 1956 civil rights bill to the Judiciary Committee, a traditional graveyard for such legislation, was an unfortunate miscalculation that resulted in a pigeon-holing of the bill within the rules. Douglas' actions as chairman of the 1961 conference committee on the depressed-areas bill, on the other hand, constituted a shrewd use of the rules for his own advantage.

2. Yet the rules are not independent of the power struggle that lies behind them. There is very little that the houses cannot do under the rules—so long as the action is backed up by votes and inclination. Yet votes and inclination are not easily obtained; and the rules persistently challenge the proponents of legislation to demonstrate that they have both resources at their command. Thus, there is little to prevent obstruction at every turn except the tacit premise that the business of the house must go on.

3. The rules cannot always be invoked with impunity. If they are resorted to indiscriminately or flagrantly, there is the risk that they will be redefined and the prerogative taken away or modified. Fulbright was made to realize this during the 1958 Banking and Currency Committee fight;[19] Judge Smith certainly understood

[19] Fulbright's successor as Banking and Currency chairman, A. Willis Robertson (D. Va.), proved less successful in controlling his committee. His re-

this in the 1958 incident, though repeated flirtations with the marginal extremes of his authority in 1960 led to its redefinition in 1961, when Speaker Rayburn was able to "pack" the Rules Committee.

4. A corollary principle is that rules and precedents often develop a life of their own. They may be valued for their own sake, and may not be subject to cynical machinations of the moment. There are two reasons for this. First, routinization itself has value in a conflict-laden body such as a legislature, for it confines conflict and settles many questions that might otherwise be troublesome. Secondly, a member who breaches the rules today may expect to have them used against him at some future date. It is this ghost that haunts senators when they are confronted with the issue of cloture and that reinforces the congressional folkway of deference to the rules.

---

peated use of the chairman's prerogatives against Douglas' "truth-in-lending" bill resulted in serious challenges to his authority during the Eighty-eighth Congress (see Chapter 5).

THE EXECUTIVE
AS LEGISLATOR

7

THE ECONOMIC OPPORTUNITY ACT OF 1964

Nine months after his sudden succession to the presidency, Lyndon B. Johnson signed the Economic Opportunity Act of 1964 —one of the most controversial of the "Great Society" programs. Earlier, Johnson had declared an unconditional "war on poverty," and now he re-emphasized the significance of this decision. "Today for the first time in all the history of the human race," he remarked expansively, "a great nation is able . . . and willing to make a commitment to eradicate poverty among its people."

The Economic Opportunity Act actually consisted of several distinct programs, loosely tied together in the enabling legislation and placed under the aegis of a new agency, the Office of Economic Opportunity (OEO). The Act's six substantive titles included several work and training programs for youth and persons on relief; self-employment loan programs for marginal farmers and would-be small businessmen; a "domestic Peace Corps" under the name of "Volunteers in Service to America" (VISTA); and an open-ended program for federal grants to community-wide organizations, designed to stimulate and coordinate a variety of local social and welfare services. Few persons thought the first-year

219

price tag of $962.5 million was adequate to relieve that one-fifth of our nation living below the poverty threshold; and more than one economist had called the Act a "band-aid program."

Few pieces of legislation in recent years, however, have generated more publicity or promised more revolutionary changes in the structure of communities and their social services. The Economic Opportunity Act signalled the elevation of poverty to a major public issue for the first time since the New Deal. "When did poor people ever make the headlines before?" asked the program's director, R. Sargent Shriver. The emergence of poverty as a public issue was all the more remarkable because it occurred without the goading of a public "crisis" and because it involved a clientele with relatively little political voice. The language of the Act, moreover, suggested that the poor themselves would be regarded as permanent participants in planning and implementing the programs, and not merely as recipients of government largesse. This explosive issue was to threaten existing patterns of community leadership, welfare services, and federal relationships.

The most significant feature of the Economic Opportunity Act, from our point of view, was that it was "legislated" almost entirely within the executive branch and, indeed, virtually without prodding from congressional or other "outside" clienteles. The draft bill that President Johnson sent to Congress on March 16, 1964, was the product of almost a year of discussions and negotiations among high-level administrators and economists. The process was culminated by a barnstorming five weeks of work by a special task force headed by Shriver. Ill-prepared congressmen opened hearings a day after the bill was sent to Capitol Hill; and the congressional amendments were, at most, marginal to the substance of the legislation. Thus, the war on poverty forms an instructive contrast to the Area Redevelopment Act of 1961—a measure that, although in an adjacent policy area, was initiated and refined largely by Congress.

Rediscovering the "Invisible" Poor

"There is an ugly smell rising from the basement of the stately American mansion," the Swedish economist Gunnar Myrdal wrote in 1963, referring to the paradox of poverty within an affluent society.[1] But though more than one-fifth of our nation's population may be classified as impoverished, their plight is strangely invisible to their more well-off neighbors. Generalized prosperity itself works to dull the concern of the nonpoor. High-speed interstate highways bypass both the back roads where the shanties of the poor are found and the crowded urban streets with their tenements. Even encountered on the street, the poor are less distinguishable than they once were: mass-produced clothing and color-fast fabrics have accomplished that feat. Ironically, the poor are the victims of the economics of affluence that makes them indistinguishable from their fellow citizens even as it sets them apart.

The poor are invisible in political terms also. They are notorious nonparticipants in politics: they tend to vote less often and to join fewer political groups than the nonpoor. Hence, few, if any, lobbies work for the interests of impoverished citizens. Urban political machines once took a certain interest in the poor, herding them to the polls to collect their votes. In exchange, the machine performed a variety of social services, dispensing minor favors, procuring jobs, even giving out food baskets. The benevolence of the urban bosses should not be exaggerated, and it hardly served to eliminate poverty; but the intimate relationship of the voter and the machine gave the poor some minimal leverage in politics. For a variety of reasons, most of the urban machines have withered away. Even the "log cabin" image of the politician of humble beginnings has faded: campaigns for major political office are costly affairs, and personal affluence has become a useful asset for a candidate. These and other factors have probably made policy-makers less sensitive to the interests of the poor. As John Kenneth Galbraith wrote in 1958, "any politician who speaks for the poor is speaking for a small and also inarticulate minority." [2]

Recent political history seemed to reinforce Galbraith's contention. Although the spectacle of massive unemployment formed the background for an impressive array of New Deal legislation, "poverty" was not a conspicuous political issue in the 1940s and 1950s. Widespread fears over anticipated manpower surpluses following post-World War II demobilization led in 1946 to passage

[1] Gunnar Myrdal, *Challenge to Affluence* (New York: Pantheon, 1963).
[2] John Kenneth Galbraith, *The Affluent Society* (Boston: Houghton-Mifflin, 1958), p. 328. See also Myrdal.

of the Employment Act, with its goals of high employment, production, and purchasing power. But general prosperity prevailed during the postwar years, and the Act remained largely unimplemented.

Two developments aided in the rediscovery of poverty. As we have seen in the depressed-areas case, it became apparent during the 1950s that certain geographic regions were not sharing in the nation's prosperity. These areas of hard-core unemployment showed up strikingly in the Labor Department's labor market statistics, especially during periods of generalized economic slack. Naturally sensitized to these problems, the "depressed-areas congressmen" soon became an identifiable bloc and evolved the series of loan and grant proposals described in the preceding chapter.

Another development, more pervasive in its impact, was the increasing national preoccupation with the problems of Negro citizens. Though initially fought in terms of social and political rights, the civil-rights issue inevitably led to the phenomenon of poverty. Not all Negroes were below the poverty threshold, and not all of the impoverished were Negroes. But the burgeoning amounts of statistics generated on the Negro question made transparently clear that a disproportionate number of Negroes were found in the ranks of the unskilled, the unemployed, and the poverty-stricken. The riots that broke out in Negro ghettoes of northern cities in the summer of 1964 were widely interpreted as protests against generalized deprivation. Thus, the Negro problem was gradually recast as the "poverty problem"—a transmutation that somehow seemed to assuage the tensions implicit in racial warfare.

The intellectual community was slow to take an interest in the problem of poverty. Though economists largely ignored the issue (Galbraith, for example, complained that no one had read beyond the title of his celebrated book, *The Affluent Society*), an increasing stream of articles and books began to appear. The Joint Economic Committee produced an important study in 1959, and soon other voices began to be heard—including economists Robert Lampman, Gabriel Kolko, Oscar Ornati, and Herman Miller, as well as journalists Ben Bagdikian and Harry Caudill. The year 1962 saw the publication of Michael Harrington's *The Other America*, an angry book in the best muckraking tradition, written by a gifted social critic.[3] A scholarly study by the liberal economist Leon Keyserling also appeared that year.[4] These two works were only indicative of the increasing ferment, but they became especially significant because they found their way into the hands of President Kennedy.

Kennedy and Poverty

It was the vagaries of politics that propelled John F. Kennedy into the West Virginia presidential primary to do battle with Senator Hubert Humphrey in 1960. Kennedy knew of the depressed regions of his native Massachusetts, and in the Senate he had been an early supporter of Senator Paul Douglas' area-redevelopment bill. But to the wealthy young Bostonian, the first-hand view of poverty in West Virginia was a new and jarring experience. Kennedy's political debt to the voters of that state, who aided so strategically in his drive for the presidency, was partially repaid with the passage of the Area Redevelopment Act and the designing of a regional development program for Appalachia. But the memory of the deprivation he had seen in West Virginia was apparently never completely erased from his mind.

Kennedy's early economic program emphasized the expansion of over-all demand, under the theory that prosperity would reduce hard-core unemployment and alleviate poverty through the creation of new jobs. During 1963 Kennedy and his advisors devoted their attentions to a comprehensive tax reduction designed to invigorate the economy further by placing more dollars in the hands of consumers. The tax cut was pending before Congress when Kennedy died, but under pressure from President Johnson it was enacted the following year. As early as May of 1963, Presidential aide Kenneth O'Donnell was assuring Walter W. Heller, the Minnesota economics professor who was serving as chairman of the President's Council of Economic Advisers, that "the tax cut is going to pass—and pass big. So worry about something else." [5]

[3] (New York: Macmillan, 1962). Also significant was Dwight Macdonald's review, "Our Invisible Poor," in *The New Yorker* (January 19, 1963).
[4] *Poverty and Deprivation in the United States* (Washington: Conference on Economic Progress, 1962).
[5] The Council of Economic Advisers (CEA) consists of a chairman and two

Meanwhile, Kennedy showed interest in the problem of poverty. As early as December 1962 he asked Heller for copies of the Harrington and Keyserling books (Heller never got them back), and a month later he was reading Dwight Macdonald's *New Yorker* article. The President then gave tentative approval to a theme of "widening participation in prosperity" for his 1964 legislative program. Thus in mid-1963 Heller and the Council turned their attentions from the expansion of demand to programs aimed directly at the poor.

The considerations that lay behind the interest in poverty were both political and intellectual. Kennedy was casting about for new programs to highlight his 1964 legislative program. If a "war against poverty" (Kennedy had used the phrase in the 1960 campaign) proved to have public appeal, it would be an important weapon in his re-election campaign. Such an issue could be especially effective if, as Kennedy apparently hoped, the conservative Senator Barry M. Goldwater (Ariz.) were the Republican nominee.

Meanwhile, many liberal economists were expressing dissatisfaction over what they interpreted as the Administration's preoccupation with improving the over-all "business climate." Such demand-expansion measures as the tax cut, they argued, would aid only those workers prepared to enter the labor market, and would not "trickle down" sufficiently to help the hard-core poor. As Galbraith had written, "growth is only for those who can take advantage of it."

Objectively, the problem of poverty was becoming increasingly stubborn, even in the face of generalized prosperity— a view urged especially by Robert Lampman, a University of Wisconsin economist serving on the Council staff during 1962-1963. According to a memorandum prepared by Lampman and forwarded to the President on May 1, there had occurred "a drastic slowdown in the rate at which the economy is taking people out of poverty." All in all, an estimated one-fifth of the population was

---

other members who are selected by the President. Created by the Employment Act of 1946, the Council prepares annual reports on the state of the economy and advises the President on over-all economic policy. The chairman has come to function as a personal adviser to the President; and the relationship between Heller and Kennedy was especially close. It is relevant to note that the Council (along with the Budget Bureau) is organizationally a part of the Executive Office of the President; and that physically the two agencies are located in the Executive Office Building directly west of the White House.

living below the poverty threshold (defined as $3000 per family per year, but later refined by government economists). This was some improvement over the "submerged third" referred to by President Franklin D. Roosevelt, but was nonetheless alarming in view of the over-all prosperity.

As Heller expressed it, "this led to some basic soul-searching" by the Council during the summer of 1963. How much would the poverty problem yield to a successful tax cut and full employment? The answer was encouraging—up to a point. Projected long-term economic growth, the Council staff believed, would reduce poverty at a faster rate than during the 1957-1961 period. But the realization that many of the poor would be untouched by over-all growth led to further queries. What antipoverty measures were already in operation? What lines of action might be proposed for 1964? And what new types of data would be needed to measure the extent of poverty and the impact of federal programs? Throughout the summer and fall, the Council generated a flurry of papers on these questions, drawing upon the White House and Bureau of the Budget staffs when necessary.

Not everyone was enthusiastic. In June Heller launched a trial balloon in a speech to the Communications Workers of America (AFL-CIO), and was disappointed with the response. A background discussion with journalists failed to produce more than a few stories. In midsummer the Council arranged a luncheon to explore the idea with a number of high-level government policy-makers. Reactions ranged from cautious approval to distinct lack of interest. Several officials pointed to the political liabilities of an antipoverty program: Kennedy had waged his 1960 campaign on the promise of "getting the country moving again," and to stress poverty after three years would appear to concede failure. As one policy-maker put it, an administration in power that elects to point up economic problems invariably ends up talking against itself.

Yet interest within the Council remained high, and the President kept giving encouragement. In early November Heller issued a formal request to members of the "domestic Cabinet" [6]

[6] At this point, the Secretaries of Commerce, Labor, and Health, Education and Welfare; the Administrator of the Housing and Home Finance Agency; and the Director of the Bureau of the Budget. Later, the Interior Department was drawn in.

in order to generate program suggestions. The departments and agencies were asked to examine their existing programs, suggest new programs or redirections of old ones, and estimate the added funding or reorganization of current programs that would be needed. The agencies were to range widely in suggesting a framework for a program termed variously "human conservation and development," "access to opportunity," and "attack on poverty."

The Council intended to report back to the White House by Thanksgiving, but by mid-November it was inundated with proposals, including a 150-page document from the Labor Department. The Bureau of the Budget was called in to process and evaluate the papers, an operation similar to its normal annual budgetary review. Predictably, each agency was preoccupied with its own bailiwick: training and employment from Labor, education and welfare services from HEW, rural development from Agriculture, and so on. But the sheer number of ideas (more than one hundred distinct proposals) was impressive. As one staff aide expressed it, "they snowed us under with an agenda for social programs which would keep Congress busy for a decade."

The size of the task made it unlikely that the Council-Bureau group could submit a definitive report by Thanksgiving, but time was short. Proposals for new legislation could be delayed until early 1964, but any references to a poverty program in the President's mid-January budget message or Economic Report would have to have White House clearance sometime in December. Heller needed a definite commitment from the President. Before departing with the Cabinet for a trip to Japan, Heller obtained a hurried interview with President Kennedy. He asked whether work should go forward under the assumption that an antipoverty measure would be included in the 1964 legislative agenda. Kennedy's answer was immediate: "Yes, and let me see your proposals in a couple of weeks." This was on November 19, as Heller and the Cabinet departed for Japan and Kennedy for Dallas.

Three days later, a Budget Bureau group was meeting to continue its evaluation of the departmental proposals when news of Kennedy's assassination reached Washington. Having no heart for further discussion, the group silently drifted out of the conference room. Like most other governmental affairs on that November 22, the poverty program was suspended, awaiting the response of the new Chief Executive.

Johnson Declares War on Poverty

Any doubts about the new President's interest in the poverty question were soon removed. On the evening of November 23— the Cabinet members had turned back from their trip in midflight—Heller briefed Johnson on the current work of the Council. When the pending antipoverty program was mentioned, Johnson responded quickly: "That's my kind of program. It will help people. I want you to move full speed ahead on it."

Spurred by this assurance, the Council embarked on what Heller described as "a most intensive period of hammering the program into shape." By mid-December a section on poverty was inserted in the President's Economic Report and a "line item" of $500 million included in the draft budget for fiscal 1965. The Council-Bureau task force, however, temporarily had no specific legislative proposal. Limited by time and preoccupied with their own policy concerns, the departments and agencies had proposed limited-purpose programs for their own areas. Many of the suggestions appeared meritorious. But with only a half-million dollars in new funds, which programs should be recommended? And even if the best suggestions could be culled out, would they constitute an integrated war on poverty?

At this point, a Budget Bureau official hit on the idea of a limited number of general-purpose grants to help localities develop their own community-wide poverty programs. This "Community Action Program" concept (as it came to be known) actually originated in the 1950s as a means of dealing with juvenile delinquency through concerted action in deteriorated neighborhoods. The Ford Foundation had supported broad-based community organizations in the "gray areas" of several northern cities; and President Kennedy's Commission on Juvenile Delinquency and Youth Crime, created in 1961 with a small staff in the Justice Department, had sponsored a limited program of demonstration grants aimed at developing neighborhood attacks on juvenile delinquency. It was this latter program that intrigued the Budget Bureau official, who immediately asked a staff member of the

President's Commission on Juvenile Delinquency to prepare papers on how the concept might be applied to the poverty question.

Others in the Council-Bureau task force bought this idea, and it soon became the keystone for the evolving poverty program. By December 17 an initial proposal was transmitted to the White House and various Cabinet members. According to the proposal, the key element in a realistic attack on poverty would be a series of grants aimed at local poverty areas and relying on organized local initiative: in the words of a Labor Department aide, "a pot of money which local people could ask for." Initially, demonstration grants would be directed to ten areas (five urban and five rural). The program would be administered by a Council on Poverty, consisting of a presidentially appointed chairman (someone who could "knock heads together to get cooperation") and appropriate department and agency chiefs. New funds would be redirected from the agencies' specific-purpose programs in order to follow up the initial community planning.

The community-action concept was attractive on at least two grounds. First, it was a way of experimenting with the poverty problem with limited funds and under the traditional framework of "grass-roots initiative." Secondly, the idea suggested a new way of coordinating and funding federal programs. Multipurpose grants to community organizations could bypass agency jurisdictions and avoid duplicating federal programs and personnel at the local level. These grants could be used for a variety of purposes suggested by local officials: educational upgrading, job-creation and work-training, health services, consumer counseling, and urban renewal and public housing.

The departments and agencies were not happy with this solution. It was true that much of the $500 million allocated for the community-action programs would eventually be spent through existing federal programs. And to boost the new programs to a "really dramatic" figure of $1 billion, the Council was proposing that an extra amount of up to $625 million be reallocated to the war on poverty from the agencies' current budget requests for fiscal 1965. The agencies, however, wanted to retain control of their own funds and programs, and the intervention of a "poverty council" posed a threat to their autonomy. Moreover, most agencies felt that their proposals had gotten short shrift from the Council-Bureau group. Even one official who was not happy with his own department's contributions remarked wearily, "we didn't come up with anything very useful and what we proposed wasn't accepted."

The agencies thus exhibited a certain ambivalence toward the war on poverty: they wanted to be included, but they feared that their own programs would be submerged in the new arrangement. The Labor Department, for example, wanted more emphasis on youth employment, but felt that too much emphasis might jeopardize the prospects for its own youth employment opportunities bill, then pending before Congress. The Department of Agriculture was interested in developing local leadership in mounting rural poverty programs; and Commerce thought that the role of local business leaders had been inadequately stressed. Spokesmen for Interior protested that their Bureau of Indian Affairs was also in the poverty business. HEW had perhaps the most to gain from the proposal, since specifications drawn up for the community-action programs were heavily weighted to welfare, health, and educational services. But even HEW feared that local community-action agencies might bypass their important clientele groups, the state and national federations of teachers and social workers.

These differences came to the surface during a White House meeting called on January 23, 1964, to discuss a draft bill that the Council had asked HEW to prepare. Labor Secretary W. Willard Wirtz bitterly attacked Heller over the entire proposal. Wirtz saw clearly that the bill's emphasis was likely to elevate local educators and welfare workers, for whom HEW serves as the natural spokesman within the federal government. At the same time, Labor's traditional concerns in minimum wages, job training, and employment would be difficult to emphasize within the community-action framework. Wirtz was able to couch his argument in general terms that Heller, Budget Director Kermit Gordon, and HEW Secretary Anthony Celebrezze found difficult to oppose. He therefore had support when he argued that the proposal be "broadened out" as essentially an expansion and redirection of ongoing federal activities administered by existing agencies.

The January 23 meeting indicated that a stalemate was threatening the war on poverty even before it began. The Council-Bureau group had general support from the White House, but short of direct presidential intervention it was clear that these staff agencies could not force a resolution of the conflict. The CEA and Budget Bureau staffs had long assumed that a strong "poverty czar," working by personal force and close access to the President, would be needed to coordinate the legislation once it was enacted. This person, whoever he might be, would be needed sooner than anyone had anticipated.

The Shriver Task Force

President Johnson announced on February 1 that Peace Corps Director R. Sargent Shriver would lead the assault on poverty.[7] Shriver's first job would be to hammer out the Administration's antipoverty legislation. The reasons for the President's choice were not hard to fathom: a businessman, a local school board chairman (in Chicago), and a brother-in-law of the late President, Shriver had gained a reputation as a strong and innovative administrator since joining the "New Frontier" in 1961. In guiding the Peace Corps, he had demonstrated acute political sense and rare ability to charm conservative congressmen. One commentator described Shriver as the only foreign aid administrator capable of appearing before Appropriations Subcommittee Chairman Otto Passman (D. La.) and getting "not just almost as much as he wants, but almost as much as he asks for."

Shriver lost no time in launching the process of fashioning the final bill. The same day his appointment was announced in the newspapers, he summoned a small group to his office to brief him on the work of the preceding four months. Two days later (February 4), he convened a full-scale meeting of departmental representatives, personal associates, and a few nongovernment observers.

This meeting witnessed a re-enactment of the conflict that had stalemated the Council-Bureau proposal. In opening the session, Heller presented an hour-long report of the work to date, devoting most of his time to the community-action concept. Secretary Wirtz followed with a half-hour statement attacking both Heller and the Council-Bureau bill. The war on poverty, he de-

[7] Two other names which figured seriously in the discussions were Governor Terry Sanford of North Carolina and Mayor Richard Lee of New Haven. However, both held elective offices whose terms would not expire for some time; and President Johnson wanted someone on the job immediately.

clared, could hardly be fought with a single weapon in only a few "demonstration" areas across the country. More jobs were what was needed, since job scarcity caused unemployment that in turn produced poverty.

As the discussion went around the table, it became obvious that Wirtz's notion of a broad-based and multifaceted war on poverty had many allies. Spokesmen for departments whose proposals had been pushed aside in favor of the community-action concept expressed their unwillingness to wait another fiscal year before funding their program ideas. Two nongovernment people, Donald Petrie, chairman of Avis Rent-a-Car Co., and Virgil Martin, vice-president of Carson Pirie Scott Co., a Chicago retailer, were strongly in favor of Wirtz's viewpoint. Acting as referee, Shriver presently indicated that he thought the poverty program should have a scope and glamour equal to the concept of a "war on poverty" that was being sold to the public through the communications media.

When the meeting adjourned, the notion that the war would consist of a few community-action programs on a pilot basis had been completely destroyed. Clearly, the new poverty bill would be a "package" of several legislative proposals, some of which were already before Congress.

For the next five weeks, a Shriver task force, working out of the Peace Corps Building, shaped the contents of this legislative package. The group had no legal status, and its staff members were either volunteers or on loan from their departments or agencies. Office expenses were covered from the White House contingency fund. The group used stationery emblazoned with the words, "War on Poverty." Even after the Administration's bill had been put together and sent to Capitol Hill, the task force remained in existence for many months to plan for implementing the law. Finally, in August 1964, the remnants of the group merged into the new Office of Economic Opportunity.

The task force was an extremely fluid group and consisted of many types of persons. Representatives were detailed by their departments and agencies to work with the task force, focusing their attention particularly on matters of interest to their agencies. Prominent among these were Labor Assistant Secretary Daniel Patrick Moynihan, HEW lawyer Harold Horowitz, Agriculture Deputy Under Secretary James Sundquist, and Commerce aides

James Adler and Hyman Bookbinder. Not all were physically located in the Peace Corps offices (where Shriver was continuing to serve as director), and scores of others from various agencies were drawn in at various times to assist with certain sections of the bill. Though responsible mainly for the provisions dealing with their agencies, these officials nonetheless met frequently to discuss the bill generally.

Another group, Shriver's personal friends and associates, was even more amorphous. This group consisted of, in Shriver's words, "the kind of people you like to bat an idea against." Prominent among these were Adam Yarmolinsky, a special assistant to the Secretary of Defense; Christopher Weeks, a former Peace Corps aide then with the Budget Bureau; Frank Mankiewicz of the Peace Corps; authors Paul Jacobs and Michael Harrington; and streams of businessmen, mayors, professors, and local welfare officials called to Washington to offer suggestions.

The Shriver task force represented a legislative work group fairly unique within the executive branch; its general structure is outlined in Figure 4. By the time the group had finished its work, one could identify individuals who had played key roles in preparing certain of the six titles of the Economic Opportunity Act.[8] These individuals, however, consulted continuously with one another, and with the scores of others who were called in for specific advice. Generalists like Weeks and Bookbinder provided overall coordinating and "kibitzing" functions. Three "intellectuals" attached to the task force, Harrington, Jacobs, and Mankiewicz, made no substantive contribution to the Act, but explored long-range topics and produced a series of "philosophic memos" (as they were called) for Shriver. Decisions were reviewed by Shriver and Yarmolinsky, with the latter serving as Shriver's alter ego and chief of staff during the five-week period. In several instances in which major departmental disputes were involved, the issues were referred to the President. About a week after the task force began its work, a legal drafting team was mobilized. This group, headed by Assistant Attorney General Norbert Schlei, was able to resolve a

[8] For example, Moynihan for work-training (Title I) and the domestic Peace Corps (Title VI); Richard Boone of the White House Office for community action (Title II); Sundquist for agricultural loans (Title III); Harold Galloway of the Small Business Administration for small business loans (Title IV); Adler for work-experience programs (Title V); and William Cannon of the Budget Bureau for organization of the new agency (Title VI).

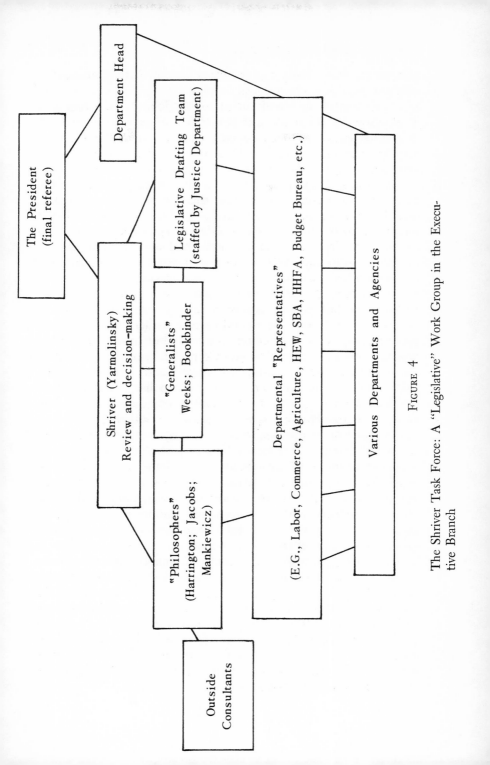

FIGURE 4

The Shriver Task Force: A "Legislative" Work Group in the Executive Branch

number of minor issues by consulting and mediating among the substantive experts on the task force.

Shriver seemed well suited to the job of evaluating and combining the proposals into an attractive legislative package. "I've never known anyone as open to ideas as Shriver," said James Sundquist of the Agriculture Department. "If a new idea came up in a meeting, the burden of proof would lie with the opposition rather than with the proponents." Shriver himself described the process to a reporter: "I came into this with an open mind. I've been learning, sifting, and consulting—just the way I did when I was trying to organize the Peace Corps." Yet some experts complained that Shriver lacked an intellectual understanding of the problem. "School-girl enthusiasm and dilettantism" was the way one intellectual summed up the Shriver approach.

Because Shriver wanted a broad-gauged and spectacular package, the task force recanvassed the agencies for suggestions, plowing over much of the ground covered earlier by the Council-Bureau group. Several pending Administration bills were woven into the new legislation. The Job Corps camps and work-training programs in Title I, for example, were previously embodied in the youth employment opportunities bill, which had been passed by the Senate and reported by the House committee before languishing in the House Rules Committee. Another Title I provision, the work-study programs for college students, had been considered but was dropped in 1963 as part of the National Defense Education Act amendments. The domestic Peace Corps, which naturally interested Shriver, had previously been proposed by the Administration as the "National Service Corps." In selecting such programs as these, Shriver was alert for ideas that could be sold to Congress and the public and that would yield visible results in a relatively short time period.

Many liberals distrusted Shriver's approach as too conventional, too parsimonious, or too permeated with middle-class values. Shriver continually emphasized that the bill would provide training and rehabilitation but not relief. "Let me tell you," he said to a reporter, "I'm not at all interested in running a handout program, or a leaf-raking program, or a 'something for nothing' program. I don't know what we're going to come up with, but when we do, it will be a practical program." [9] Outside economists

[9] *Newsweek*, February 17, 1964, p. 38.

criticized the task force for producing merely conventional federal services; and at one point, a group of liberals associated with the Americans for Democratic Action (ADA) threatened to denounce publicly the war on poverty as inadequate to the needs of the poor. Inside the task force, the three "philosophers" were equally critical. Harrington told Shriver that the program was "nickles and dimes" compared to the immensity of the problem. Staring in disbelief, Shriver answered: "Mr. Harrington, perhaps you've spent a billion dollars before, but this is my first time around." To his left-wing critics, Shriver had a stock response: "I don't want anybody to get the idea that [with this bill] we're going to cure the poverty problem in this country. Nobody thinks that. But we can do something."

Explicit attention was devoted to outside clienteles, for one of the task force's functions was to consult and win over numbers of businessmen, economists, local officials, and welfare workers. Thus, the working group was often forced to halt whatever they were doing and receive out-of-town visitors who had been summoned by Shriver. A few useful ideas were obtained, but the main idea was to make the visitors feel that they had participated in the evolution of a practical and far-reaching piece of legislation. When the final draft bill was unveiled, the White House released a list of 137 names, described as "a partial list of people Mr. Shriver has consulted in developing the poverty program."

Shriver was especially proud that he had consulted more than thirty business and farm leaders. ("Wait 'til I show them the list of businessmen who've helped us with this program," he remarked on the eve of the House hearings.) At one point, in fact, Shriver's preoccupation with neutralizing conservative opposition almost alienated potential supporters from the labor movement. Already fearful that a poverty program might dislocate union workers from their jobs, labor leaders temporarily lost communication with the Shriver group. Word was filtered back to the task force, and an effort was made thereafter to keep in touch with them.

In addition to screening a vast number of existing proposals, the task force was called upon to resolve several major conflicts. The first of these was what importance to give to the community-action programs, which had been the heart of the earlier bill. Many persons believed these were the only unique product of the poverty discussions—a sentiment not confined to the Council or Budget Bureau. Shriver did not share their enthusiasm, preferring instead a limited number of specific-purpose programs. Upon the urging of people in the Budget Bureau and the Juvenile Delinquency Commission, however, Attorney General Robert Kennedy, who had taken an interest in the juvenile delinquency approach, contacted Shriver and persuaded him to emphasize the community-action programs as Title II of the new bill. No less than $315 million was allocated for this purpose.

The task force also inserted the stipulation that community programs should be "developed, conducted, and administered with the maximum feasible participation of residents of the area and members of the groups served." Staff people from the President's Commission on Juvenile Delinquency proposed this wording, understanding clearly that it might serve as a wedge to pry loose existing local power structures. To most members of the task force, however, the provision simply permitted inclusion of Negro leaders in planning antipoverty campaigns in southern communities. Whatever the motivations, the task force accepted the provision casually, few of them foreseeing it implied that the poor themselves were to participate in decision-making.

Once the poverty program was under way, however, this "maximum feasible participation" clause (Section 202[a][3]) became a rallying cry for those who wished to involve the poor in policy-making and not merely as objects of welfare programs. Local radical activists and self-proclaimed spokesmen for the poor, backed up by some of the more enthusiastic spirits within the Office of Economic Opportunity, attempted to use this provision to wage a war against City Hall—an effort that provoked retaliation from local politicians of both parties. For the time being, however, few in the executive branch were aware of the revolutionary potential of these words; and those who were, remained silent.

The task force spent some time drawing up detailed specifications for the community-action programs, under the assumption that Congress would be reluctant to approve such a large amount of money for unspecified purposes. But the various welfare groups soon began jockeying to obtain high priority for their programs. There were too many claimants for the funds available. Finally, the legal drafting team decided to resolve the issue by removing all the specifications from Title II. The lawyers were unhappy about this legal untidiness, but as it turned out Congress did not seem to notice the omission.

Conflicts over administration of the legislation were not so subtle. Once it became inevitable that a special agency (presumably under Shriver's direction) would coordinate and administer portions of the package, the leading question was which, if any, programs would be assigned to existing agencies. The Labor Department was most vocal on this issue, with Secretary Wirtz holding that the war on poverty should be implemented and coordinated through established agencies. At the very least, Wirtz hoped to administer the youth employment and work-experience programs himself. He had an established claim to the former, including the Job Corps, in the pending youth-employment bill.

Shriver himself decided to locate the Job Corps in the new OEO and give the Neighborhood Youth Corps to the Labor Department in exchange. Apparently attracted by the potential glamour of the Job Corps camps, he determined to run them himself, along with the community-action programs and the domestic Peace Corps (VISTA). Wirtz was unhappy with this solution, and the final decision was referred to the President, who elected to stand behind Shriver. It was informally agreed that other programs would be delegated to the relevant agencies with vaguely defined supervision by the new poverty office.[10]

If it were decided that the poverty office would have operating as well as supervisory functions, there remained the question of whether poverty would be independent or a part of the Executive Office of the President. Shriver opted for the latter alternative, under the reasonable theory that he would need the weight of the presidential office to coordinate the activities of other departments and agencies. Budget Bureau canons, however, hold that operating and staff agencies should be separated, with only the latter located in the Executive Office. Again the final decision was taken to the President, who once more ruled in Shriver's favor.

In allocating funds, the Shriver task force had only limited freedom. Many of the programs were already "locked in" by budget proposals in pending legislation. Also inflexible was the $500

---

[10] This is the so-called "delegate agency" concept, in which an agency will contract, or delegate, certain of its programs to another agency. Thus, for example, rural poverty programs remained technically under OEO's jurisdiction, but in fact were implemented and controlled by the Agriculture Department.

million listed in the budget's line item for poverty. The final bill had a definite youthful flavor: of the $962.5 million in new obligational authority, $412.5 million was allocated to various youth opportunity projects. With the $315 million allotted to community-action programs, this left only $75 million for programs to aid subsistence farmers and would-be small businessmen (the latter being referred to as "the teeny tiny loan program").

On March 16 the President transmitted to Capitol Hill the draft bill for the Economic Opportunity Act, along with a message urging "total victory" in the war against poverty. He announced that he proposed to appoint Shriver "my personal Chief of Staff in the war" as head of the proposed Office of Economic Opportunity. In less than a year's time, the executive branch had generated a major domestic policy departure, initially in the virtual absence of expressed outside interest. It had canvassed the technical constituencies represented by the various federal welfare agencies, and had endeavored to consult external clienteles—such as local officials, the social welfare groups, businessmen, community developers, and the academic community. And it had combined a number of specific-purpose programs into a legislative package designed to draw support from most of the groups currently engaged in social welfare activities. Finally, the Administration had endeavored to sell the program as responsible and consistent with the American traditions of local initiative, voluntarism, and self-help. The public had appeared to be enthusiastic. It remained to see how Congress would react to such an initiative.

The Congressional Phase

The process of shaping the poverty package was legislative in character though executive in locus. Thus, Congress was asked not to draft the war on poverty, but rather, to ratify a fully prepared Administration program, and invited, though hardly encouraged, to propose marginal changes.

The Johnson Administration constructed a favorable setting for the passage of this legislation. Shortly after assuming office, Johnson began to cultivate the image of fiscal frugality, when he asked Defense Secretary McNamara to cut defense production costs, called for an over-all curb in federal jobs, and underscored the point by personally turning out lights in the White House.

The President encouraged the notion that these savings might be utilized for social welfare legislation. In announcing a billion-dollar slash in the defense budget late in 1963, for example, it was suggested that the move would pay for the initial year of the war on poverty. Johnson told reporters that this would be a "redistribution in wealth" that would "come from those who have it, to those who don't have it." Congressional constituencies were reminded of their stake in the poverty program. Early in 1964, Mrs. Johnson toured depressed coal-mining regions in Pennsylvania, and in April the President himself made the first of two flying tours of Appalachia. Meanwhile, the Administration dangled the prospect of forthcoming funds before mayors and other local officials.

Potential opponents had little time to gather their forces. Congressional hearings were launched on March 17, the day after the Administration's draft bill (H.R. 10440) was introduced. Major attention was focused on the House, where the most strenuous opposition was expected. Representative Adam Clayton Powell (D. N.Y.), chairman of the Committee on Education and Labor, quickly named an Ad Hoc Subcommittee on Poverty, with himself as chairman, to take testimony. Powell took an active interest in the bill, though he agreed to the Administration's tactical suggestion that a respected southern moderate, Representative Phil M. Landrum (D. Ga.), serve as the bill's principal sponsor.

The hearings were designed to advertise broad support for the poverty bill. Shriver appeared as the lead-off witness to outline the program and describe it as responsible, comprehensive, and the product of many individuals and groups. Then Heller presented the Council's statistics on the extent of the problem. Like Shriver, he stressed the program's self-help features, arguing that it would permit individuals to "earn" their way out of poverty. For the next two weeks the Administration's top brass—the Secretaries of Defense, Labor, Commerce, Agriculture, Interior, and Health, Education and Welfare; the Attorney General; and the Administrators of HHFA and SBA—appeared before the committee to amplify the case for each provision. Later, spokesmen for an impressive range of civic, welfare, and religious groups appeared to endorse the bill. AFL-CIO President George Meany and the National Urban League's executive director, Whitney Young, Jr., led off, followed by representatives of such groups as the National

Council of Churches, the National Catholic Welfare Council, the National Education Association, the American Public Welfare Association, the National Farmers Union, the National Grange, the American Friends Service Committee, and the General Federation of Women's Clubs. The Administration also procured five mayors, five governors, and several local welfare officials to testify in the bill's behalf. And of the 139 "advisors" to the Shriver task force, no less than thirty-three appeared or filed statements with the House Committee.

The bill's opponents were hopelessly outnumbered in the hearings, as the figures in Table 13 demonstrate. Of the seventy-

TABLE 13   PRIMARY* WITNESSES IN THE HOUSE HEARINGS ON THE ECONOMIC OPPORTUNITY ACT OF 1964

Category	Favored	Opposed	Advisory—no opinion
Executive Branch	12	0	2
State, local officials	14	0	1
Business groups	0	3	—
Business individuals	3	0	—
Labor groups	2	0	—
Religious, welfare groups	14	0	—
Farm groups	5	1	—
Scholars	3	3	—
Members of Congress	3	2	1
Totals	56	9	4

* Only the "primary" spokesman for each group or agency was counted. Secondary, advisory, or back-up witnesses were excluded when several individuals appeared together.

nine witnesses who appeared during the twenty days of House hearings, only nine were in opposition to the bill. Of these, four were from groups traditionally opposed to governmental spending in social welfare: the U.S. Chamber of Commerce, the National Association of Manufacturers, the American Farm Bureau Federation, and a state (Illinois) manufacturers' association. Of the remaining five, two were Republican members of the Joint Economic Committee whose minority report had accused the Council of Economic Advisers of exaggerating the extent of poverty. The final three objectors were professors who argued that the bill's focus was unclear.

The pace of the hearings was accelerated by Powell and by the two next-ranking subcommittee members, Landrum and Carl Perkins (D. Ky.). Republicans complained that the sessions were scheduled at irregular hours and without proper notice, and that members were being gavelled down before finishing their questioning of witnesses. One morning the Republicans were able to call as witnesses a group of statistical experts from the Labor Department and the Census Bureau, in an effort to show the need for further study of the nature and extent of poverty. Powell's gavel became so heavy that protests of being "stampeded" came from Representatives Peter Frelinghuysen (R. N.J.), and Charles Goodell (R. N.Y.). "I am the chairman," Powell retorted. "I will run this committee as I desire." [11]

Committee Republicans explored for breaches in the Administration's defenses, and several promising issues developed. An obvious target was the bill's unique administrative arrangement and the broad authorization under Title II. Frelinghuysen, the ranking Republican on the full committee, asserted that OEO would be resented by existing agency heads and would duplicate their programs. Obviously feeling for a sensitive nerve, Frelinghuysen, Goodell, and William Ayres of Ohio (ranking minority member of the subcommittee) pursued the point vigorously, asking several Cabinet members their reactions to becoming subordinates to a "poverty czar." Even Labor Secretary Wirtz replied blandly that "I do not think of it in terms of any diminution or enlargement of the power in the department." [12] One by one the Cabinet members pledged fealty to the new arrangement.

Another line of attack concerned the issue of states' rights and the future of the American federal system. The Republicans noted that the poverty program would bypass the states and create new functional relationships between the federal government and public and private entities in the localities. Fearing that poverty projects and the potential patronage they embodied might be used to undermine the position of an incumbent governor (especially if he were a Republican), the congressmen argued that governors should at least have some review powers over projects in

[11] U.S. House of Representatives, Committee on Education and Labor, *Hearings on the Economic Opportunity Act of 1964*, III (Eighty-eighth Congress, 2d session, 1964), p. 1150. (Cited hereinafter as *House Hearings*.)
[12] *House Hearings*, I, p. 201.

their own states. Because of the obvious relevance of the war on poverty to disadvantaged Negroes, the bill also stirred traditional states' rights concerns.

More broadly, the Republicans charged that the bill was not needed, that inflation, and not welfare, was the prime problem, and that in any event more research into the question was needed. In the presidential primary fights, candidates Barry Goldwater and Nelson Rockefeller held that the Administration was "playing politics with poverty." And two Republican congressmen, M. G. (Gene) Snyder (Ky.) and David T. Martin (Neb.) made a well-publicized flying tour of Mrs. Lyndon Johnson's Alabama farm—which they described as a "pocket of poverty." They returned to display photographs of the six Negro sharecroppers and tenants living on the Johnson land, and to say that "We saw people living in deplorable poverty, with little evidence of concern by their millionaire landlords." (The White House issued an explanation: the land was inherited, and when cotton became an unprofitable crop Mrs. Johnson decided to use most of the land for timber. But some of the tenants were reluctant to leave, and Mrs. Johnson allowed them to remain.)

On April 28 Frelinghuysen introduced an alternative bill (H.R. 11050) reflecting Republican criticisms. The Frelinghuysen version authorized $1.5 billion for a three-year program run by the states and coordinated by HEW. Except for deletion of the Job Corps, the bill included many of the same programs as the Administration proposal, but gave more powers to the states in planning, implementation, and financing. The bill also authorized further research into the poverty question, including exploration of the feasibility of giving Selective Service examinations to sixteen-year-olds to identify those needing remedial education and training.

Committee Democrats were by this time encountering their own troubles in reaching agreement on the more than twenty proposed compromise amendments. On April 29 they held a lengthy caucus, after which Chairman Powell announced suspension of hearings for a week due to members' "other responsibilities." But the caucuses continued throughout the first week in May. The most troublesome issue was aid to sectarian schools under the community-action programs. The Administration's drafting team had given much thought to this problem, concluding that local programs should not be administered by parochial schools but that their pupils should be included in programs of the public schools. This implied that parochial school pupils would be included through a "shared time" arrangement—a position consistent with HEW's handling of the general school aid problem. But Representative Hugh Carey (D. N.Y.), a Roman Catholic, would not accept such a flat prohibition of funds to parochial schools. Finally, an acceptable compromise was reached under which parochial schools could receive aid for nonsectarian "remedial noncurricular" programs.

Another focus of the discussions was the Title III program of grants to enable nonprofit corporations to buy up land, redevelop it into family farms, and sell it to low-income farm families. Though vigorously defended by Secretary Freeman, this landreform scheme smacked of socialist "collective farming" to many congressmen, Democrats as well as Republicans. Though the committee retained this provision, the Senate struck it from the bill during floor debate. Other provisions that came under close scrutiny included a Title V program to train unemployed fathers, the method of allocating funds among the states, the question of including women in the Job Corps, and the addition of an adult literacy program.

By the second week in May another series of hearings could be scheduled, and on May 26 the full committee approved, by a straight party-line vote (19–11), the Johnson Administration's bill as amended by the Democratic caucus. The committee omitted a Title IV program of incentive loans designed to encourage businesses to hire the hard-core unemployed. But two new programs were added—aid for adult literacy education (Title II) and assistance to migrant farm workers (Title III). And at the insistence of Representative Edith Green (D. Ore.), the Job Corps was opened to women as well as men.

As minor concessions to Republicans and southern Democrats, the committee bill included a formula for allotting funds among the states for certain programs, as well as a requirement that the OEO utilize existing federal agencies wherever possible. Still, every Republican on the committee voted against the bill. They explained that their amendments had been ignored—especially their proposals for deletion of OEO, revamping the domestic Peace Corps, and sponsoring Selective Service examinations for sixteen-year-olds.

Landrum reported a "clean" bill (H.R. 11377) to the House on June 3, petitioning the Committee on Rules for a rule governing floor debate.[13] At a June 16 hearing, Rules Committee Chairman Judge Howard W. Smith (D. Va.) indicated he was "doubtful" about the legislation because it was "too vague and indefinite for me." Smith said he was worried that the Job Corps camps would be coeducational and integrated. As for coeducation, Landrum replied that "common sense" would dictate separate camps for men and women. Under questioning, however, he acknowledged that the camps would probably be integrated. But he stressed that enrollment in the camps would be voluntary, telling Smith that integration was "a matter of law on which neither you nor I can prevail." But Smith allowed the bill to languish before his committee for another six weeks: on July 28 a rule for debate was finally granted by an eight to seven vote.

While the Rules Committee was temporizing, the Senate was considering and approving its version of the poverty bill. The Administration's bill (S. 2642) was introduced by the late Senator Patrick McNamara (D. Mich.) and referred to a select subcommittee of the Labor and Public Welfare Committee. McNamara was chosen by Committee Chairman Lister Hill (D. Ala.) to head the *ad hoc* group. After four days of hearings featuring many of the same witnesses who had appeared earlier before the House groups[14] the full committee revised the measure and on July 7 ordered it reported. The vote was thirteen to two, with only Republicans Barry Goldwater (Ariz.) and John Tower (Tex.) in opposition.

The Senate version was similar to the House committee bill (H.R. 11377), but differed in several minor respects. Three of the Senate committee's contributions were especially noteworthy. Senator Jacob K. Javits (R. N.Y.) successfully sponsored an amendment permitting federal aid to state Job Corps camps.

[13] House Report 1458.
[14] June 17, 18, 23, and 25. U.S. Senate, Committee on Labor and Public Welfare, *Hearings on the Economic Opportunity Act of 1964* (Eighty-eighth Congress, 2d session, 1964).

Several states were then supporting their own Job Corps programs, but neither the Administration nor the House committee bills included an aid provision. Javits' goal, as he put it, was "to encourage and facilitate the full cooperation of the states, and the integration wherever possible of this program with existing state and community public and private agency activities." [15] A second amendment by the committee tightened up House provisions for aid to local groups in the absence of community-wide antipoverty plans. And Senator Goldwater sponsored yet another formula for resolving the church-state issue—an amendment that made its way into the final Act. Other amendments were technical in nature.

The two days of Senate floor debate (July 22 and 23) centered around the issues of states' rights and the agricultural programs. In a series of close roll-call votes, the Administration forces turned back attempts to require the governors' approval of all poverty programs in each state; but two compromise states'-rights amendments sponsored by Senator George Smathers (D. Fla.) were accepted by the bill's floor manager, Senator McNamara. These amendments, which provided for a governor's veto of Job Corps camps and contracts with private agencies, were later accepted by the House and included in the final act.

Two controversial farm provisions were eliminated. By a forty-nine to forty-three roll-call vote, the Senate adopted Senator Frank J. Lausche's (D. Ohio) amendments eliminating the "socialistic" farm development corporations. This vote was the Administration's only real defeat in the Senate. Another controversial Title III provision, direct grants to poverty-stricken farm families, was deleted and a loan program was substituted by Majority Whip Hubert Humphrey (D. Minn.), in a move endorsed by the bill's sponsors.

The Senate passed S. 2642 on July 23 by a sixty-one to thirty-four roll-call vote. Among the northern Democrats, only the conservative Lausche voted "no." The southerners were evenly split, and ten Republicans crossed party lines to vote for the bill. The measure now awaited only final House action.

The three days of House floor debate (August 5-7) had a highly partisan flavor. Goodell charged that the Administration was

[15] U.S. Senate, Committee on Labor and Public Welfare, *Report on S. 2642* (S. Rept. 1218. Eighty-eighth Congress, 2d session, 1964), p. 87.

subjecting members to "unprecedented pressure" to gain votes, and other Republicans noted that they had been coerced. "We have been blackjacked, gagged, threatened, and bulldozed into accepting something that we know is not good," Frelinghuysen declared. For their part, Democrats accused Republican leaders of instructing their members to oppose the bill without even reading it.[16]

Both sides attempted to lure southern votes. Republican floor managers attempted to characterize the OEO's powers as an invasion of states' rights. The bill's proponents made a concession to this argument by offering a floor amendment permitting governors to veto community-action projects. Not all southerners were placated by this action. Referring to the "integrated camps" of the Job Corps, Judge Smith declared: "I want to say to any southerners who plan to vote for this bill, you are implementing the civil rights bill that you opposed." Landrum, the bill's floor manager, responded by describing the measure as "the most conservative I've ever seen."

A subsidiary issue was raised during the final day's debate when Ayres mentioned the name of Adam Yarmolinsky, who "is really running this show under . . . Shriver." Yarmolinsky's name was calculated to provoke southern ire, for as Special Assistant to Defense Secretary Robert McNamara he had helped draw up a 1963 directive aimed at off-base discrimination against Negro servicemen stationed in the South. Now the Administration was faced with a quick decision, for it was widely assumed that Yarmolinsky would serve as Shriver's deputy in the OEO. The Administration felt it needed southern votes, and a number of powerful southerners were pressing Shriver to sacrifice Yarmolinsky. So Shriver gave the word, and Landrum—with Yarmolinsky sitting, unaware, in the House gallery—announced: "I have been told on the highest authority that not only will he not be appointed, but that he will not be considered if he is recommended for a place in this agency." [17] It seemed a simple concession at the time, but many never forgave Shriver for making it.

[16] The House floor debate is found in *Congressional Record* (Eighty-eighth Congress, 2d session; August 5, 6, 7, 1964, daily edition), pp. 17610-17652, 17672-17739, 17932-18025.
[17] *Congressional Record* (August 7, 1964, daily edition), p. 17996.

The outcome of the debate became a foregone conclusion on August 7, when Judge Smith's motion to "strike the enacting clause" (a routine motion to kill a bill) was defeated. The Smith motion first carried by a 170 to 135 teller vote, but the Administration hustled its forces to the floor to win the roll-call, 225 to 197. After this vote, the Democratic floor leadership imposed tight reins on debate. In order to avoid a conference with the Senate, Landrum substituted for the committee bill (H.R. 11377) an amended version of the Senate-passed bill (S. 2642). Before the final voting on August 8, Frelinghuysen moved to recommit the bill to the committee with instructions to report out the Republican version; but this motion was defeated by a 295 to 177 party-line roll-call vote. Then, on final passage, the vote was 226-185. Every northern Democrat was recorded in favor of the bill, along with forty southerners and twenty-two Republicans.

Several amendments of some significance were accepted during the House debate. In addition to the Senate's gubernatorial veto, the House approved without debate an amendment by John Bell Williams (D. Miss.) requiring loyalty oaths or disclaimer affidavits of all aid recipients. In addition, two GOP amendments were adopted: one preventing solicitation of funds for political purposes from aid recipients, and a "conservationist" amendment requiring that at least forty percent of Job Corps enrollees be assigned to conservation camps. [This latter amendment was sponsored by Representative John P. Saylor (Pa.), ranking Republican on the House Interior Committee.]

Three days later, the Senate approved the House changes by a voice vote, and the bill was sent to the White House for President Johnson's signature.

In retrospect, the congressional contributions can hardly be viewed as of major importance to the Economic Opportunity Act. The governor's veto, though used only a few times, gained prominence after Alabama's Governor George Wallace used it as a weapon to substitute his own "lily white" poverty organization for an integrated group that had been established earlier. Governors of both parties regarded the veto as a protection for their own political position, and opposed its elimination in the 1965 amendments to the Act. But in light of the larger exclusion of state governments, and the revolutionary provision for "maximum feasible participation" by the poor (not discussed on Capitol Hill), the gubernatorial veto paled in importance as an instrument for preserving established federal relationships.

Perhaps the most significant congressional contributions were the addition of three new programs: aid for migrant farmers, an adult literacy education program, and an unrelated "rider" authorizing indemnity payments to dairy farmers whose milk had been ordered removed from the market by the federal government because of the presence of chemical residues. In addition, Congress vetoed two items in the Administration's draft bill: the Title IV business-incentive loans, and the "socialistic" farm land corporations provision in Title III. The other controversies that occupied the bulk of the legislators' time represented typical (though not necessarily trivial) "political" concerns on Capitol Hill: aid to church-related schools, the inclusion of women, solicitations for partisan political advantage, and loyalty to the nation. The remainder of the congressional amendments were in the nature of minor technical adjustments of one sort or another.

Conclusion: Executive Legislation

Traditionally Americans have paid allegiance to the constitutional dictum that "all legislative powers . . . shall be vested in a Congress of the United States" (Art. I, Sec. 1). Yet an increasingly powerful springboard for legislative authority is another of the Constitution's provisions: the President "shall from time to time give to the Congress information of the state of the Union, and recommend to their considerations such measures as he shall judge necessary and expedient" (Art. II, Sec. 3).

Primarily a twentieth century phenomenon, the emergence of the President as "chief legislator" has received almost continuous attention from commentators since the era of Theodore Roosevelt. Until well after World War II, the President's legislative program was apparently a casual affair in which the Chief Executive merely lent his support to a few of the many proposals floating around Capitol Hill. Gradually the President's legislative role became institutionalized, not only for setting the congressional agenda, but also for proposing the specific content of bills.[18]

[18] See Richard Neustadt's articles, "Presidency and Legislation," *American Political Science Review*, XLVIII (September 1954), pp. 641-671, and

Until 1961, the fiction was observed that the President himself did not sign the draft bills sent to Congress, and friendly members were solicited to introduce the Administration's measures as their own. After 1961, the President's signature began appearing on draft bills, even though formal introduction must still be by a member of Congress. President Johnson has attempted to institute long-range planning of legislative programs, an indication that presidential legislation has not reached its final stage of development.

The President's ability to function as chief legislator stems from the capacity of the executive branch to articulate and resolve many, if not all, of the demands being pressed upon government in a particular policy area. In the modern "service state," the vast and diverse bureaucratic apparatus offers to outside interests a multiplicity of effective access points to public policy. These interests often find that their viewpoints are faithfully represented by the executive agencies with which they normally do business. When this phenomenon is multiplied, the interplay of outside clienteles and executive agencies produces a process of negotiation, bargaining, and conflict among the various agencies and groups.

An Administration bill may therefore be viewed as a treaty among the several interested parties that is negotiated through lateral bargaining within the executive branch. If the conflicts remain unresolved, the President, or his political advisors, may step in to effectuate a bargain or to select one alternative over the others. If the issue is too low in priority to warrant direct intervention, however, it may lie dormant until some kind of bargain can be reached. The Economic Opportunity Act of 1964 was a classic case of executive legislation. The bargaining process was originally sponsored and stimulated by the White House, acting through the Council of Economic Advisers. When the Council (working with the Budget Bureau) proved unable to conclude the negotiations, the President intervened by appointing Sargent Shriver to act as a broker among the quarreling interests. With the force of the President behind him, Shriver was able to resolve the conflicts and hammer out a multipurpose bill.

The classic legislative function—bringing political combatants together to hear their claims, and then resolving these

---

XLIX (September 1955), pp. 930-1021. The narrative is continued in Neustadt's "Politicians and Bureaucrats," in David B. Truman (ed.), *The Congress and America's Future* (Englewood Cliffs, N.J.: Prentice-Hall, 1965).

claims—is becoming, in the complex modern polity, less and less the exclusive domain of Congress. Huntington's conclusion concerning decision-making in military strategy applies, in varying degrees, to other policy areas:

> No congressional committee is competent to [select military programs], not because it lacks the technical knowledge, but because it lacks the legal authority and political capability to bring together all these conflicting interests, balance one off against another, and arrive at a compromise or decision. . . . No congressional body gets more than a partial view of the interests involved.[19]

Military and foreign policy decision-making is particularly troublesome for Congress, because the interested parties are almost without exception embodied in executive agencies. In domestic policy-making, Congress has typically shown more dexterity in articulating and integrating the relevant interests. We have already seen this pattern in the history of the Area Redevelopment Act of 1961. Yet the case of the war on poverty demonstrates the full potentialities of the "executive" pattern in domestic as well as foreign and military policy-making. And it must be observed that this pattern is becoming more the rule than the exception.

The ability of the executive to perform the traditional legislative functions has profound consequences for the future of Congress. As Arthur F. Bentley foresaw in 1908,

> If the group interests work out a fair and satisfying adjustment through the legislature, then the executive sinks in prominence . . . when the adjustment is not perfected in the legislature, then the executive rises in strength to do the work . . . the growth of executive discretion is therefore a phase of the group process.[20]

According to constitutional theory, political bargains will be struck by the legislature; executive agencies ratify these bargains when the President signs them into law and when bureaucrats act to implement them. But when the bargains are struck within the

---

[19] Samuel Huntington, *The Common Defense* (New York: Columbia University Press, 1961), pp. 131-132. It might be added, however, that in many cases Congress also lacks "technical knowledge," at least in comparison with the superior information-gathering and processing facilities of the bureaucracy.
[20] Arthur F. Bentley, *The Process of Government* (Chicago: University of Chicago Press, 1908), p. 359.

executive branch, these institutional roles tend to be reversed. Congress becomes a ratifier, modifier, a lobbyist, and even a court of appeals for policies originating in the executive. It is this pattern that we have seen at work in the origins of the war on poverty, and that causes greatest fear among those with a stake in the future vitality of the legislative branch.

CONGRESS IN THE YEARS AHEAD | 8

As an institution, Congress is neither unchanging nor uncontroversial in its interplay with the various forces of the larger American political system. Uniquely exposed and intensely political, Congress is subject to the combined respect and denigration with which Americans view their elected officials. Since World War II Congress has come under increasing criticism from both scholars and citizens for its inefficient procedures, its undemocratic structure, and its political shortcomings, whether real or imagined. Together with the rising executive participation in legislative functions (discussed in the preceding chapter), these criticisms have called into question the very survival of our national legislature as a viable instrument of policy-making.

In recent decades institutional changes have taken place on Capitol Hill. The landmark Legislative Reorganization Act of 1946, which was preceded by extensive investigations by a joint committee chaired by Senator Robert M. La Follette, Jr. (Progressive. Wis.) and then-Representative A. S. Mike Monroney (D. Okla.), produced ambitious innovations in congressional practices, especially in additional staff resources and reduction of the number of standing committees. Numerous minor innovations since World War II have been in response to the increasing work load of individual members. The unique political complexion of the Eighty-ninth Congress produced a number of changes in both houses. (Some of these are discussed in Chapter 4.) A few of these innovations were no doubt transitory and reflected simply unusually large Democratic majorities; but other changes promised to leave their imprint on Capitol Hill long after the Eighty-ninth Congress passed into history.

One of the more notable creations in 1965 was the second Joint Committee on the Organization of the Congress, which, as we have noted in Chapter 4, was included in the Democratic Study Group's reform package. The Joint Committee's work provides a typical illustration of the political dimensions of congressional reformism and will serve to open our consideration of the future of Congress. Yet its necessarily cautious and limited approach did not resolve the fundamental controversies over Congress. As the committee completed its work, many thoughtful observers were wondering aloud whether Congress, if left to its own designs, could ever hope to reverse the antiparliamentary forces at large in the last half of the twentieth century. (The impact of these forces is discussed in Chapter 1.)

THE JOINT COMMITTEE AND THE "REFORM MOSAIC"

The senior senator from Oklahoma rapped his gavel briskly and called the Joint Committee to order. For the second time in twenty years, Senator Monroney was serving as cochairman of a major effort by Congress to examine its own rules and procedures. Following this initial session on May 10, 1965, the old Supreme Court Chamber in the Capitol's Senate wing was witness to three months of hearings featuring senators, congressmen, scholars, interest-group spokesmen, and government officials. "From time to time," Monroney observed in opening the hearings, "pressures for reform within and without the halls of Congress have caused us to stop and take a searching look at the legislative edifice. The result has normally been a strengthened and revitalized institution, better able to cope with the myriad problems of its times." [1]

Monroney's strategy of reform had been indicated the preceding November, when he called a press conference to announce

---

[1] U.S. Congress, Joint Committee on the Organization of the Congress, *Hearings, I* (Eighty-ninth Congress, 1st Session), p. 4.

his intention of introducing a resolution for a successor to the LaFollette-Monroney committee. He spoke particularly of the appropriations process and showed reporters the piles of weighty documents that had to be digested by legislators in reviewing the annual federal budget. Congress follows "an obsolete system inherited from the Gay Nineties," he declared, comparing present procedures to "a group of farmers sitting around a cracker barrel and a pot-bellied stove and trying to run a $100 billion business." Monroney also said he wanted to study changes in scheduling and in committee structures and work loads.[2] His remarks did not betray the "public-policy" bias of many legislators who are often prominently identified with reformism. He told the reporters, for example: "We will, I hope, not start out with one single purpose to achieve a single objective. Such an approach, or suspicion thereof, has frustrated many well-intentioned efforts of the past to modernize Congress." Stressing the theme of "modernizing" Congress, Monroney indicated that a piecemeal approach would be needed to attract votes for reorganization. He was fond of pointing out, for example, that the 1946 act was approved partly because it was accompanied by a pay-raise bill desired by most members.

Many reform-minded congressmen, especially the liberals, found this approach too cautious. This difference of opinion came to the surface during the brief but spirited floor debate on Monroney's proposal (S. Con. Res. 2). For, according to the resolution, the new Joint Committee, like its 1945 predecessor, was to be prohibited from recommending changes in House or Senate rules. This limitation was supported by the Senate Rules and Administration Committee, which reported out the proposal. Monroney argued that contentious rules fights, such as that over the Senate's cloture rule, should be avoided. "The intent of this resolution," he told the Senate, "is to seek solutions to the problems of Congress on which there is a consensus that something should be done."[3]

Many of the changes Monroney had in mind, such as reformulation of committee jurisdictions, obviously involved amending the rules; but these alterations could be stimulated by the Joint Committee's work (as occurred in 1945-1946) and then be

[2] *New York Times*, November 26, 1964, p. 42.
[3] The Senate debate over S. Con. Res. 2 is found in *Congressional Record* (Eighty-ninth Congress, 1st Session; March 8-9, 1965, daily edition), pp. 4223-4429.

processed by the two houses separately. Monroney's sense of propriety directed him to honor the constitutional provision that each house be the judge of its own rules, though he explained that the Joint Committee could still hear testimony concerning rules changes. Several senators, led by Joseph S. Clark (D. Pa.), charged that reform would be meaningful only if the committee were free to probe what Clark called "our present iniquitous rules." "I find myself unable to agree," Clark declared, "that the resolution as he [Monroney] has caused it to be drawn would accomplish what the body of the resolution purports to do." Those who drafted the resolution, he continued, "do not wish to put their support behind any investigation . . . which might conceivably overthrow the balance of power in the Senate." He went on to estimate that the limitation would cut out two-thirds to three-fourths of the work that the committee ought to accomplish. During the Eighty-eighth Congress, Clark himself had proposed no less than twenty-seven rules changes, and "not one of these . . . changes in the rules . . . could be the subject of recommendation by the joint committee under the resolution of the Senator from Oklahoma."

Clark even offered to exclude specifically the Senate cloture rule from the Joint Committee's jurisdiction—though Clark's colleague, Clifford Case (R. N.J.) objected that even this limitation would shackle the committee. Clark's general position was supported by statements from Jacob K. Javits (R. N.Y.) and Wayne Morse (D. Ore.), in addition to Case. But Clark's amendment to the Monroney resolution was defeated on March 9 by a twenty-nine to fifty-eight roll-call vote.

Yielding to the DSG's demands for a Joint Committee, Speaker McCormack meanwhile designated Representative Ray J. Madden (D. Ind.) to sponsor the Monroney resolution in the House (H. Con. Res. 4). Two days after the Senate adopted the Joint Committee plan, the House approved it quickly by a voice vote.

The committee's twelve members (six from each chamber divided equally by party) illustrated again the complex political considerations that conditioned its work. The members were designated by the House and Senate majority and minority leadership. Madden, who led the House delegation and was named cochairman, was chosen by Speaker McCormack. His credentials were that he was a liberal and a member of the House Rules Committee, which would have to pass on the Joint Committee's recommendations. Another member of Rules, Representative Richard Bolling (D. Mo.), had been more prominently identified with reform than Madden; but Bolling had opposed McCormack's succession to the Speakership three years earlier, had written a book containing slighting comments about McCormack,[4] and in any event was distrusted by conservatives. The only House delegate with a long-term interest in reorganization was Representative Thomas B. Curtis (R. Mo.), who since 1961 had been a leader of a quiet bipartisan study group on the subject. The other members chosen by Speaker McCormack and Minority Leader Gerald Ford (R. Mich.) represented faithfully the various ideological viewpoints in the House: liberal Ken Hechler (D. W. Va.), moderates Jack Brooks (D. Tex.) and Robert P. Griffin (R. Mich.), and conservative Durward G. Hall (R. Mo.). Many "reformist" members were deliberately passed over, and the DSG played no role in the appointments.

Monroney, who headed the six-man Senate contingent, was a moderate who was acceptable to conservatives as well as liberals. Case was named to the committee, but Clark was passed over. Other members from the Senate were John J. Sparkman (D. Ala.), former DSG chairman Lee Metcalf (D. Mont.), Karl E. Mundt (R. S.D.), and J. Caleb Boggs (R. Del.). Mundt had served on the LaFollette-Monroney Committee as a congressman.

Selection of the committee's four professional staff aides was divided among the four delegations. Monroney designated a young Oklahoma attorney to be chief counsel, while the House Democrats picked Professor Nicholas A. Masters of Pennsylvania State University—the only political scientist on the staff. Two other staff members served the Senate and House Republican delegations, respectively. A ceiling of $150,000 for expenditures was placed on the committee's operations through January 1966, when a supplemental appropriation was voted to allow the committee to finish its work. The dispersion of committee assignments and the shortage of funds were not conducive to the coordinated research and staff work that had marked the LaFollette-Monroney Committee's operations.

Starting off under these handicaps, the committee organized itself and inaugurated hearings on May 10. During 31 public ses-

[4] See Bolling's *House Out of Order* (New York: Dutton, 1965), esp. p. 72 ff.

sions, testimony was heard from 83 members of Congress, 19 scholars, 26 interest-group spokesmen, and 9 government officials —137 witnesses in all. "I think just about every reasonable and constructive idea for the reorganization of Congress—plus a few silly ones—is in our files," Monroney reported.

On July 21, 1966, the Joint Committee was ready to announce the results of its deliberations. Nearly fifty proposals received the unanimous backing of the committee, which immediately turned to the problem of incorporating the reforms into an omnibus "Legislative Reorganization Act of 1966." [5] The committee hoped to ask for permission to report its bill directly to the floor of each house before the close of the Eighty-ninth Congress.

Perhaps the most publicized of the Joint Committee's recommendations was its "committee bill of rights," which included: recognition of the majority's right to call meetings and report bills in the event that the chairman refused to do so; more frequent use of open hearings; broadcasting and telecasting of hearings at the committee's discretion; participation of all committee members in preparation of reports; and elimination of proxy voting in committees. Three staff positions on each committee would be allotted to the minority party, upon its request. An additional staff member, designated as a "review specialist," would be assigned to each standing committee to handle oversight functions. Such reform proposals were obvious attempts to deal with problems of the committee system discussed in this volume—for example, the sometimes arbitrary powers of chairmen (see the Senate Banking and Currency Committee cases in Chapters 5 and 6), and the problem of minority-party rights (as in the instance of the House Education and Labor Committee, Chapter 7). Another committee-oriented reform suggested by the Joint Committee was the creation of new Committees on Education within each house. These new committees would assume jurisdiction over many mat-

[5] U.S. Congress, Joint Committee on the Organization of the Congress, *Organization of Congress* (Senate Report 1414, 89th Congress, 2nd session, 1966). Though the Committee's recommendations were unanimous, the Republican delegates from the House filed supplemental views urging, among other things: minority party control of an investigatory committee when the same party controls both houses of Congress and the Presidency; curtailment of lobbying by the Executive branch; disclosures of assets and income by Members; and provisions relating to financing of political campaigns. Representative Hechler (D. W.Va.) also called for reforms going beyond the report—including provision for electronic voting for roll-call votes.

ters now handled by the Senate Committee on Labor and Public
Welfare, and by the House Committee on Education and Labor,
in addition to other education matters now under the jurisdictions
of other committees.

From an extensive study of Congressional work loads and
schedules, the Joint Committee proposed to limit committee assignments and chairmanships. It also recommended that no
senator serve on more than one of the Appropriations, Armed
Services, Finance, and Foreign Relations Committees.

Fiscal controls and congressional review of the budget were
also the subjects of numerous proposals. Automatic data processing was advocated to expand the amount of budget information
available to members. Specific alterations in the presentation of
the budget were also suggested. Provision would be made for the
appearance of executive officers before the appropriations committees within 30 days after the submission of the budget, to discuss overall budget guidelines. The appropriations committees
were enjoined to expand their study of multi-agency programs and
to hold more hearings. Now operating units within the General
Accounting Office were urged to assist committees in program
evaluation. Such proposals, and others, were indicative of concern
over failure to perform adequately the oversight function (see
Chapter 5).

One of the more far-reaching suggestions was for the creation of a Joint Committee on Congressional Operations to conduct continuing studies of the organization of Congress and to
protect legislative prerogatives. Other proposals included: an enlarged Legislative Reference Service (to be called the "Legislative
Research Service"); a five-day work week for legislative business;
a recess during the month of August; and changes in the content
and format of the *Congressional Record*.

It is clear from this listing that the Joint Committee's report was a laundry-list of relatively detailed and specific items. The
Committee did not, predictably, strike at the issues dear to the
hearts of many dedicated congressional reformers—the seniority system, party responsibility, filibusters in the Senate, and so forth.
While conceding that some of the recommendations were "very
useful," the liberally oriented *Washington Post*, for example,
editorialized that the report as a whole was "disappointing" because it failed to "touch the major weaknesses in the power struc-

ture of Congress." [6] In light of the Joint Committee's limited mandate and broad ideological mixture—not to mention its limited time and resources—the omissions were understandable. Indeed, the tone of the report reflected perfectly the piecemeal approach of its cochairman, Senator Monroney. "A lot of little reforms add up to a big reform," he remarked during one of the hearings. "If we are going to get an up-to-date, modern Congress, it will be a mosaic you build from lots of little improvements." [7] Neither chamber, however, in the rush of last-minute business during the closing days of the Eighty-ninth Congress, acted upon the Joint Committee's recommendations. Further action and maneuvering on congressional reform was therefore put over until the new Ninetieth Congress convened after the 1966 mid-term elections.

THE CRISIS OF CONGRESSIONAL GOVERNMENT

Such congressional efforts at piecemeal reform, necessarily circumscribed by political exigencies, fail to satisfy those observers who believe that Congress is in need of radical reconstruction if it is to survive. In the face of what they have diagnosed as severe hardening of the arteries, reformers have bombarded Congress with all manner of nostrums. No less than 316 separate reorganization proposals were offered during the first 26 days of the Joint Committee's 1965 hearings. Many of the proposals were surrounded by the urgent yet unarticulated premise that the very future of legislative institutions is in the balance. As veteran legislator F. Edward Hèbert (D. La.) was in the habit of declaring, "Every day in every way the power of Congress is being diluted."

This concern over the status and functions of Congress is indeed ironic, in view of the past glories of legislative institutions. "The energy of legislatures," Sir Henry Sumner Maine wrote one hundred years ago, "is the prime characteristic of modern societies." In the United States, the framers of the Constitution clearly viewed Congress as the keystone of the democracy: It was no accident that Article I of the Constitution is devoted to enunciating the powers of Congress. Reflecting upon the prolonged period of

---

[6] *Washington Post*, July 23, 1966.
[7] *Joint Committee Hearings*, I, 75.

legislative ascendancy following the Civil War, Woodrow Wilson concluded that "Congress is the dominant, nay, the irresistible power of the federal system. . . . In a country which governs itself by means of a public meeting, a Congress, or a parliament," he stated, "the only real leadership in governmental affairs must be the legislative." [8]

Hardly any observer in the mid-twentieth century would describe Congress in terms of its "irresistible power." Its decline is universally commented upon—by friends as well as detractors, and by members themselves as well as by academic observers. In 1964 Senator Clark, one of the most articulate proponents of thoroughgoing reform, published a book entitled *Congress: The Sapless Branch*.[9] The pessimistic assessment of George Galloway, written on the eve of the Legislative Reorganization Act's passage in 1946, would be accepted by most observers:

> Overworked and underpaid, often lampooned by the press and unfairly criticized by the thoughtless, our national legislature had fallen from its once high estate. . . . With Congress overwhelmed by its great responsibilities, operating under its ancient ritual, the streamlined age . . . seemed to have passed it by.[10]

As we have explained in Chapter 1, however, it would probably be incorrect to assert that congressional powers have declined in any absolute sense. The twentieth-century Congress involves itself in a host of governmental functions that in earlier days were performed by local or private entities—or else not performed at all. As President Kennedy was fond of recalling, the legislative giants of the nineteenth century—the Clays, Calhouns, and Websters—could afford to devote a whole generation or more to refining and debating the few great controversies of the Republic. The contemporary legislator cannot take such a leisurely approach; he finds himself beset daily by a staggering number and range of public problems, both large and small. And the rising size, complexity, educational level, and mass media exposure of constituents have greatly increased the volume of communications handled by congressional offices (a phenomenon noted in our discussion of the

---

[8] See his *Congressional Government* (New York: Meridian, 1955), esp. p. 23.
[9] New York: Harper & Row.
[10] George B. Galloway, *Congress at the Crossroads* (New York: Crowell, 1946), pp. 5-6.

work load of members in Chapter 3). The quantity and diversity of legislative business create their own frustrations for Congress, to be sure; and it is debatable whether congressional involvement is as decisive as it once was. But the fact of this involvement itself cannot be questioned.

It is in relation to the executive branch that the influence of Congress is most in jeopardy. Few would disagree with the judgment offered by Edward S. Corwin that, "taken by and large, the history of the presidency is a history of aggrandizement." [11] And in the past generation, a quiet constitutional revolution has resulted in executive leadership in the initiation of legislation. The depressed-areas legislation, discussed in Chapter 6, was noteworthy in that the major impetus for its passage came originally from congressional representatives of the depressed areas. For six years these members sparred with the Eisenhower Administration, which evolved more modest measures of its own and vetoed two "Democratic" bills. With the advent of a Democratic Administration committed to passage of depressed-areas legislation, Senator Douglas and his colleagues were faced with a quite different problem. For, once passage was virtually assured, the executive branch assumed leadership in laying out specific provisions—sometimes in opposition to Douglas' objectives.

If the Area Redevelopment Act illustrated the influence of executive leadership in a congressionally originated issue, the Economic Opportunity Act of 1964 demonstrated the full dimensions of executive "legislation." Here the intricate processes of interest articulation and consensus-building were concentrated almost wholly within the executive branch. The stream of individuals and group representatives that poured through the Peace Corps Building during the Shriver Task Force's deliberations constituted a legislative process in almost every sense of the term. Congress quickly ratified the resulting package, understanding little and altering less. This case is extreme, perhaps, but it suggests the directions that executive initiation of legislation can take.

Many of the controversies raging over the future of Congress relate to its ability to compete with the executive establishment in participating in the complex policy-making tasks of our age. Can Congress effectively process the specialized economic and

[11] Edward S. Corwin, *The President: Office and Powers*, 4th ed. (New York: New York University Press, 1957), pp. 29-30.

sociological data that went into the drafting of the Economic Opportunity Act? Further, is Congress capable even of providing intelligent supervision over those who are implementing the Act's revolutionary programs? Various schools of congressional critics are inclined to offer differing answers to these questions.

Those who would answer in the negative include many who welcome the growth of executive power. Two clusters of values are probably at work here. First, those who profess a preference for executive approaches to issues are motivated in part by "liberal" policy considerations. Contemporary Presidents have become spokesmen for the forces of urbanism, minority rights, social welfare legislation, and internationalism—policy values typically associated with "liberalism." When viewed alongside the presidency, Congress to many liberals appears reactionary, parochial, small-townish, and an impediment to the "progressive" policy objectives of the executive. James M. Burns contends, for example, that the congressional power system places leadership in the hands of "those members . . . least aware of the problems of industrial society and least equipped to deal with them." [12]

Preference for executive institutions may also be a function of one's stylistic approach to problem-solving. Bureaucratic institutions, at least in theory, represent the application of organized rationality to public problems. To those who are attracted to planning and orderly structure, therefore, the executive branch is far more congenial than Congress. Many observers, schooled in the management techniques of large-scale organizations, look with undisguised horror upon what they interpret as the messy inefficiency of Capitol Hill. As an overtly political body, Congress frequently engages in symbolic or even ritualistic behavior to facilitate the processes of conflict resolution. Coupled with the intensive personalism found on Capitol Hill, these practices are jarring to efficiency-minded critics, who tend to overlook the ad hoc, political character of such executive bargaining processes as were involved in producing the Economic Opportunity Act of 1964 (see Chapter 7).

Such considerations as these motivate many critics to advocate executive dominance in decision-making. "The executive is the

[12] James M. Burns, *Congress on Trial* (New York: Harper & Row, 1949), p. 59.

active power in the state, the asking and the proposing power," writes Walter Lippmann, a well-known proponent of this view. In turn, Congress must be acknowledged as "the consenting power, the petitioning, the approving and the criticizing, the accepting and the refusing power." [13] This viewpoint usually emphasizes the oversight function of Congress, as expressed in the 1946 Legislative Reorganization Act's injunction that congressional committees exercise "continuous watchfulness" over executive agencies. To assure that legislators do not "meddle" in the implementation of programs, however, it is usually specified that congressional review should be directed to generalized policy decisions rather than to details.

Most advocates of executive leadership are confident that history is on their side. "The cause of the opponents of a strong Presidency," Clinton Rossiter writes with finality, "is ill-starred because they cannot win a war against American history. The strong Presidency is the product of events that cannot be undone and of forces that continue to roll." [14] The post-World War II policy environment, it must be conceded, lends impressive confirmation to this interpretation. The past few decades have witnessed a new ascendancy of foreign affairs and national defense in public discussions and federal expenditures. Presidential initiative in these areas is clearly indicated by the Constitution and validated by historical experience. If these concerns are enhanced by events, then the President and the executive establishment are enhanced in turn. An era of constant semicrisis has merely served to reinforce this historical tendency, because every contemporary President is required to be "strong."

Many congressmen and senators are willing to accept the implications of this interpretation, at least in terms of presidential initiation of legislation. "It is the natural thing," declares Representative Chet Holifield (D. Calif.), "for the executive branch to take the initiative, to make proposals and to present us with programs." [15] As we have seen, executive initiation of legislation provides Congress with an agenda—something it cannot easily provide

[13] Walter Lippmann, *The Public Philosophy* (Boston: Little, Brown, 1954), p. 30.
[14] Clinton Rossiter, *The American Presidency* (New York: New American Library, 1956), p. 151.
[15] *Joint Committee Hearings*, II, p. 185.

for itself. And congressional leaders are quick to criticize the President when he fails to provide adequate leadership, just as they are equally prone to complain about executive "pressuring."

Proponents of executive dominance maintain that the legislature's prime task is to ratify, modify, and legitimize executive initiatives. However Congress disposes of these proposals, it should act upon them. It should also supervise and oversee administration of programs. And perhaps at the fringes of policy-making, it can provide fresh initiatives of its own. In terms of specific institutional changes, this implies more assurances that presidential proposals will be acted upon, and wider latitude for the executive in implementing laws. It may also involve efforts to nationalize the party system and to shape congressional constituencies more in the image of the presidential constituency—through strengthening national party bodies and reapportioning legislative districts on a strict population basis.

While fascination with executive institutions may be characteristic of the liberal intelligentsia, it is by no means the only viewpoint extant in the current debate over congressional functioning. An increasing number of observers, concerned over the attrition of legislative influence, hold that Congress should exercise more, rather than less, power than it now does.

The defenders of Congress come in many shapes and sizes, and range from those who talk in terms of reinstating "congressional supremacy" to those who are merely interested in restoring the constitutional balance of power. As a group, they are as concerned over Congress' "give-away" of power as the liberals are critical of its "obstructionism." James Burnham has declared that

> What the American government system now needs is
> . . . a very considerably strengthened Congress: strengthened in the political sense of gaining (regaining, in historical fact) increased relative weight within the political equilibrium. On this assumption . . . the performance of Congress will be judged much less than stellar.[16]

[16] James Burnham, *Congress and the American Tradition* (Chicago: Henry Regnery, 1959), p. 276. A somewhat more optimistic assessment from a similar ideological vantage-point is found in Willmoore Kendall's *The Conservative Affirmation* (Chicago: Regnery, 1963), chapter 2.

The decline of Congress, so this theory runs, can be attributed fundamentally to the advent of the sprawling welfare state. The compelling popular image of the President, together with academic and journalistic carping at Congress, have conspired to dissolve public support for legislative institutions. Congress, moreover, has failed to "stiffen its spine" against intrusions upon legislative prerogatives by the executive and the judiciary.

The pro-Congress forces look to Capitol Hill for a reversal of the long-term trends of centralism and paternalism. Congress seems to them to be the repository of such policy values as free enterprise, states' rights, intellectual and religious conservatism, nationalism, and rural and small-town interests. They have identified executive ascendancy as the enemy of these values. "As Congress is the bulwark of [the Constitutional] system," a spokesman of the Americans for Constitutional Action asserted, "the goal of the socialist planners is to be won by rendering Congress ineffectual." [17]

Congressmen and senators have reasons quite apart from ideology for resisting the dissolution of their power and influence. Many are understandably frustrated, when, upon arriving in Washington, they discover that their expectations for exerting influence upon policy-making are not met. Thus Senator Abraham Ribicoff (D. Conn.), certainly no conservative in policy matters, complained bitterly in 1964 that Congress had "surrendered its rightful leadership in the law-making process to the White House." [18] And upon taking over as chairman of the House Armed Services Committee, Representative Mendel Rivers (D. S.C.) had imprinted on the dais in the committee chambers those constitutional phrases giving Congress the power to raise and equip armies, so that executive witnesses would be mindful of his committee's prerogatives.

Advocates of congressional power thus stress revitalizing the national legislature as the prime representative of the diverse interests of the nation, and as the formulator of national policies. Congress should not be reduced to saying "yes" or "no" to executive initiatives, because law-making is a complex process through which numerous and shifting minority claims must be digested. Neither speed, nor efficiency, nor "passing a lot of laws" are indica-

[17] *Joint Committee Hearings*, VII, p. 1090.
[18] *Saturday Evening Post*, March 21, 1964, p. 10.

tive of congressional effectiveness in performing these functions. Even the refusal to pass laws may often be a positive act. When Congress acts, however, the executive should faithfully implement. Thus, legislative mandates should be as precise as possible, and oversight must be detailed and continuous. The courts must likewise be prevented from usurping lawmaking functions. Specific reforms that will maximize congressional influence in lawmaking, representation, and oversight are advocated.

These diverse prescriptions for congressional functioning indicate that there is a lack of agreement concerning the appropriate future role of our national legislature. This absence of consensus is perhaps to be expected in a complex society marked by numerous and often conflicting demands upon the institutions of government. Those who urge an interventionist, problem-solving role upon the federal government will desire a legislature far different from that seen by those who advocate a passivist, consensus-building government. "In point of fact," one eminent student concludes, "the struggle over the powers of the Presidency as against Congress . . . is only a secondary campaign in a political war over the future of America." [19]

The pervasiveness of the debate over Congress extends far beyond substantive policy controversies, however. A person's stance in the debate over Congress calls into play his assumptions concerning the nature of political man, the style and behavior of political institutions, and the priorities of traditional normative theory, and can be answered only through an insightful examination of one's own political values. So long as the twentieth century continues to produce confusion and conflict over these values, the national legislature will remain at the center of a prolonged institutional dialogue.

[19] Clinton Rossiter, *The American Presidency* (New York: New American Library, 1956), pp. 150-151.

FOR FURTHER READING

Reflecting the national legislature's importance, vitality, and complexity, the literature on Congress is rich and varied. No attempt is made here to mention all the books and articles on Congress. This listing is selective. It presents some of the best literature categorized to permit the student to identify materials on topics of particular interest. Books available in paperback have been marked with an asterisk (*).

GENERAL DISCUSSIONS OF CONGRESS

Probably the best short and analytic discussion of Congress is David B. Truman (ed.), *Congress and America's Future* (Englewood Cliffs, N.J.: Prentice-Hall, 1965).* This is a collection of essays in which respected contemporary scholars analyze why Congress functions as it does and assess the prospects for congressional reorganization.

Among the better texts on Congress are William J. Keefe and Morris S. Ogul, *The American Legislative Process: Congress and the States* (Englewood Cliffs, N.J.: Prentice-Hall, 1964); Malcolm E. Jewell and Samuel C. Patterson, *The Legislative Process in the United States* (New York: Random House, 1966); George B. Galloway, *The Legislative Process in Congress* (New York: Crowell, 1953), a comprehensive institutional discussion; Bertram M. Gross, *The Legislative Struggle: A Study in Social Combat* (New York: Mc-Graw-Hill, 1953), an analysis from the perspective of the group struggle; and Roland Young, *The American Congress* (New York: Harper & Row, 1958), a functional analysis. A concise and critical interpretation of the best literature on Congress written in a readable and personalized style is Nelson W. Polsby's *Congress and the President* (Englewood Cliffs, N.J.: Prentice-Hall, 1964).* Theodore Lowi's *Legislative Politics U.S.A.* (Boston: Little, Brown, 1965)* contains selected readings dealing with the role of the legislature in the political process and important phases of congressional life. A collection of readings for advanced students is *Legislative Behavior: A Reader in Theory and Research* (New York: Free Press, 1959) edited by John C. Wahlke and Heinz Eulau. *The Legislative System: Explorations in Legislative Behavior* by John C. Wahlke, William Buchanan, Heinz Eulau and LeRoy C. Ferguson (New York: Wiley, 1962) utilizes role theory to provide fresh insights into legislative behavior. The focus for this ground-breaking study is state legislatures, but its findings have applicability to Congress.

First published in 1885, Woodrow Wilson's *Congressional Government* (New York: Meridian, 1956)* remains a classic critical study of Congress. This edition contains an essay by Walter Lippmann on the evolution of Wilson's ideas concerning Congress and the presidency. An analysis of various theories of Congress, the role of public attitudes, and views of congressmen toward the institution is found in Roger H. Davidson, David M. Kovenock, and Michael K. O'Leary, *Congress in Crisis: Politics and Congressional Reform* (Belmont, Calif.: Wadsworth, 1966).*

George B. Galloway's *History of the House of Representatives* (New York: Crowell, 1962) traces the development of House institutions and practices in a scholarly manner, while Neil MacNeil provides a journalistic and anecdotal discussion of the chamber's history in *Forge of Democracy: The House of Representatives* (New York: McKay, 1963).*

CAMPAIGNS AND ELECTIONS

Since every member of Congress must live with the need to win a nomination and an election, the electoral arena is a basic part of the congressional system. The best summary discussions of congressional nominations and elections are V. O. Key's *Politics, Parties, and Pressure Groups* (New York: Crowell, 1964), Chapters 16 and 20; and H. Douglas Price's short but perceptive essay in Truman (ed.), *The Congress and America's Future*, pp. 52-76.

The impact of presidential coattails on congressional elections is analyzed in Malcolm Moos' *Politics, Presidents and Coattails* (Baltimore: Johns Hopkins, 1952); by Warren E. Miller in "Presidential Coattails: A Study in Political Myth and Methodology," *Public Opinion Quarterly*, XIX (Winter 1955-1956), pp. 353-368; and by Charles Press in "Presidential Coattails and Party Cohesion," *Midwest Journal of Political Science*, XII (November 1963), pp. 320-335.

The extent of interparty competition in congressional elections is analyzed by Charles O. Jones in "Inter-Party Competition for Congressional Seats," *Western Political Quarterly*, XVII (September 1964), pp. 461-476.

LEGISLATIVE LIFE AND ROUTINE

Excellent scholarly discussions of Senate life are found in the articles of Ralph K. Huitt: "Democratic Party Leadership in the Senate," *American Political Science Review*, LV (June 1961), pp. 333-344; "The Morse Committee Assignment Controversy: A Study in Senate Norms," *American Political Science Review*, LI (June 1957), pp. 313-329; "The Outsider in the Senate: An Alternative Role," *American Political Science Review* LV (September 1961), pp. 566-575; "The Internal Distribution of Influence: The Senate," in Truman (ed.), *The Congress and America's Future*, pp. 77-101.

The most complete book-length treatment of the Senate is Donald R. Matthews' *U.S. Senators and Their World* (Chapel Hill, N.C.: University of North Carolina Press, 1960).* Matthews espouses the "inner-club" theory that a small, close-knit, bipartisan "club" runs the Senate. Joseph S. Clark in *The Senate Establishment* (New York: Hill & Wang, 1963)* gives a senator's account of the inner club's operation, while a journalist's version of the club theory is William S. White's *Citadel: The Story of the United States Senate* (New York: Harper & Row, 1956). In Chapter 3 of Nelson W. Polsby's *Congress and the President* there is a sharp critique of the inner club theory.

Robert L. Peabody and Nelson W. Polsby have assembled in *New Perspectives on the House of Representatives* (Chicago: Rand McNally, 1963)* an excellent collection of articles dealing with activities in the House. Congressmen's own accounts of their work and their problems are found in Charles L. Clapp's description of life in the House, *The Congressman: His Work as He Sees It* (Washington: Brookings, 1963). A perceptive account of the job of a representative is also provided by the late Congressman Clem Miller's letters which have been compiled and edited by John W. Baker in *Member of the House: Letters of a Congressman* (New York: Scribner, 1962).* More critical of the House is *House Out of Order* (New York: Dutton, 1965) by Representative Richard Bolling, who provides an intimate account of the late Speaker Sam Rayburn's leadership.

By analyzing roll-call votes and the characteristics of congressional districts, Lewis A. Froman has provided new insights into congressmen's relations with their constituencies in his *Congressmen and Their Constituencies* (Chicago: Rand McNally, 1963).* Warren E. Miller and Donald E. Stokes also discuss the impact of constituency in their "Constituency Influence in Congress," *American Political Science Review*, LVII (March 1963), pp. 45-56.

Three excellent short discussions of the milieu within which representatives must function are Lewis Anthony Dexter's "The Representative and His District," *Human Organization*, XVI (Spring 1957), pp. 2-13; Richard F. Fenno's "The Internal Distribution of Influence: The House," in Truman (ed.), *The Congress and America's Future*, pp. 52-76; and Edward A. Shils' "Congressional Investigations: The Legislator and His Environment," *University of Chicago Law Review*, XVIII (Spring 1951), pp. 571-584.

An important aspect of Senate and House operations is the work of the congressional staff personnel. A critical examination of congressional staffing practices is Kenneth Kofmehl's *Professional Staffs of Congress* (Lafayette, Ind.: Purdue University Press, 1962). A more politically oriented study of staffing practices is James D. Cochrane's "Partisan Aspects of Congressional Committee Staffing," *Western Political Quarterly*, XVII (June 1964), pp. 338-348.

PARTY LEADERS AND FOLLOWERS

The classic study of the influence of party on congressional voting behavior is Julius Turner's roll-call analysis, which assesses the influence of various factors on congressional voting, *Party and Constituency: Pressures on Congress* (Baltimore: Johns Hopkins, 1951). David B. Truman in his *The Congressional Party: A Case Study* (New York: Wiley, 1959) describes and analyzes party structure and leadership through use of cluster-bloc analysis. The history, operation, and impact of the House Republican Policy Committee is found in Charles O. Jones's *Party and Policy-Making: The House Republican Policy Committee* (New Brunswick, N.J.: Rutgers University Press, 1964); while a GOP leadership fight is described by Robert L. Peabody in *The Ford-Halleck Minority Leadership Contest, 1965* (New York: McGraw-Hill, 1966).

Among the better articles on party leadership are Ralph K. Huitt's "Democratic Party Leadership in the Senate," *American Political Science Review*, LV (June 1961), pp. 333-344; Lewis A. Froman and Randall Ripley's "Conditions for Party Leadership: The Case of the House Democrats," *American Political Science Review*, LIX (March 1965), pp. 52-63; Nelson W. Polsby's "Two Strategies of Influence: Choosing a Majority Leader, 1962," in Peabody and Polsby, *New Perspectives on the House of Representatives*, pp. 237-270; and Randall B. Ripley's "The Whip Organization in the United States House of Representatives," *American Political Science Review*, LVIII (September 1964), pp. 561-576.

THE CONGRESSIONAL COMMITTEE

There is a growing literature of thorough and sophisticated studies of congressional committees. Among the best is *The Government and the Atom: The Fusion of Powers* (New York: Atherton, 1963) by Harold P. Green and Alan Rosenthal. This work is an intensive study of why the Joint Committee on Atomic Energy has been able to exert a powerful influence in the Congress and on the Atomic Energy Commission. An analysis of the powers and functions of the House Rules Committee is James Robinson's *The House Rules Committee* (Indianapolis: Bobbs-Merrill, 1963).* The most comprehensive study of committee politics is Richard Fenno's analysis of the appropriations process, *The Power of the Purse* (Boston: Little, Brown, 1966).

A pioneering behavioral analysis of committees using role theory is Ralph K. Huitt's "The Congressional Committee: A Case Study," *American Political Science Review*, XLVIII (June 1954), pp. 340-365. Other leading articles on committee politics are Richard Fenno, "The House Appropriations Committee as a Political System: The Problem of Integration," *American Political Science Review*, LVI (June 1962), pp. 310-324; George Goodwin, "The Seniority System in Congress," *American Political Science Review*, LIII (June 1959), pp. 412-436; George Goodwin's "Subcommittees: Miniatures of Congress," *American Political Science Review*, LVI (September 1962), pp. 596-604; Charles O. Jones, "Representation in Congress: The Case of the House Agriculture Committee," *American Political Science Review*, LV (June 1961), pp. 358-367; Charles O. Jones, "The Role of the Congressional Subcommittee," *Midwest Journal of Political Science*, VI (November 1962), pp. 327-344; and Nicholas A. Masters's, "Committee Assignments in the House," *American Political Science Review*, LV (June 1961), pp. 345-357.

HOW A BILL BECOMES A LAW

There are a series of detailed case studies of a major bill's passage through the congressional labyrinth. Each provides much of the atmosphere of Congress, sharply criticizes the legislative process, and illustrates the liberal's displeasures with congressional operations. Among the best case studies are Stephen K. Bailey, *Congress Makes a Law* (New York: Columbia University Press, 1950);* Robert Bendiner, *Obstacle Course on Capitol Hill* (New York: McGraw-Hill, 1946)*; and Daniel M. Berman, *A Bill Becomes a Law: The Civil Rights Act of 1960*, 2d edition (New York: Macmillan, 1966).* A more analytic treatment of problems of pushing legislation through

Congress is Frank J. Munger and Richard F. Fenno, Jr., *National Politics and Federal Aid to Education* (Syracuse: Syracuse University Press, 1962).*

THE PRESIDENT AS LEGISLATOR

An excellent historical account of congressional-executive relations is *President and Congress* (New York: Vintage, 1962) by Wilfred E. Binkley. The most original work on the power of the President and his impact on the Congress has been done by Richard E. Neustadt. His *Presidential Power* (New York: Wiley, 1960),* a discussion of how Presidents acquire, use, and maintain power, contains perceptive insights into why some Presidents are successful in leading Congress. He has also traced the development and analyzed the impact of two important tools of presidential power in "Presidency and Legislation: The Growth of Central Clearance," *American Political Science Review*, LIX (September 1954), pp. 641-671; and "Presidency and Legislation: Planning the President's Program," *American Political Science Review*, XLIX (December 1955), pp. 980-1021. The nature of present-day relationships among the President, Congress, and the bureaucracy is developed in Neustadt's essay "Politicians and Bureaucrats" in Truman (ed.), *The Congress and America's Future*, pp. 102-120.

INTEREST GROUPS AND THE LEGISLATIVE PROCESS

The best modern-day discussion of interest group theory remains David B. Truman, *The Governmental Process* (New York: Knopf, 1951). The factors that affect access to legislatures and the techniques of influence are discussed in Chapters 11 and 12. Some of the most original and enlightening research on interest group activities and the groups' relationships with the executive and legislature are found in *American Business and Public Policy* (New York: Atherton Press, 1963) by Bauer, Pool, and Dexter. *The Washington Lobbyists* (Chicago: Rand McNally, 1963) by Lester Milbrath is an analysis of lobbyists—who they are and what they do—based on extensive interviews of lobbyists and congressional recipients of lobbying.

More general, descriptive discussions of lobbying are found in Matthews, *U.S. Senators and Their World*, Chapter 8, and in Keefe and Ogul, *The American Legislative Process*, Chapters 9 and 10.

CONGRESSIONAL CONTROL OF ADMINISTRATION

With the initiative for legislation continuing to shift to the executive, the oversight function has taken on increased significance.

There is, however, a dearth of literature systematically analyzing legislative oversight. Green and Rosenthal's *Government and the Atom* presents the most thorough analysis of how a congressional committee has been able to assume a strong position vis-a-vis an executive agency. *The Political Process: Executive Bureau-Legislative Committee Relations* (New York: Random House, 1965)* by J. Leiper Freeman analyzes the subsystem of committee-agency relations to demonstrate the reciprocal nature of influence, and Aaron Wildavsky's *The Politics of the Budgetary Process* (Boston: Little, Brown, 1964) describes the strategies involved in securing approval of the budget.

In addition, some of the best work in the field of oversight has been done by Seymour Scher. See his "Congressional Committee Members as Independent Agency Overseers," *American Political Science Review*, LIV (December 1960), pp. 911-920; "Conditions for Legislative Control," *Journal of Politics*, XV (August 1963), pp. 526-551; "The Politics of Agency Organization," *Western Political Quarterly*, XV (June 1962), pp. 328-344. See also John F. Bibby's "Committee Characteristics and Legislative Oversight of Administration," *Midwest Journal of Political Science*, X (February 1966), pp. 78-98.

REFERENCE WORKS

The publications of Congressional Quarterly provide a wealth of data on Congress so accurate and complete that they are relied upon heavily by members of Congress, newsmen, and scholars. The major Congressional Quarterly publications are *Congressional Quarterly Almanac*, an annual compendium of biographical and organizational data, summaries of actions taken in each session of Congress, roll-call votes and analyses of congressional voting; *Congress and the Nation* (1965), a summary of all major postwar legislation, biographical index to members of Congress (Seventy-ninth through Eighty-eighth Congresses), report on postwar elections, and key roll-call votes; *Congressional Quarterly Weekly Report*, a weekly summary of important congressional news, roll calls, and analyses of congressional voting.

Indispensable to the student of Congress are the *Congressional Record*, an almost verbatim account of activities on the floor of the House and Senate, and the *Congressional Directory*, containing biographical data on members of Congress, organizational data on Congress and the executive branch, and election statistics.

INDEX